My friends Gary Lovejoy and Greg Knopf have written a fresh and insightful book on a vitally important subject. They view depression as an alarm system that alerts us to issues we should address, as interdependent people who need God and each other. Having finished *Light in the Darkness*, I am left appreciating their handling of true and false guilt, the need for authenticity, how depression has been stereotyped, and their thoughtful depiction of biblical characters who faced depression. I found this book warm, helpful, biblically solid, and full of hope.

—RANDY ALCORN, author of *Heaven*, *The Treasure Principle*, and *Deception*

This book, like the Psalms of Lament from which it draws in part, presents real issues that affect many, many people. It addresses the problem of those who would challenge the spirituality, even the salvation, of people who are beset with depression. But depression has ranged through time barriers and is no respecter of persons (Christian or not). In *Light in the Darkness*, there is help for many, even for troubled critics.

—DR. RONALD B. ALLEN, senior professor of Bible
exposition, Dallas Theological Seminary

In the past thirty-five years, I have witnessed too many pastors who have lost their passion for ministry due to depression. I strongly recommend this book for all leaders who want to maintain their zeal for ministry in their forties, fifties, and sixties. What's more, I highly recommend it for everyone in their congregations, especially those who are hurting and wondering how their faith relates to their pain.

—JOHN BRADLEY, president, IDAK Group

Knowing Gary Lovejoy and Greg Knopf, I expected their book to be filled with deep psychological and medical wisdom backed by years of clinical experience. I was not disappointed! But I hadn't quite expected the depth and breadth of biblical and theological insights. Now I don't know how to categorize the book. Is it a fine theology text, an excellent commentary on the whole Bible, or the best Christian book on depression I've ever read? Perhaps all of the above!

—GERRY BRESHEARS, PhD, professor of theology, Western Seminary,
and coauthor of *Vintage Jesus* and *Vintage Church*

After pastoring for over thirty years, I have come to the conclusion that many followers of Christ struggle with depression. Drs. Lovejoy and Knopf have recognized the important balance of integrating the roots of depression and the important principles and tools (backed by sound biblical doctrine) that people can use to respond more effectively in overcoming their depression. This book is long overdue and I know it will have a profound impact on the many people who desire to be free of the emotional battle that haunts their daily lives.

—DALE E. EBEL, senior pastor emeritus, Rolling Hills Community Church

The complex interactions of spiritual, psychological, and physical factors that contribute to depression need real and understandable answers. Good news! Here is hope and insight. This book is a guide, not down a road of guilt and shame, but provides a path into freedom and wholeness.

—MARCUS "GOODIE" GOODLOE, Catalyst, Mosaic Church

At last! Here is an extraordinary blend of fresh, empathetic, biblical counsel for all who struggle with depression. If you are looking for a pathway out of the darkness, you will want to read *Light in the Darkness*. Its pages are brimming with practical tools and powerful messages of hope. The updated medical information adds a dimension rarely seen in books of this nature. I know *Light in the Darkness* will be a treasure for anyone struggling with depression.

—ALICE GRAY, coauthor of *The Worn Out Woman*

Aptly named, *Light in the Darkness* offers hope to those whose lives have been disrupted by the common cold of human suffering: depression. In this book, Drs. Lovejoy and Knopf provide biblical, theological, psychological, and medical counsel that is both sound and practical. It is a valuable resource for those who suffer with depression, as well as the clinicians who work with them.

—GENE HARKER, MD, PhD, physician, psychologist, and professor

Drs. Lovejoy and Knopf have spent decades providing guidance and medical support for people in the "fog" of depression. Now, through sound biblical teaching and psychological and medical insight, *Light in the Darkness* delivers a reason to hope for believers with depression who have often suffered in silent darkness.

—DENNIS HENDERSON, PsyD, licensed psychologist and vice president of Western Psychological and Counseling Service

This book is impressive! Clearly thought-out and researched. It is a study in depression that will help those who read it better understand themselves and how God will cause growth in the worst of times (when it really doesn't feel like he is). It is also the best biochemical interpretation of depression that I have read, and the appendix info is very helpful as well.

—REG P. MARTO, PhD, clinical psychologist

Depression is a significant roadblock to being conformed to the image of Christ. It is time we gave people permission and skills needed to embark upon a holistic journey of healing in Christ in this crucial area. I believe this book can play a significant part in that journey.

—DR. RICK MCKINLEY, pastor of Imago Dei Community, author of
This Beautiful Mess and *Jesus in the Margins*

Too often there is misunderstanding in the Christian community regarding mental illness—its meaning and interpretation—with harsh consequences for those lacking understanding. This book presents a wonderful integration of psychological and spiritual insight offering real hope to those suffering from depression. Highly recommended.

—JON MESSINGER, MD, psychiatrist

I read this manuscript on a day when I felt troubling thoughts tugging at my heart. I found challenge, clarity, concrete hope, and—best of all—some moments of "Aha! That's what's going on!" Teens and adults, men and women, husbands and wives, sons and daughters, dads and moms—all can be helped by the God-honoring view of depression contained in these pages.

—ELISA MORGAN, CEO of MOPS International and publisher of *FullFill* magazine

If you or a loved one is suffering from the ravages of depression, Drs. Gary Lovejoy and Gregory Knopf are the ones you would want to guide you through the experience. This book is the synthesis of over thirty years of practice and teaching by men of deep integrity with a unique sensitivity to the human heart. It is a captivating integration of psychological issues and theological perspectives that evokes an entirely new appreciation for the emotionally healing role of a person's faith.

—WILLIAM H. MULLINS, PHD, clinical psychologist

Most of us who pick up a book and see the word *depression* initially think, "Hmmm, not for me!" But do yourself and those you love a big favor and read this. You'll be surprised at what you learn about yourself while at the same time learning how to help others. You will find that it is very insightful and contains lots of useful information.

—DR. GEORGE POWELL, senior pastor, Abundant Life Church

If you have never sunk beneath the waves of depression, you can be very grateful. If you are now feeling overwhelmed by your emotions and even feeling guilty about them, this book can serve as a life preserver for you. If you are a Christian physician or a pastor or you have a friend experiencing depression, *Light in the Darkness* will help you to help them. It contains advice about depression that almost everyone can use.

—DR. HADDON ROBINSON, Gordon-Conwell Theological Seminary

Finally a biblical view of depression that makes sense! All of us have visited the dark hole of despair and depression—some of us have lived there too long. This book is a must-read for anyone who wants to climb out of that hole or help someone else out. Drs. Lovejoy and Knopf in *Light in the Darkness: Finding Hope in the Shadow of Depression* not only focus a biblical and informed professional light on depression, but chart the biblical course out of the storm into the calm.

—DR. RICH ROLLINS, coauthor of *Redeeming Relationships*

Where was this book when I hit the wall? Drs. Lovejoy and Knopf open the door to understanding and walking through the real pain of depression. It's clear, practical, and points to the Source of all hope. If you or someone you care about is experiencing depression, read this book.

—RANDY SHAW, director of Northwest Church Planting and founding pastor of Mosaic

What a great book! I couldn't put it down until I reached the final page. Lovejoy and Knopf combine a solid biblical worldview with a medical and psychological insight to create one of the best books on the human struggle I've read in years. If you care about people, you must read *Light in the Darkness*. This is a book about faith, hope, and health. It's a book that will help you help others and help yourself.

—DR. STEVE STEPHENS, coauthor of *The Worn Out Woman*, *20 Rules and Tools for a Great Marriage*, and *Risking Faith*

Drs. Lovejoy and Knopf have written an easy-to-approach book that will help us better understand the nature of depression and exercise our spiritual circuits to help restore wellness. The authors explain how there is a fog present, not only from the illness, but from self-imposed guilt, doubt, shame, and uncertainty. They illuminate a clear path for the believer to regain hope. *Light in the Darkness* is precisely on target. This is a book I will want all of my patients of faith who struggle with depression to read. Indeed, I am pleased to recommend it to everyone, including family members, pastors, and counselors as an excellent study of the path to recovery from depression through a spiritual journey from legalism to grace through faith. This uplifting guide will help many back onto the path of healing of both mind and spirit.

—WARNER B. SWARNER, MD, medical director, Cornerstone Clinical Services

I highly recommend the book *Light in the Darkness: Finding Hope in the Shadow of Depression* by Drs. Gary Lovejoy and Gregory Knopf. It is a must-read for counselors, pastors, and those struggling with depression to help them find a greater understanding of the struggles of depression. It also explains that we do not have to live in despair but can live with joy if we understand what depression is telling us and don't ignore it. I am looking forward to referring the book to many to find incredible healing.

—JULIE WOODLEY, founder and director of Restoring the Heart Ministry

LIGHT
IN THE
DARKNESS

FINDING HOPE IN THE
SHADOW OF DEPRESSION

GARY H. LOVEJOY, PhD
GREGORY M. KNOPF, MD

wphonline.com

Copyright © 2014 by Gary H. Lovejoy and Gregory M. Knopf
Published by Wesleyan Publishing House
Indianapolis, Indiana 46250
Printed in the United States of America
ISBN: 978-0-89827-825-5
ISBN (e-book): 978-0-89827-826-2

Library of Congress Cataloging-in-Publication Data

Lovejoy, Gary H.
  Light in the darkness : finding hope in the shadow of depression / Gary H. Lovejoy,
PhD, Gregory M. Knopf, MD.
      pages cm
  Includes bibliographical references.
  ISBN 978-0-89827-825-5 (pbk.)
  1. Depression, Mental--Religious aspects--Christianity. 2. Depressed persons--
Religious life. I. Knopf, Gregory. II. Title.
  BV4910.34.L68 2014
  248.8'625--dc23
                              2014001456

We dedicate this book to our clients—once-hurting people who invited us into their lives for a short time, whose transparency helped us to see the conflicts that often exist between spiritual understanding and emotional experience—that is, between faith and adversity. We commend their courage to challenge their thinking with the truth—something that God has bid us all to do. Above all, we thank them for the ways they encouraged us to reexamine our own faith, to make it more real and relevant to the issues God's Word has addressed, and to do so with compassion and tenderness.

CONTENTS

FOREWORD

If you want advice about fixing your car, you seek an experienced mechanic; if you want advice about selling your home, you seek a successful real estate agent; and if you want to know more about the weather, you seek the reports of a trained meteorologist. But if you want to understand something as deeply personal as your experience of depression, you would seek not merely a competent therapist but one whose mature Christian faith is evident and whose values are similar to your own. In all the years I have known him (and that goes back to our college days together), Dr. Gary Lovejoy has been and is such a person. His unwavering belief in God's healing power, his deep love for people, his intellectual curiosity, and his understanding of the paradoxical traps others find themselves in make him uniquely compassionate about the Christian's struggle with depression.

Always a man to thoroughly prepare himself for something, Gary is well-educated and trained as a therapist who systematically explores every dimension of a problem. After many years of private practice in which he has counseled several thousand depressed people, many of them believers, Dr. Lovejoy has come to some important conclusions about integrating spiritual and emotional insights that reframe the issues clients most often struggle with. In *Light in the Darkness: Finding Hope in the Shadow of Depression*, he answers the question that is so commonly found on the lips of troubled Christians about how to relate their depressive experience to their faith. Many of them feel guilty about being depressed or believe they have somehow failed God by not being sufficiently "happy"—and so have become even further depressed. But Dr. Lovejoy fits their struggles into the larger picture of the image of God in each one of us. He does this in an intensely engaging style, using many relevant examples that bring his ideas into the living room of our experience. By identifying how depression, like anger and fear, is a key emotional alarm system signaling that something in our life needs our attention, he has removed the stigma so many people I have known place on emotional struggles.

Like pain in the physical body, the authors argue that depression is not itself the primary problem but rather a signal calling attention to that problem. To this end, Dr. Lovejoy debunks many of the myths Christians believe (and the church sometimes teaches), which serve to inhibit them from even seeking the help they need in the first place. He accurately reveals how God has actually responded to his servants' episodes of depression, episodes that are described in detail in the Bible. He points out that most of the great characters of redemptive history suffered depression at one time or another, and yet God used them mightily for his glory.

Without a doubt, *Light in the Darkness: Finding Hope in the Shadow of Depression* is a book that provides the proper basis for understanding self-acceptance, even during the most trying of times. It provides, too, an eye-opening discussion on the misguided perceptions about God that weigh many of us down and the uplifting alternative rooted in the intimacy we all desire. Along the way, Dr. Lovejoy makes many useful and practical suggestions for dealing with the various depression-generating strategies we sometimes employ to solve our problems. For this reason alone, he has provided a much-needed volume in a critical area of emotional life. For the believer, myself included, it especially addresses those troubling questions that create as much distress for our spiritual life as they do for our emotional health.

Included in this meaningful integration of psychological and theological concepts is a thorough discussion by coauthor Dr. Gregory Knopf concerning the current scene of antidepressant medications. He helpfully points out how each of these medications is used and when they may be contraindicated. As a medical professional, he gives us a peek into the physiology of depression that puts our mind at rest about the conditions under which antidepressant medication is most needed and effective.

All in all, this book should be available for reference in every Christian home. Besides being a great read, it is an invaluable aid in keeping our heads straight about God's view of our struggles. I could not recommend it more highly for our depressed brothers and sisters, and for those who work with them.

Dr. Gary Smalley
author and speaker on family relationships

PREFACE

We were doing a series on the Psalms in our church, and I was due to speak on Sunday. As I looked over the psalm chosen for that week, Psalm 22, I could only think of the folks I had counseled just the week before who struggled with the emotional pain conveyed in this psalm. As they poured out stories of hurt, I could see this psalmist nodding his head in empathy. Indeed, his feelings of abandonment are all too familiar: "My God, my God, why have you forsaken me? Why are you so far from saving me, so far from the words of my groaning? O my God, I cry out by day, but you do not answer, by night, but I find no rest. . . . But I am a worm and not a man, scorned by everyone and despised by the people" (vv. 1–2, 6).

Many of us have felt something like this at some point in our lives. Some of these words were even uttered by our Lord in his agony on the cross. But they were originally King David's deeply felt words of despair.

Low points. We all have them. The trouble is, we usually don't know what to do when we're there or how to make sense of them in light of our faith. In fact, we tend to think they indicate that we're spiritual failures.

One day, some time ago, Dr. Knopf and I were caught up in a conversation about the frequency of this kind of thinking among our Christian patients. We had both come to the same conclusion: what makes depression difficult for many Christians is their confusion over what it reflects about their spiritual life. Over the years, we have watched countless believers wrestle with self-hatred and self-blame, convinced they are useless to God and a burden to others. They struggle with the idea that God actually wants them to treat themselves with grace and to see themselves for what they are: the marvelous result of his compassionate handiwork. This is what Christian psychologists and others variously call "self-esteem" or "self-acceptance." But God calls it simply knowing the truth.

As Psalm 139 points out in beautiful poetic terms, if anyone knows us, God does. He created us with strengths in order to testify of his glory and honor. He has designed everything about us down to the smallest detail. Nothing was left to chance.

It should not surprise us, then, that depression is part of that design.

What? How is that possible? Because depression exposes the ways we are thinking and behaving that are unhealthy for us. It dramatizes how far we have drifted in our faulty processing of the past. Depression is unpleasant because it is a purposefully uncomfortable alarm system designed to get our attention. We don't need to be afraid of it or use it as a weapon to dump judgment on ourselves. These reactions only undermine the real purpose of the experience.

Understanding what God has to say about depression and how he responds to us when we are going through a dark period tells us a lot about the God we serve. It also tells us how we can use the experience of depression as a means of growth that will, in time, strengthen our relationships with others and deepen our faith in God. Looking at depression from this perspective gives us a way of seeing that it has, indeed, a divinely designed purpose. This purpose provides the hope that is our inheritance in Christ for all who are suffering with depression (or who know someone who is). After all, for both the Christian psychotherapist and the Christian physician, the prism of a mutually held faith is the crucial lens through which true healing must begin and through which it must triumphantly end.

This book is the result of ongoing discussions about these things over many years and is intended as a guide to stimulate further thinking about an emotional struggle that is much more common than most people believe. We hope it enlightens and lightens you. Our journey through life is meant to be shared in community, so we warmly invite you into the conversation.

Gary H. Lovejoy, PhD
Gregory M. Knopf, MD

ACKNOWLEDGEMENTS

We want to thank those whose timely insights over the years have stimulated our thinking, especially the folks in our covenant group. These dear friends, whom we have known and fellowshipped with for nearly twenty-five years, have, throughout our professional careers, provided their unwavering emotional and spiritual support. We also want to thank our families for enduring the time-intensive responsibilities of such a project. Their interest, patience, and encouragement reassured our efforts to stay the course until we completed our work.

Also deserving of our gratitude are those who have given their time and energy to review (or listen to) various parts of the book and give us invaluable feedback about its content. These have included Cheryl Adelman, Roger Greene, Linda Streger, Dr. Don Harris, Himon and Nellie Cradduck, Betty Holmlund, Ken Aust, and Kathy Ward. We are also indebted to David Sanford, who worked with us and provided unstinting support for our project.

Special thanks go to Brian Smith, whose herculean efforts to edit the manuscript will never be forgotten. His sensitive spirit and undeniable expertise uplifted the entire enterprise. We must also mention the invaluable advice we received from Jeff Pederson (president/CEO of JPED Consulting). His creative spirit, dynamic energy, and incredible ability to see the larger picture have provided an enthusiasm for this project few could ever match. Special thanks are given to the wonderful staff at Wesleyan Publishing House, whose commitment to our vision of addressing the emotional needs of the Christian community has been unstinting and whose work on our behalf has demonstrated unparalleled excellence. Finally, the list would not be complete without recognizing along the way the editing work done by Doug Schmidt. His ability to refine a manuscript and capture the voice of the author is remarkable.

Lastly, how can we ever thank enough the tireless efforts of Sue Lovejoy (Dr. Lovejoy's wife) in tackling the seemingly endless task of typing one draft of the manuscript after another. Her indefatigable spirit made possible what few volunteers could have done. We should not fail to mention, too, the assistance of professional typist Karen Weitzel, whose able hand and inspiration made the task easier for us all.

PART 1

BEHIND THE SCENES OF DEPRESSION

UNRAVELING THE MYSTERY

OUR BUILT-IN
ALARM SYSTEM

Our problems are not here for us to solve them but for them to solve us.

—Salvador de Madariaga, Spanish writer

A couple I (Gary) counseled had recently watched their new, five-thousand-square-foot home burn to the ground. A shrieking smoke alarm had startled them awake that night. They jumped out of bed and ran into the hallway to find the entire back of the house ablaze. Fighting a choking cloud of smoke, the wife rushed to their son's bedroom, scooped him up, and ran out the front door. Her husband called the fire department, grabbed what possessions he could, and raced out after his family. Dazed, they watched as the flames destroyed their dream home.

They'd lost so much. But they were forever grateful that their smoke alarm had worked. It had saved their lives! They still had their son. They realized, as never before, the importance of warning signals. We may dislike the shock associated with warning signals, but they do push us into action, sometimes preventing the unthinkable. As it turned out, this experience was indeed a turning point for this couple.

The world is filled with alarms—fire alarms, theft alarms, intruder alarms, maintenance alarms, and a host of others. Our car dashboards sport an array of warning lights signaling trouble with oil pressure, water temperature, or the battery. Gauges tell us when to get gas, when we're pushing the engine's rpms too high, even when a door is ajar. We can hardly take a step without some alarm system protecting our best interests.

Should it surprise us then that a powerful, wise God would equip our bodies in a similar way? We're wired with alarm systems that prepare us for the myriad of things that menace our well-being. As one scientist aptly observed, such bodily alarms are convincing evidence of our grand design. Indeed they are!

THE PARADOXICAL VALUE OF EMOTIONAL PAIN

As dreadful as depression is, you might be startled to hear that it is actually one of those alarm systems, and that it, in fact, has the same protective purpose as other alarms. It protects you by signaling damaging problems that may have escaped your notice. If you do nothing about these problems, your defenses will disintegrate. Depression alerts you to do something about the problems before they destroy your chances for meaningful living in the future. In one way or another, they involve issues that reflect a frustrated search for love and significance.

Depression can warn you that certain emotional attachments are harmful or that something going on inside you is emotionally destructive; or it may simply reflect the normal distress of grief from the death of a loved one. It may also be telling you that your circumstances (or your internal narratives about them) need to change. Even in the experience of grief, if the depression does not abate, your internal narrative may need intervention.

As an emotional warning system, depression is but one of four alarms you have that regulate your quality of life. The other three are fear, guilt, and anger. These signals tell you that something important is amiss in your relationships with others, yourself, or both.

Fear is the alarm system that alerts you to physical or psychological danger, calling for immediate defense. This is different than constant or recurrent anxiety, which sounds a false alarm in the absence of concrete danger, therefore sending a false signal. Guilt is geared to issues of moral compromise, warning you of spiritual injury if alternative action isn't taken. Anger is a common reaction to someone who has hurt you or created some sort of loss in your life.

Anger is one of the most frequently triggered alarm systems, partly because it signals immediate injury. Quite often, you can become angry because you are reciting internalized messages about yourself—messages that originated with your parents or other significant childhood figures, messages that are just as mistaken now as they were then. Such anger is especially likely to occur when you have endured a history of rejection in a dysfunctional family. It's typically manifested in high levels of defensiveness in a relationship.

Anger can also reveal your frustration when you don't get what you want when you want it. When this is the case, it arises from self-centered interests and can become ruinous to your relationships. Alternatively, anger can be a secondary reaction to another signal, such as guilt or fear, essentially serving as cover for an emotion you don't want to acknowledge. Or, the other way around, it can itself be threatening enough to be repressed, serving instead to trigger a different emotion, even a stoic reaction.

Whatever the source, anger, when it functions according to design, can prompt you to reevaluate your communication patterns or change something in yourself. In fact, without periodic expressions of legitimate anger, your relationships likely would not change much at all. Instead, they would become stagnant and sterile, remain stuck in a rut of boredom, and be unfulfilling to everyone.

Many people wish they handled anger differently. The apostle Paul taught that although anger itself isn't sinful, many things we say or do when we're angry are (Eph. 4:26ff). He distinguished between anger as an emotional state and the rage that is at the root of most destructive attitudes. For example, he encouraged us to admit to our emotion of anger while avoiding the wrath (lashing out) and bitterness that can so easily follow.

Understanding anger is particularly important, because it's an early warning indicator that your present emotional state could possibly descend into depression if things remain unchanged. Anger tends to be more sudden, even if sometimes subliminal; depression, on the other hand, usually develops more slowly and manifests its warnings more persistently over time.

Depression is usually elicited by chronic, unresolved issues, which may go underground because they're too threatening to deal with openly. Maybe someone hurts you, so you become angry. Then you feel guilty about your anger ("I really *shouldn't* be angry"), so you bury the feeling (and sometimes the guilt) and the slow inner burn feeds the self-hatred of depression. These kinds of interactions between emotions can become quite complex — and deadly to the quality of your life.

One thing is certain: depression, like all emotional alarm systems, has a way of creating such discomfort that it *dominates* your attention. You're forced to acknowledge that a problem exists; otherwise the internal havoc will stubbornly persist until you confront and resolve it.

Never forget, its purpose is to point to the value of change. It's only when it finally succeeds in prompting this change and producing growth that you then discover the real reason for viewing depression optimistically. The truth is that depression is really meant to be your *ally*, not your enemy, even if that sounds incomprehensible to you at the moment.

This understanding may be contrary to all you have been taught; nonetheless, it's the inescapable conclusion about every emotional alarm — including this one.

WITH FRIENDS LIKE THIS . . .

The positive potential of depression can be seen in a powerful way in a book by journalist Andrew Solomon in which he describes his nearly lifelong battle with despair. Solomon concluded from the drama of his experience that depressive episodes, though painful, also have the upside of providing opportunities for examining life more deeply: "The opposite of depression is not happiness but vitality, and my life, as I write this, is vital, even when sad. . . . Almost every day I feel momentary flashes of hopelessness and wonder every time whether I'm slipping. . . . I hate those feelings, but I know that they have driven me to look deeper at life, to find and cling to reasons for living. I cannot find it in me to regret entirely the course my life has taken. Every day, I choose . . . to be alive. Is that not a rare joy?"[1]

Mr. Solomon's experience forced him to understand his own freedom more fully, to exercise the "rare joy" of making life-changing choices. It provided him with greater wisdom and new meaning. It may seem strange to you, but it also gave him reasons to celebrate the challenge of adversity.

His experience presents a challenge to everyone who struggles with depression: you can make choices any way you want to—wisely or poorly—but no one can take away your opportunity to make them. Even when facing conditions you cannot change, the choice of attitude is always *yours*—no one else's.

Even though depression can have a beneficial purpose, nobody, of course, ever wishes for it. I'm not saying anyone should. But when depression does strike, you stand to gain more from life by learning its lessons. Remember, this is why James encouraged us to accept the testing of our faith, because such experiences can, in effect, strengthen our stamina for hard times (James 1:2–8).

Testing can also give you wisdom to recognize the dangerous instability James referred to as "double-mindedness," the habit of vacillating between conviction and cynicism. This instability gradually allows helplessness and fatalism to creep in, and that provides the grounds for depression to follow. When emotional endurance replaces this instability, it produces character, the kind that results in steadfast hope in who God is (Rom. 5:3–5).

You might be thinking, "Yes, but how can I keep a strong faith when everything in my life is crashing down around me and I'm depressed out of my skull? Am I supposed to feel guilty now because I'm questioning everything?" The simple answer to the latter question is an unequivocal *no*. God doesn't expect you to have superhuman emotional strength— he knows you can become overwhelmed by life's adversities. He knows, too, that you may lapse into doubt and anxiety. All he asks is that you be honest, both with yourself and with him. Remember that although God rebuked Job's friends for their false legalism, he praised Job for his honesty about his anger and confusion.

God's ways will at times no doubt be difficult to discern, especially when your experience contradicts your expectations. But responding with cynicism only blinds you to seeing God's presence and purpose in the midst of your hardship. Persistent faith, on the other hand, calls you to depend on God's goodness. Some people put God on trial for their suffering, attacking his character—a tendency Paul confronted in Romans 9. But without a righteous God, nothing about faith or hope makes sense. Truly, the existence of *any* goodness in the world is attributed to God's righteous presence and sovereign purpose. Evil will not forever prevail, because God refuses to abandon you to the shipwreck of your own circumstances.

Author Edith Schaeffer once noted that if you argue for an impersonal universe—one without a personal God intimately invested in us—then the very existence of human personality would be tragically, logically absurd. It would be futile to understand why people enjoy reflecting on the human condition, why they engage in interpersonal communication, or even why they love one another. As Schaeffer put it, these pursuits would be as meaningless as "fish developing lungs in an airless universe."[2] The deepest longings of humankind would be reduced to merely illusion.

But if you attribute the universe to a personal God, your experience becomes intelligible—and purposeful. Your desires and behaviors can fit into a sensible pattern. Life is complex; it can't always be reduced to simple, predictable terms. But God, in his mercy, has equipped you with emotional signals to help you adapt to the world's complexity—and, after the fall, to its dangers.

These signals, difficult though they may be to manage, are necessary for healthy functioning. That's why I have likened the alerting role of depression to the biological alarm system of pain. In other words, depression is to the psychological self as pain is to the physical self. It's obvious that almost no one enjoys pain. It's usually the last thing people would call beneficial. Many would prefer to be completely numb to it. But that rare individual born partially or wholly unable to feel pain holds a different opinion. As unpleasant as it is, pain is perhaps the most valuable sensory system you have. It warns you of the potential for damage to your body, even fatal damage, unless you immediately change what you're doing. When you turn an ankle, the pain drives you to remove weight from the injured foot, so you limp. If the pain continues, you seek medical diagnosis and care. Otherwise you might further injure the ankle, perhaps severely.

The great missionary physician Dr. Paul Brand described what happens to leprosy patients who lose the sense of pain in their extremities. He watched in horror as an African man reached his pain-deadened hand into a fire pit to retrieve a fallen yam from the red-hot coals.[3] This failure of the pain warning system explains why leprosy often leads to disfiguring damage to hands, feet, and other body parts.

Pain is necessary to call attention to disease and injury. It helps guard your long-term physical health.

Depression performs a similar role regarding your emotional wounds. Its distressing persistence bears testimony to its significance. Like pain, you can't merely will it away. It's there to tell you something, which means you ignore it at your peril. But heeding it can lead to valuable insight and the resolution of sometimes longstanding problems that have compromised the quality of your life.

Why, then, might you resist allowing depression to serve its purpose? One reason is that contributing factors often lie deep within you, involving issues you've avoided for a long time. In your efforts to survive painful past events, you may have insulated yourself from their impact by denying them. Though you don't want to be depressed, you may not want to face the truth either.

Sometimes, too, acknowledging the sources of your despair may seem to endanger relationships or threaten to shatter your sense of identity. What's more, your depression may come out of events that seem unrelated but that you nonetheless associate with earlier grievous wounds.

You can see this pattern in Barbara's struggle with depression. Coming from a turbulent alcoholic home, she couldn't wait to escape from her family. Barely out of high school, she married an older man she thought understood and cared for her—a person quite unlike her father. She dismissed her husband's history of repeated job firings and two divorces. She accepted this man's explanations about tyrannical bosses and controlling women, which portrayed him as a victim.

Within weeks of their wedding, however, she discovered the lies behind the explanations. He became increasingly abusive. She feared for her life. His drinking, which she hadn't known about before they married, only made things worse. She sometimes cowered before him, praying to survive his verbal attacks, praying he wouldn't hurt her . . . or kill her. Her desperate attempts to placate him did nothing to quell his rage. "When he starts drinking, it doesn't matter if I'm nice to him," she said. "I think he just *wants* to attack me. I think he gets a kick out of seeing me scared to death. . . . I'm afraid that one of these times he's not gonna stop with just words."

She became anxious and depressed because she found herself in the same never-ending nightmare, this time with a reincarnation of her violent father. Here was yet another destructive relationship with a man. She felt as trapped as she had when she was a child.

Barbara sought help from her church but said nothing about her husband's behavior, fearing the leaders would confront him, making things worse in the prison she called home. So the pastoral staff never really learned about the pathetic state of her marriage. The consequences of her silence were devastating.

Barbara accepted her husband's accusations that she was "rebellious" and "selfish"—after all, she already believed she was worthless. She mistakenly assumed responsibility, resigning herself to bear her burden alone, bolstered only by the tenacity of her legalistic faith. She had not dared seek counseling with her husband. As a result, he was never held accountable for his abusive behavior. Not surprisingly, she felt abandoned to perpetual fear of injury and despair for the future.

She needed to listen to her depression and its message. At the very least, she needed to seek a new direction for herself.

OF LEMONS AND LEMONADE

It's always useful to draw upon your own natural strengths— resources you already have for making a difference—especially when you're depressed. Using existing abilities makes the change process feel more familiar and doable.

I'm reminded of psychiatrist Milton Erickson's "African violet therapy." Visiting a depressed and suicidal woman who had withdrawn from everyone, he noted her interest in African violets. These delicate flowers are difficult to grow, but the woman had a knack for nurturing them. Erickson suggested that she use her talent by giving violets to the principals of her church's weddings, funerals, baptisms, and the like. She followed his suggestion, and it changed her life. When she died years later, more than a thousand people attended her memorial—people who had been moved by her quiet, generous spirit.

She thought depression meant that her life was worthless. But her depression was, in fact, a window of discovery. She had a gift perfectly matched to the world of need. Speaking of our country, but in terms applicable to the individual as well, the poet Robert Frost wrote, "Something we were withholding made us weak until we found out that it was ourselves."[4] Your unique gift, freely given, opens up unforeseen possibilities for you and for those you touch. The past may shape the present, but so also does a healthy anticipation of the future.

Depression represents the challenge of your feelings of helplessness, your sense of shame, and your burden of guilt. It forces you to rethink your perceptions of a world that seems at times to demand more than you can give. It pushes you to consider new insights about yourself, changes that will help you cope more effectively with adversity. Depression can prompt you to discover how to grow, not in spite of but *because of* your pain. If you can learn a more meaningful way to live—and to give—your depression will have served its purpose.

Through the years, God has moved mightily through servants who were prone to depression. For example, some of the great luminaries of church history—such as Martin Luther, Charles Spurgeon, and D. L. Moody— suffered major depressive episodes. Depression is no stranger to God's people. We shouldn't pretend that it is. It's far better to be honest about our struggles as believers, to bring a refreshing transparency to the Christian community before a culture that already constantly questions our credibility.

But most believers share a powerful fear of shedding their façades. They're terrified of being judged, especially by their churches. So they go on living their people-pleasing, sanitized lives, calling it Christian love and believing it pleases God.

AN INVITATION FOR ALL SEASONS

All bold responses to pain share something in common: a deeper sense of purpose that gives meaning in the face of apparent meaninglessness. Viktor Frankl revealed this as the secret to his survival of the horrors of the Nazi death camp at Auschwitz. The apostle Paul also alluded to it as the enigma of strength through weakness in the midst of his persecution (2 Cor. 12:9). Paul found unusual strength not in himself, but in a dependency upon God made necessary by the persistence of his own failures. The success of the gospel—despite Paul's obvious imperfections—simply made the Lord's victorious hand more visible to the early church.

Isn't it interesting that we are likely to attribute success to God when it happens in spite of weakness? For example, contrary to a well-delivered sermon by a great preacher, aren't we more likely to give the glory to God when an inexperienced speaker gives a testimony that spiritually moves the audience? It's not the speaker's performance but God's power that makes the difference. It's neither eloquence nor position that wins hearts and minds. Not even martyrdom provides triumph. Rather, the love only God can supply drives home the message of hope.

That same love stands ready to transform your life, but you may not be able to see God's hand through the veil of your pain. Sometimes you may despair over your limitations, which hinders your understanding of the bigger picture. If this is the case, you are likely inhibited from fully experiencing the kind of relationship God desires to have with you.

It's very easy to become bogged down by memories of failed relationships that have diminished your aspirations. Yet God is persistent, continuing to invite you into intimacy, a banquet of love that often seems too good to be true. It seems that way only because it's an unconditional love that comes from a God who doesn't need your attention but nevertheless desires you more deeply than you can ever imagine.

You're not going to be perfect in your efforts to walk with God; nor should you expect to be. God knows your limitations, which is why he grieves when you reject yourself because of them. It's because of your proclivity to sin in the first place that he gave you the Holy Spirit to guide and transform you in ways you can't do on your own. So, instead of emotionally beating yourself up, he wants you to have joy in your journey. He has no desire for you to live life merely with a grim determination to make it to the end. Rather than agitating against your failings (real or imagined), take comfort in his complete understanding of your humanity. Turning your frustration and wrath on yourself is no better than turning it on others. Try training your eye on the goal of learning what God can teach you through your struggles. You might be surprised at what the residuals of pain can reveal.

A gifted client of mine had long been laboring to understand the nature of this kind of relationship with God. She came to liken it to the intimacy between a loving father and his child. She arrived at this conclusion as she worked through her depression:

> It is the question of God's hand as an intervening, directive force, or as something resting gently on the believer's shoulder, infusing him with the power to see the mysteries that abound. . . . I wonder if feeling God's hand on my shoulder is like a father touching a child to get his attention so he can point out something the child otherwise would have missed. So it seems that the sense of loss I've experienced is but a part of something much bigger that is happening to me, like a window of opportunity to understand things that the mind can never know, only the heart.

I'm convinced that God is honored when you struggle to understand him. Faith in him means freely admitting your ignorance and your questions—just like when the desperate father, seeking Jesus' help for his son, cried, "I do believe; help me overcome my unbelief" (Mark

9:24). God wants you to acknowledge your doubts and fears, because it prepares you to receive the truth. Arrogant certainty will never motivate you to seek God's face because it cannot stir the passion to look beyond the limits of your own mind.

I recently attended a memorial service for a wonderful Christian woman. She had died from complications related to Hodgkin's disease. Her early family environment had been particularly dysfunctional, resulting in the neglect or rejection of nearly everyone who was supposed to love her. Over the years, she grew remarkably through her suffering, so much so that she went on to touch the lives of many other troubled people. You see, she was an excellent therapist, highly respected for her ability to get past the defensive façades of her patients. She was particularly effective with troubled youth, partly because she uniquely understood their pain. God used her in a way she never would have dreamed of as a child.

Although she did not have a loving family around her, her impact was measured by the large crowd who came to pay tribute to her abbreviated life. Sitting there listening to the many people testifying to her influence in their lives, I was reminded once again that God never lets an experience go to waste. Surely the God who enabled her victory is the same one who can enable yours.

If you persevere in your sacred journey of discovery, you will be drawn into the accepting, redemptive heart of God himself. There you will find—perhaps with some surprise—that your weakness is made strong by his love. Paul described this phenomenon as a strange and otherwise inexplicable peace that wells up within the soul (Phil. 4:4–7).

Contentment doesn't just happen. Contentment is learned.

INSTRUMENTS OF LOVE

Notice that we keep running again and again into the concept of connection—of loving and being loved—that survival kit for the human heart. Even under the most desperate conditions, intimacy's appeal lingers in the air, luring each of us with its promise of healing.

Viktor Frankl described love as an important conduit of meaning—that loving someone is a primary reason for feeling emotionally alive.[5] As long as German death camp prisoners could attribute meaning to their experience, even if only by treasuring an imagined liberation date, they could survive the Nazis' worst. This triumph of the spirit was not possible, however, without reaching beyond the suffering, lifting their eyes to a hope connected to the relational requirements of the heart. These formidable conditions—the common ground of pain—fostered some of the prisoners' deepest connections with each other. Frankl saw prisoners at Auschwitz bond with their fellow prisoners, often giving of themselves to meet one another's survival needs. One would give his ration of bread to an ailing friend. Or he might complete a chore for a weaker comrade rather than see him beaten for "dereliction of duty." These heroic deeds in the courageous, pain-forged bonds of intimacy momentarily removed them from their suffering. Their suffering freed them to be vulnerable and sacrificial toward one another. It brought out the best. It endowed with nobility people who were otherwise stripped of dignity.

When people reach out of their isolation to others, seeking relief from their suffering, they inevitably go beyond head knowledge and appeal to the heart. In this way, the deepest human need is addressed by the solace of love. Notice that Jesus connected his message of redemption to the passion of his Father for his people. By his sacrifice, he demonstrated that God's purpose cannot be vanquished. Through his pain, he revealed the power of divine intimacy, which is far greater than the meager offerings of the secular world.

Because our Lord has shared your earthly pain, you can find in him the healing opportunity to view your suffering through the window of a loving Father's empathy. A relationship with him fills the spiritual void that makes suffering so much worse, freeing you to rebuild from your losses on a new foundation. Remember, depression is not merely sadness; it's profound emptiness.

Even with those losses, God's love will inspire you to make the most of what you have left, to assemble the remaining pieces of your life into a new arrangement. Itzhak Perlman, arguably the world's finest violinist, once demonstrated such triumph. His passion for music enabled him to craft a magical moment from the shards of apparent misfortune. Read syndicated columnist Jack Riemer's account in the *Houston Chronicle*:

On November 18, 1995, Itzhak Perlman, the violinist, came on stage to give a concert at Avery Fisher Hall at Lincoln Center in New York City.

If you have ever been to a Perlman concert, you know that getting on stage is no small achievement for him. He was stricken with polio as a child, and so he has braces on both legs and walks with the aid of two crutches. To see him walk across the stage one step at a time, painfully and slowly, is an awesome sight. He walks painfully, yet majestically, until he reaches his chair. Then he sits down, slowly, puts his crutches on the floor, undoes the clasps on his legs, tucks one foot back and extends the other foot forward. Then he bends down and picks up the violin, puts it under his chin, nods to the conductor and proceeds to play.

By now, the audience is used to this ritual. They sit quietly while he makes his way across the stage to his chair. They remain reverently silent while he undoes the clasps on his legs. They wait until he is ready to play.

But this time, something went wrong. Just as he finished the first few bars, one of the strings on his violin broke. You could hear it snap—it went off like gunfire across the room. There was no mistaking what that sound meant. There was no mistaking what he had to do.

People who were there that night thought to themselves: "We figured that he would have to get up, put on the clasps again, pick up the crutches and limp his way off stage—to either find another violin or else find another string for this one."

But he didn't. Instead, he waited a moment, closed his eyes and then signaled the conductor to begin again. The orchestra began, and he played from where he had left off. And he played with such passion and such power and such purity, as they had never heard before.

Of course, anyone knows that it is impossible to play a symphonic work with just three strings. I know that, and you know that, but that night Itzhak Perlman refused to know that. You could see him modulating, changing, and recomposing the piece in his head. At one point, it sounded like he was de-tuning the strings to get new sounds from them that they had never made before.

When he finished, there was an awesome silence in the room. And then people rose and cheered. There was an extraordinary outburst of applause from every corner of the auditorium. We were all on our feet, screaming and cheering, doing everything we could to show how much we appreciated what he had done.

He smiled, wiped the sweat from his brow, raised his bow to quiet us, and then he said—not boastfully, but in a quiet, pensive, reverent tone—"You know, sometimes it is the artist's task to find out how much music you can still make with what you have left."

What a powerful line that is. It has stayed in my mind ever since I heard it.

And who knows? Perhaps that is the [way] of life—not just for artists but for all of us. . . . So, perhaps our task in this shaky, fast-changing, bewildering world in which we live is to make music, at first with all that we have, and then, when that is no longer possible, to make music with what we have left.[6]

This is the artist's heroic pursuit of the finest he can produce. God, the Artist of life, is the creator of the best in you. Even when badly wounded, you can find new strength in the concerto of his compassion. Only the music he performs on the instrument of your soul can fulfill you because it alone resonates with who you were created to be. No broken heartstring need cause you to fall silent and withdraw from the stage of life. God teaches you to play your damaged instrument with a new intensity—modulating, changing, and recomposing the music of your life. When played to the tempo of God's grace, your song inspires praise from the hosts of heaven.

THE MUSIC OF DISCOVERY

In therapy, Barbara painfully reviewed her confining relationship patterns and began to see herself in surprisingly new ways. Her healing didn't happen overnight. But in time, she understood why she had willingly accepted abuse from her husband and herself and how that had contributed to her depression. She learned a more effective, more assertive approach to dealing with her husband. She now knows that no one has to silently endure someone else's sins in a kind of lifelong purgatory. She sees the distinction between real and false guilt and consequently no longer carries the burden of misguided devotion. Freedom in Christ has a new ring to her.

She accepts God's love and grace, and her faith now serves to nurture, not injure, her mental health. She recognizes her power to make genuine choices. During our last session, she commented, "Sometimes I'm amazed how lost I had become—I didn't think I even had the right to live, but I was also scared to die because I never felt I had done enough to get to heaven. At one point, I actually thought God had sent my husband to punish me for what a disappointment I had been to him. But I would never go back there in a million years. My days of being abused are over. Now I know what God *really* wants for my life." In pursuing professional help, Barbara courageously waded against the strong current of dysfunctional messages. Such courage is rare.

Understanding depression helps you make sense of your emotional design, which can lead you to greater self-acceptance. It also puts you in closer touch with your inherent longing to be loved. Without the experience of love, life rapidly becomes empty and meaningless. When cut loose from this essential mooring of life, you become adrift in a sea of misleading beliefs about yourself and the world around you. Little seems left to guide you other than cruel chance.

Millions of people exist like this, directionless and without purpose. They don't have to. But still they betray their own souls, forsaking their heart's true desire. They blame others, though their life's pain is often a result of their abandoning their own dreams. As a result, they live lives of disengagement. Only when they realize that depression is a clarion call to change do they begin mending their broken hearts. Depression may be the only way to distract them from their deadening routines long enough to consider something different.

Barbara accepted depression as an ally. It rescued her from a war between emotional exhaustion and the dictates of a legalistic faith by showing her that it's a needless war. Her depression was, in fact, a consequence of wrong thinking and flawed theology.

Only when you return to the music of your faith will you find the melody of your healing. In his endless love, God seeks you out even at your lowest ebb; and he finds you, even if you're not really looking for him. The question is: What choices will you make when he does? Will you opt to play his composition of life or one composed by your dysfunctional world? Will you see your depression as a signal to change or a sign of defeat? The choice is yours.

I like to think that while God supplies the lyrics and the tune to a life well-lived, we counselors have the rare privilege of helping to repair the instruments that can uniquely play his arrangements.

FINDING HOPE

1. The discomfort of your depression has a positive signaling purpose: to prompt you to take action on an unattended problem.

2. God has given you the freedom to make choices that change your world and address your pain.

3. You are physically and psychologically designed for a purpose. Your longings to be loved reflect that purpose, a purpose that is both personal and interpersonal.

4. Depression gives you the opportunity to discover something important about life: although the past may influence the present, the way you anticipate the future does so as well.

5. If you aspire to live a productive life, you are in a position to discover God's principle that strength can be found through weakness.

6. Depression can be the hopeful prelude to something better.

THE LANDSCAPE OF DEPRESSION

I am poured out like water, and all my bones are out of joint; my heart has turned to wax; it has melted within me. My mouth is dried up.

—Psalm 22:14-15

Have you been depressed but feared admitting it openly to yourself or to others? Do you think that admitting it means you have failed God? Do you see depression as proof that you are a wayward believer? Do you believe that only happy Christians are "good" Christians who have a strong faith? Are you convinced that you are either beyond help or not worthy of it?

If you believe any of these things, then what follows in the remaining chapters will be eye opening to you. You will see, for example, that most of God's faithful servants in the Bible suffered episodes of depression, sometimes even suicidal depression. God did not reject, rebuff, or lecture them, as if they had somehow failed him. Instead, he loved, encouraged, and gently guided them to a new understanding of themselves or their circumstances. And many times he took the opportunity to reveal to them more about himself.

You see, God *never* deviates from his nature. Your emotional ebbs and flows are not a sign of failure, but rather a sign of his creative genius and his great mercy.

This book is a story about God's unfailing love and compassionate guidance in hard times, guidance that reveals his complete understanding of your psychological makeup. The good news is that *you* are always his focus, no matter whether you are joyful, depressed, or somewhere in between.

Such love is seen not only in his redemptive acts, but also in creation itself. As we discussed in the first chapter, you are designed with built-in alarm systems to protect you from ignoring continuing injury to body, mind, and spirit. If nothing else, this surely tells you that you matter to God.

In fact, you matter a lot.

That's why depression is perhaps the most durable, if not the most important, emotional signal you have.

So it turns out that depression not only *isn't* a sin; it's actually, by design, a warning light, indicating that your life needs to change in some consequential way. Contrary to popular belief, depression occurs to mercifully alert you about something more damaging than you may even realize. Ultimately, depression is there to help you, not destroy you.

Depression tells you when hope has died and when you need to make a significant shift in what you think and do in order to revive it.

SEARCHING FOR THE HOPE IN HOPELESS

In the midst of your confusion and pain, hope can sometimes seem like an elusive promise, a hoax, a vapor that lasts for a little while and then vanishes without a trace. In that moment, every unhappy event that has ever happened to you seems to converge into one desolate landscape of injustice. Life becomes pointless and cruel. Nothing seems to make sense anymore. You feel like giving up.

Depression is like that, isn't it?

Consider, for instance, the case of Jeff, a recent client. He was a financial advisor who had to take a medical leave from his job. He was no longer emotionally functional. In fact, he had been hospitalized just weeks before with severe depression. As he sat in my (Gary's) office, fidgeting with his coat buttons, he rambled on in disjointed sentences about how miserable and hopeless life had become. "Life seems like one meaningless routine after another," he complained. "It's a dog-eat-dog world out there where people are just looking for ways to sucker-punch someone. What's the point? Is that all there is to life?" Jeff was normally quite affable, indeed, the life of the party at times. But now he had become quiet and withdrawn, even shutting out his wife of twenty-five years.

As the session progressed, he revealed that his company, where he had become a vice president several years earlier, had recently demoted him. His closest friend in the company—another vice president—had turned on him and falsely reported to the president that Jeff was courting offers from a rival company. Jeff felt betrayed by someone he had fully trusted. And that's when the bottom fell out.

He said, "My father betrayed me when he ran off with another woman; my roommate in college got caught cheating in a class and blamed me for writing his paper, which almost got me kicked out of school; and my best friend in high school stole my girlfriend. I could go on, but you get the idea. You can't trust anybody." For the first time in his life, he started drinking heavily, alarming his wife. As she described it, he was becoming a stranger in their house, pulling away from the entire family. Depression was clearly an unwelcome guest in their household, posing a threat to Jeff's job, marriage, and relationships with his children.

Like many people who are depressed, you may follow a similar pattern. Your life may be marked by lethargy and isolation. In the meaningless montage of your bitter disappointments, you are likely unaware of just how many share your dark experience. Instead, you're probably convinced that no one else could possibly understand what you're feeling.

Making matters worse, you may have no clue as to your real problems. Even if you do, you probably don't know what to do about them. Ironically, your emotional or physical withdrawal may have only deepened your desperation and feelings of helplessness. In search of relief, whether you're conscious of it or not, you're more prone to emotionally numb yourself, either by self-medicating or by retreating into a world of denial, anything that serves to insulate you from further pain.

Getting out of bed is often a major accomplishment. It's hard to generate much enthusiasm for anything, least of all for any activity that requires even a modicum of concentration. You may notice that friends and family are becoming increasingly upset by your behavior, particularly if you're becoming more irritable with them. If you start compulsively overeating or if you lose interest in food altogether, that concern only grows.

It's easy to become even more depressed when you see your family becoming frustrated by the seemingly endless nature of your struggles. In fact, you're likely to feel all the more guilty for making life difficult for them. It may be hard to understand that they are feeling helpless too. The bottom line is they want you to *do* something rather than merely feeling bad all the time. They don't seem to get the idea that depression's tightening grip feels like a vise that squeezes out every drop of initiative to do anything. This inhibiting effect, depending on your personal history and response patterns, can sometimes seem overwhelming. Yet, ironically, taking some sort of action is *exactly* what your emotional alarm is telling you to do.

Despite the platitudes of others, you're probably wondering how anything that feels so bad can still produce any good. How can an experience that is so negative still hold promise for a positive future?

When you're depressed, that's really the only question that matters.

Yet no one seems to have the answer—or at least not one that makes more sense than the faulty belief you already have. So in the absence of answers, what happens? That's right. You usually see no choice other than to persist in your passive, self-inflicted paralysis.

This is the double bind in which you can often find yourself. On the one hand, your inaction and isolation is making you miserable (by making you lonely and providing lots of time for self-defeating rumination). But on the other, you intuitively avoid seeking possible solutions to your problems, most likely because you believe that a solution, if it exists at all, is beyond your control.

The compromise is to instead blame your fatigue and insomnia on some undefined physical illness and to seek a diagnosis from your physician. But when the doctor rules out any medical cause—which is frequently the case—you feel even more adrift in a sea of confusion.

If you're like most people I see, what you probably want more than anything else is just to find hope in something. That doesn't mean, however, that you're necessarily looking for personal change. It just means that you simply don't want to hurt anymore.

Sometimes your behavior can become so disturbing, even reckless, that it forces others to intervene. But if no one heeds the warning signals and takes some kind of action, sometimes the unthinkable can happen: suicide. That's when impulsive action turns the prospect of violence inward to the self and the specter of trauma outward to the survivors. Both are thrust into the harsh light of tragedy. No one escapes untouched.

Have your thoughts ever taken you there?

If they have, you're not alone. However, it's important to remember, that's when you most need others to help you break the trance of self-destruction. Unfortunately, that's also when you are least likely to seek assistance.

In reality, as an emotional alarm system, depression is a wakeup call to corrective action, not a pretext for oblivion. By corrective, I mean productive in the sense of important personal change—change that will free you to try new things and find new ways to connect to the significant people in your life.

Whether you like it or not, everyone is involved when your depression hits—you and all of those who care about you.

Though it may seem impossible to imagine now, especially if you're in the midst of it, depression can actually present the opportunity to find new ways of thinking and behaving that will ultimately result in a better, much more satisfying life than you have ever experienced before.

But we are getting ahead of our story. If this book is going to be helpful to you, whether you personally struggle with depression or know someone who does, then we must look more closely at what lies underneath depressive states.

WHAT ABOUT THE ELEMENT OF ANXIETY?

It's entirely possible to become so completely adapted to your soul's emptiness that you are unaware that you're actually depressed. Instead, you may think it's just life, so get used to it. Like in the film *As Good as It Gets*. Jack Nicholson's character, who had severe OCD (obsessive-compulsive disorder), had merely lowered his expectations of life. In effect, he lived a life of resignation based on the assumption that things were about as good as they were ever going to get.

Some circumstances, such as a physical disability, *are* beyond anyone's control. But believing this limits potential satisfaction in life is an assumption that ignores the power of choosing your own perspective. Viktor Frankl demonstrated through his experience at Auschwitz that our interpretation of events determines how we react to difficult situations. He argued that the attitude you take, even toward a circumstance you cannot change, is critical to your ability to not just survive these situations, but to grow through them.

You're wired to find meaning in every situation. If you're like most people, you prefer order and predictability over uncertainty and all the anxiety that creates. When you can't readily identify purpose in your circumstances, you become distressed and are likely to impose a meaning of your own. You may try to reduce your anxiety by assuming (usually incorrectly) the motives of others around you. These assumptions, especially when they are distorted by your own biases, can cause you to respond inappropriately to others.

On the other hand, you might also explain your circumstances in distorted assumptions about yourself. You may explain negative events in terms of personal inadequacy ("I never do anything right") or by claiming that you are incapable of change ("I'm hopeless") or by believing that any future happiness is forever lost ("My whole life is ruined").

It's easy to see how such pessimism and self-blame can become the foundation for depression. In fact, it's one of the most common ways depressed people interpret life's many disappointments. Jeff, our distressed financial advisor, certainly felt this way. In time, however, he began to see how his fatalism produced a false, almost hypnotic train of thought that was dismantling his every chance for happiness.

Everyone lives with some uncertainty in life. But if you have a lot of anxiety over such uncertainty and it continues to reach increasingly higher levels, you will substantially increase your risk for depression. It's common to try to control this surging anxiety, to keep it from happening, only to discover it actually gets worse. You can easily end up believing you're completely powerless. And if you do, you'll likely respond to events in ways that simply reinforce these feelings.

The good news is that at any point in this cycle you retain full autonomy over your beliefs.

Though you are free to choose hopelessness, you are just as free to believe a situation can and will change for the better, and that you can in fact be an agent of that change. If you choose the latter, you'll learn why your anxiety has continued despite your best efforts to stop it. While it may seem paradoxical, it's precisely *because* of your misguided efforts to make it go away that you are actually prolonging it. In effect, when you encounter uneasiness and respond to it as if it imperils your life, you make it more chronic and overwhelming, which is the reason you falsely conclude that you're incompetent and frightfully fragile. You can, instead, accept (or, at least stop fighting) anxiety, and simply acknowledge it while calmly anticipating its eventual decrease. Think of it as merely temporary discomfort, which is what it is. Since this frees you to focus on what you can do to make useful changes in how you live, you'll find it to be a much more productive (and relieving) use of your time. In fact, this kind of accepting outlook may enable you to see particular things you can do to alter your life that would otherwise escape your attention. Such discoveries reveal why responding positively is an exercise in empowerment. As you become less anxious and more empowered, you significantly reduce your chances of becoming depressed.

So if you observe that your usual responses to difficult circumstances aren't working—*which is what depression is telling you*—then why not heed the warning signal? Look for the exceptions. Do something different, something surprising. Consider the alternatives. Try something new. Rediscover your creativity.

WHAT DO YOU REALLY CONTROL?

The first lesson you must learn is to distinguish between what you can and cannot control. For example, you don't have the power to make others more pleasant or less obnoxious. You do, however, have the power to change your response to them. While you can directly bring about change in yourself, you can only indirectly inspire change in others.

Many chronically depressed people haven't learned these distinctions. Their depression often results from a twofold mistake: first, futilely trying to change things that *are not* under their control; and, second, failing to change the things that *are* under their control. Strangely enough, a common reason why they don't take charge of the things that are under their control is because they are too busy trying to make a difference in the things that are not under their control.

Does this sound familiar?

Are you trying to control the behavior of others—in other words, trying to get others to respond to you in the way you want? If so, you're probably going to end up chronically unhappy about the results. Worse still, you will likely be labeled a "control freak" by the very people you are trying to influence. There's really not much to commend that approach.

Is it any surprise so many people become frustrated and give up hope?

Often, part of the problem is a heavy dependence on particular emotional survival myths—like the one that says you must protect yourself at all times from a hostile world, or that if you don't control others, they'll control you. These myths usually grow out of early formative experiences in your family.

Bad things that were out of your control happened when you were a child, so you concluded that you must control everything in order for good things to happen. Usually, however, this only leads to more bad things happening—so once again, it leaves you feeling hopeless.

The past doesn't have to endlessly repeat itself. But you must first actively challenge and alter these myths. Try to remember that when you perceive that your life is out of control, you will only make things worse if you falsely believe your troubles are not only unavoidable, but also deserved. Such thinking will merely give you more reason to deny to yourself any possible strategy for a better life . . . and more reason to perpetuate your own dreadful self-fulfilling prophecies.

Critical and demeaning self-talk naturally tend to follow. You are then left to hope that others will take pity on you, since taking action on your own behalf is not even an option.

Inside you may grow puzzled, resentful, and defensive toward a world that doesn't seem to care enough to help. In fact, at times it seems only to favor those who've hurt you. A. W. Tozer described this fortress mentality: "The heart's fierce effort to protect itself from every slight, to shield its touchy honor from the bad opinion of friend and enemy, will never let the mind have rest. Continue this fight through the years and the burden will become intolerable."[1]

It's not difficult to understand why you might be caught off guard when your doctor suggests professional help. Doesn't he or she know you're already doing the best you can under the circumstances? Does he or she think you're just too "stupid" or "weak" or "crazy" to survive on your own? Is he or she just trying to get you out the door? But if you can get past this initial resistance and consider the idea that by pursuing change a better life lies ahead, you've taken the first important step toward a major therapeutic shift in your thinking.

Though you may still fear exploring unfamiliar ground, you will gradually come to see the link between your inner conflicts and your outward fatigue, insomnia, headaches, and other physical symptoms. In fact, as your problems are reframed in terms that suggest solutions, hope will begin to reemerge and fears will begin to subside.

You will finally see what has eluded you for so long, namely that your depression is a constructive, growth-directing alarm signal that has been triggered by something inside that urgently needs attention.

Recognizing depression as depression and viewing it as a useful guide is a good beginning. But it's only the beginning. Its resolution requires an examination of what's at stake and coming up with a practical plan of action.

UNDERSTANDING DEPRESSION COMING OF AGE

As mystifying as depression often seems, it's no surprise to discover that it's a much more complex warning signal than originally thought. The potential causes of depression are now understood to be so numerous that authors have written entire books to describe them. Some causal factors are related to how much your biology is responsible for the moods you experience and others to how much responsibility can be assigned to environmental events.

Have you ever wondered whether your depression is the result of something gone haywire in your brain? Or have others suggested it must be linked to some kind of painful or abusive events in your past (or ongoing in your present)? These are common questions you may encounter when you're depressed. This quandary certainly isn't new. But it can definitely be perplexing to your state of mind nonetheless. (See www.Depression outreach.com to know in more detail how professionals view the different ways depression can be caused.)

Broadly speaking, the complexity of the mind-body relationship is the reason we no longer limit ourselves to either-or questions when it comes to causes—much less make predictions based on them. Instead, we look to two general things we know that help us to determine when and how to treat depression.

First, treatment of depression that has a strong biological base usually involves at least some kind of immediate medical intervention, while depression primarily traceable to environmental events normally requires at least some kind of consistent psychotherapy. Interestingly enough, though, it tends to lead to better outcomes if *both* kinds of depression are treated with medication and counseling together rather than either one alone.

Second, regardless of its source, chronic depression, if it goes untreated, can actually harm certain structures in the brain. Very real brain cell damage can occur especially in areas vital to learning, memory, and higher thinking. This is because depression actively inhibits a certain protein in the brain now understood to be critical to cell renewal and repair. Areas in the central nervous system particularly affected by this protein literally begin to atrophy. Apparently, then, resigning yourself to a life of feeling blue can, in the long run, actually have serious neurological consequences.

The good news is that you don't have to understand the mind-body interaction to know that it's important to get help as early as possible for your depression, just as it is to take any other preemptive step to safeguard your health.

Don't be lulled by the all-too-common definition of depression as simply a "chemical imbalance," a description that is both misleading and far too limiting. Otherwise, you'll limit yourself to medication (which, despite some claims, is not a cure-all for mood disorders). Indeed, sometimes medication is too automatically (or too exclusively) prescribed. You should always consider the important value of psychotherapy. Failing to take the more comprehensive approach to addressing your depression is like a mechanic trying to repair your car with only half the necessary tools.

But treatment must not stop there. We can't forget the role of your spiritual nature. It's important to understand how faulty coping strategies can affect your relationship with God. Psychological and biological factors aren't the only things at work in your depression; spiritual factors are involved as well. Depression is an alarm system of the whole person—body, mind, and spirit.

How you struggle with adversity may stir up hidden doubts about God's faithfulness or prompt you to act out in sinful ways. How you respond to your pain can affect your concept of God as well as your Christian walk.

Humans are fully integrated beings—what happens in one area of life affects every other area. Nothing is left untouched by your emotional struggles. The sooner you realize this truth, the sooner you will understand that becoming whole again requires attention to every facet of the problem.

Most important, viewing things through the prism of faith can help you actually see the optimism—the growth potential—tucked away in your experience of depression.

A PURPOSE TO THE LOSS OF PURPOSE

Depression is always a dreadful experience. But, as we've seen, it's precisely because it is so unpleasant that depression is effective in getting us to pay attention to the fact that a problem exists.

It may still seem like a mind-bending paradox to say that depression, in the final analysis, plays a protective role. But depression may be the one crucial signal that makes all the difference in turning around a damaging situation.

Like other signals, depression was never intended to continue indefinitely without corrective action. This is important to realize, because most depression will not entirely disappear, at least not permanently, simply with the passage of time.

Only changing how we think and act will accomplish that.

Some therapists believe that depression purposefully slows down your life to a lethargic crawl, conserving energy for the changes you need to make. While that may not be depression's primary function, this perspective argues, too, for the value of depression. One thing is certain: anything that originates in the mind of God is not merely an intelligent design, but is a merciful one as well. Underlying every emotional experience, even the puzzling one of depression, is a helpful purpose to be discovered.

Sometimes this purpose may be played out in an entire family system. This can be seen when your depression influences other relationships in your home, usually creating still further stress in your environment. However, even one strategic positive change can set off a cascade of adjustments and a corresponding chain of emotional payoffs that lead to a burst of growth.

I witnessed this in dramatic fashion with one family I recently counseled. While the dad sought to rescue the mother from her chronic depression, the children forfeited playtime and time with their dad to put their energy into household chores. Everyone tiptoed around the house. Mom entered counseling and began to improve. In fact, she improved so much that she could resume her responsibilities in the home. But as a consequence, Dad lost his sense of purpose and with-drew, and the kids left their chores to Mom and spent all their time with friends.

Dad eventually learned that rescuing his wife had been a means of avoiding conflict with her. He was petrified about their differences. He found better ways to invest himself in his marriage and more effectively resolve conflict. As a result, the children reconnected with both of them. In the end, the treatment of Mom's depression led to improved relation-ships throughout the entire family. One of the children said, "At first I was scared that Mom was going to leave us. Then later I thought *Dad* was going to leave. But after they got help, they told me that they loved us too much to ever do that. I finally realized we were going to stay a family."

As unpredictable and tumultuous as these changes may seem, they're vital to healthier patterns of interaction. These extraordinary outcomes remind us just how interdependent we all really are.

THE WAR INSIDE

You are no doubt by now familiar with the various symptoms of depression. If you need help identifying your own pattern, you can con-sult the checklist in appendix A to confirm which particular symptoms you are experiencing.

It's important to know that you don't have to have all the described symptoms at once to be diagnosed as depressed; you only need four or more. To assist you further in determining whether you are clinically depressed and how severely, I recommend that you take the Hamilton Survey for Physical and Emotional Wellness (see www.Depressionout reach.com).

These symptoms of depression can, of course, vary widely in intensity and duration. Your doctor will in all likelihood determine the diagnosis of your depression by assessing these variations. Once your particular pattern has been diagnosed, your doctor will then be able to suggest a plan of treatment.

In beginning treatment, the undercurrent of your self-hatred is often the first issue to address, as it can otherwise undermine your motivation to change. Why pursue personal transformation if you think you're incapable or even undeserving? Without rekindled hope, therapy is unlikely to be productive.

When you're depressed, you're likely to feel humiliated, ashamed, worthless, and incompetent by every setback in your initial attempts to change. You must reframe what successes and failures mean in order to grow toward healthy self-respect. It's important to reach a point where such setbacks only leave you disappointed or dismayed, not ready to give up. Start being at least as good a friend to yourself as you are to others. That usually means treating yourself differently from the way you were treated growing up. How you were treated in the past is the primary reason you don't respect yourself now.

When you are self-rejecting, you generally read setbacks not as an act of failing but as *being* a failure. You view yourself as incapable of success. On the other hand, those who respect themselves allow failures to teach them how to behave differently or how to live with their strengths and weaknesses so they can fine-tune their strategies to get the most out of life. Notice that both approaches deal with setbacks and failures (no one is immune to adversity); the two just represent different responses to the same situations.

With an emotional war going on inside, your self-rejection is likely to lead you to avoid attempting anything new or doing things in a new way. Consequently, taking small steps of change is useful in slowly desensitizing yourself to the risk you fear. Even small successes can empower you to significantly alter your world—and your perspective of what's happening.

Many emotionally incapacitated Christians also overlook the strength that faith can give them—which is why they typically respond to Jesus' teachings on discipleship with guilt and pessimism. "Take up your cross" is a terrifying proposition, and yet the believer's failure to do this only leads to more anxiety and self-condemnation.

Does that describe you?

IS LIFE WITH GOD TOO RISKY?

The apostle Paul wrote that he knew the secret of being content in every situation (Phil. 4:12–13). He realized that regardless of his circumstances, he could respond to them with courage and truth. While you can't always avoid negative circumstances or the sins of others, you can successfully overcome them. It's the lure of resignation that the Holy Spirit encourages you to resist.

The apostle learned the joy of mindfulness in God's presence — it stirred him to be enterprising, willing to experiment with his options. This is what Jesus asked us to do when he told us to "seek" and to "knock" (Matt. 7:7). God's direction always follows your decision to step out and test the waters. This was what the apostle Peter discovered so dramatically one stormy night on the Sea of Galilee (Matt. 14:22–32).

God knows you are far better off when you are willing to take a risk. Nowhere does he suggest that you greet life with silence or reticence. Instead, he encourages you to take the initiative to make a difference. Yet you may be too busy fearfully running away from life.

The common refrain "I will never measure up" echoes the deep sense of personal defeat many feel when they're depressed. Underlying it is often a smoldering resentment toward the criticism received from others. When you feel inadequate, you may withdraw from situations involving even the slightest chance of failure. Or you may purposefully underperform to keep from testing your true limits, a behavior a clinical professor of mine called "studied incompetence." People who do this avoid responsibility and push tasks onto other "more capable" shoulders. In effect, they are too afraid of falling short if they assume that responsibility for themselves.

When you make avoiding risk a lifestyle, every relationship and every goal is sabotaged. And the relationships that do survive generally won't be healthy.

In marriage, for instance, it's the fear of being unable to provide something the other asks that creates distance and loneliness. Intimacy problems are addressed only indirectly (or not at all), and the relationship gradually dies of neglect—one feeling incapable of giving and the other no longer interested in responding.

Many families train their members to deny their needs and feelings and to alter reality to protect the family secrets. Above all else, they are trained never to trust themselves. The resulting denial destroys any chance for fulfilling relationships. Life is governed by robotic perfectionism, methodical discipline, and rigid convictions. Gone are spontaneity, interpersonal honesty, genuine dissent, and mercy—toward themselves or others. Under these conditions, family members have no convincing reason to pursue intimacy. It's not surprising then that marriages with these characteristics become little more than empty, loveless gestures in the name of social (or perhaps biblical) obligation.

Others are trained to see themselves as victims, unfairly martyred by everyone else. Awash in a sea of self-pity and paranoia, they unwittingly poison every relationship they enter, especially those that could be the most healing.

Still another reaction is to take on a posture of gloom and doom. In your pessimism, you are more likely to strike back angrily against everyone you think is making you feel bad about yourself. If you choose this course, you will eventually exhaust the stamina of even your most loyal friends, which will only deepen your own despair and further ravage your self-image. All this accomplishes is compounding your self-hatred. As author Theodore Rubin put it, you end up hating yourself for hating yourself.[2]

Sometimes, when such self-rejection is covered up by a superficially confident exterior, conflicting and confusing messages are broadcast to others. If you've ever felt lost in a conversation with someone who's secretly hurting, it's probably because they have mixed feelings about letting you know what's going on. Double messages, delivered through verbal and nonverbal cues, keep people's heads constantly spinning. Such double-speak may be the mind's last-ditch effort to rescue the remaining shreds of identity from self-destruction.

Have you ever heard someone say, "I can't change; you'll just have to accept me the way I am"? You are being told, in essence, that they have no intention of changing. Their refusal to even discuss any kind of change nearly always destroys the spirit of a relationship. By placing responsibility for growth entirely on the other person's shoulders, they are basically saying that facing one's own pain is far worse than facing another's angry withdrawal.

This approach mirrors a man I once saw who had lost his father to suicide early in his life. Traumatized by the experience, he withdrew into a life of self-loathing, frozen at a child's level of emotional maturity and resisting anyone's attempts to help him. Such tragedies happen, but the greater tragedy is the truncated life such reactions lead to, a life that hinders any learning or action that could reverse the legacy of the past. Most tragic of all, this approach unconsciously denies God's gentle voice of healing.

It's understandable if early traumatizing experiences have left you risk averse. But is that a justification for forfeiting the rest of your life?

If you refuse to consider change, it means that you, like the man described above, will remain stuck in your history and become a perpetual child in an adult body. Just because painful events happened to you when you were young doesn't mean life will always be the same in the future. However, if that's what you believe, you'll more easily become prey to addictions, which will only further entrap you. Or you may simply give up all ambition and wait passively to be rescued. One client's story illustrates this phenomenon:

> When I was a little boy, I used to lock myself in the bathroom, away from my brothers and parents, and bawl my eyes out. I'd cry because no one understood me. No one seemed to really care how I felt. I waited and waited for someone to knock on the door and ask me if I was OK. What I really wanted was for someone to break down the door and rescue me from my aloneness. But no one came. In many ways, I never really left that bathroom. I've been waiting and waiting for someone to rescue me—to give me direction. To save me. But no one is coming.

For years this Christian man had been living a pointless existence of dreary expectations. He had no concept of the new, more fulfilling life

God was inviting him to take. He failed to understand that he really wasn't alone after all. In fact, others were available—if he'd only been open to them. At the very least, he could have freely acknowledged his feelings of abandonment to God; but, instead, he blamed God for his family experience.

God's truth is never relative, just as his love never wavers. Nothing can change these facts—not our rebellious behavior or our accusations against God and his goodness. Not even the spiritual inertia of our self-pity. That's because the constancy of his affection is rooted in his unchanging nature.

THE UPSIDE OF BEING DOWN

The resolution of old, often festering, problems finally releases emotional energy for tackling issues in the present—energy that has long been used simply to push down feelings from the past. Until now, you may have been merely compounding your stress, building a backlog of issues demanding your attention. If things were to remain that way, the entire dam holding back your emotions would collapse from the accumulated pressure behind it. That's why it's so important that depression is there—to push you to address your unfinished business.

It takes great courage to confront the skeletons in your closet. The God who urged Joshua to be of good courage when taking the field of battle and spurred David to defeat the Philistines is the same God who invites you to heroic change in your own life. Heroism can be found on the emotional battlefield just as surely as it can be found on a military one. The goal is always the same: a sweeping triumph over the enemy.

Any honest effort leads to gain. Each new choice you make provides more evidence of God's loving hand, quietly orchestrating your gradual release from bondage. A step here, a step there. Like pieces of a puzzle, they all work together for your good. God calls you to tap in to the freedom of your spiritual heritage, to allow the provocation of his love to awaken your slumbering spirit.

Hurting people are seldom impressed by sermons on gratitude for adversity. Many wonder if God even cares. Yes, adversity *does* provide evidence of his interest and compassion—but you must first be attuned to it. You must know his voice in the darkness of your pain, much like frightened sheep who recognize the calming voice of their shepherd. Your true destiny is found in melding your fledgling faith into his unswerving faithfulness.

God's thinking is radically different from what you and I often believe. Thankfully you don't have to understand his thinking to be transformed by it (just as you don't have to know how medications work to be physically restored by them). You can simply come to appreciate his compassionate and creative work in you—which includes, if you allow it, the changes wrought by the demands of your depression.

Therein is your hope.

FINDING HOPE

1. It's important to distinguish between what you can control (changing yourself) and what you cannot control (changing others) to free yourself from frustration and emotional exhaustion.

2. Consider challenging your distorted thinking (irrational beliefs) as an invitation God has given you to experience the world in new, more useful ways.

3. With each setback or disappointment, ask yourself, "What would I say to my closest friend if he or she were in this situation?" Then determine to say those same things to yourself.

4. If you think it's unfair not to get what you want, consider experimenting with new ways to work with what you have.

5. Observe how people with healthy coping skills talk to themselves about setbacks, and try to incorporate that thinking into your own. Become more solution-focused.

DEPRESSION IN GOD'S LARGER DESIGN

Knowing ourselves teaches us what to ask. It helps us to identify the
areas of need in our lives. It also teaches us how to approach God.

—James Houston

The events of September 11, 2001, forever changed our lives. In less time
than it takes to watch your favorite morning show, almost three thousand
people in New York City and Washington, DC, died. Our nation was
stunned but resilient, in no small measure due to a reawakening of
religious sentiments. Church attendance rose. People prayed. Politicians
openly affirmed God's mercy. If only briefly, God took center stage.
Our national outpouring of emotion reminded us of the void in this
country's soul. For the moment, at least, we put off spiritual amnesia
by acknowledging God once more.

There had been warnings of an impending terrorist attack, but we
failed to heed them because we were lulled into the belief that the threat
did not exist. Only after a tragedy did we take action. In our crisis, we
awoke from our denial and developed a network of preventive detection
systems under a new Department of Homeland Security.

In the course of these events, we demonstrated our uniquely human
capacity for devising innovative problem-solving strategies. But as is so
often the case, this capacity has proven to be a two-edged sword. While
we find new and creative ways to solve our problems, we tend to regress
once again to denial—we believe that the triumphs of our ability to
reason are all we need to live successfully. One of our greatest strengths,
then, becomes a weakness, creating a false sense of security in our own
competency.

Our culture teaches that our accomplishments can replace our dependence on God. Our God-given rationality has become our Achilles' heel. We've trapped ourselves. What we have been given by God has never seemed enough. He made us a little lower than the angels, but we claim superiority over all. He crowned us with glory and honor, but we demand admiration. He loves us, but many have written him off as irrelevant. Nothing short of assuming complete authority seems to satisfy us—and even that doesn't seem to be enough. We have spurned the awe that creatures owe their Creator. We've edited the blueprint of our own design, and the original is forgotten.

Faith in scientific inquiry as the only means of understanding the world has blinded us to eternity's landscape. To remove God from life's equation is to eliminate the only ground for human significance. Denying the spiritual worldview, we fail to appreciate why we're so precisely equipped to handle threats to our well-being.

In our materialism, we have dismissed questions about the meaning of life as too religious, leaving a spiritual vacuum that the cult of science cannot fill. But we can't reduce experience merely to our biology and expect to understand the purpose for how we function. A former colleague of mine (Gary) once said to me in frustration, "This religious stuff is just superstitious nonsense that keeps getting in the way of science. Why do you persist in helping these people pursue their ignorance? Can't they (and you) see that life is nothing more than the evolution of our biology? I'll never understand you—you're educated, and you still believe in God. I think it's pretty hopeless."

In rejecting such reductionism, Viktor Frankl argued that, rather than being *pushed* toward meaning by some biological drive, we are actually *pulled* toward meaning by something that appeals to our human spirit. From this point of view, our emotional alarm systems are designed to keep bringing us back to a purposeful life—which, of course, is the life God intended—a view my colleague could never accept.

We have no difficulty explaining short-range, emotionally powerful, physiological events, such as the "fight or flight (or freeze)" response preparing the body for action. But longer-term emotional states, like depression, require a broader explanation that incorporates the divine logic behind the system. All emotional signals were originally meant to arouse our resistance to anything not coming from God and to stimulate joy in response to goodness. But after the fall, these signals were needed for damage control. The hardships of a fallen world required a design that steered us back to the purpose of loving—back to God himself.

Our emotional signals are, therefore, part of the divine image in us. Any warning system, such as depression, though unpleasant to experience, is meant to guard that image. Depression is not merely a disease to treat, but an experience that leads us to something better. It may prompt us to clear away the baggage of a difficult past, or to process a significant loss.

Clinical practice tells us that, in most cases, depression has a far more useful role than we think. It's not simply a matter of chance errors in the function of enzymes. Author Andrew Solomon agrees: "Anyone who lives through this [depression] knows that it is never as simple as complicated chemistry."[1]

Now, we are by no means dismissing the biological factors or genetic predispositions to depression. They certainly occur, and in such instances, depression signals the onset of measurable physical dysfunction. That calls for a specific, mainly medical, course of treatment.

But many cases of depression can be traced back to relational causes. Depression can prompt us to examine conflicts that we were previously too distracted or, more likely, too fearful to face. When this signal intrudes and pries open our tightly held irrational beliefs, it can open up an entirely new way of thinking.

Nothing less than the trauma of depression is likely to stimulate such change.

IN THE BEGINNING: A LIVING PARADOX

Humans were created in the *perfect* image of God—perfectly in his likeness. But Adam and Eve, denying their inferiority to God, chose the path of moral independence. And so humanity's soul was emptied, and our moral senses permanently dulled. In love, God warned Adam and Eve against this spiritually fatal step. But they still proceeded to damage the divine image in humans and, as a result, developed an abiding tendency to sin. As amazing as it may seem, even though Adam and Eve deliberately rejected their natural spiritual inheritance, God never put a single condition on his love for them.

We know that God is wholly righteous with no capacity for evil (James 1:13). Humans, however, lack power to resist evil on our own, so we are reliant on God to sustain purity. Apparently though, Adam and Eve weren't convinced. They held fantasies of moral indignation, cultivated by Satan when he openly questioned God's goodness. As a result, they took matters into their own hands.

The consequences for Adam and Eve were disastrous, ending their tenure in the garden and staining their divine image. Most tragic of all was the fact that they were cut off from their Creator's presence. They were powerless to regain any of this on their own. But God, in his mercy, took the initiative to restore this intimacy and to offer healing for a damaged divine image.

This is the story of the gospel: an incorruptible love brought to bear on a sin-corrupted need to be loved. It's just like God to create a people who need intimate fellowship, so that we might serve God and minister in love to others. But we are able to love like this *only* because he loved us first (1 John 4:19)!

That love transforms people. It allowed Stephen, the first Christian martyr, to forgive his killers. It took Saul's zealous pursuit of religious legalism and turned it into a white-hot fire for God. And it calls out to us in our meaninglessness and offers us a sense of purpose.

Why do you suppose that if you scan the books on today's best-seller nonfiction list, you will find, aside from the political hot topic of the day, mostly volumes on how to succeed, influence others, or find happiness? Do most of us feel like poverty-stricken failures, convinced that happiness is as elusive as the city of Atlantis? If we do, it's more likely because we lack any purpose other than material gain.

Don't you yearn, however, for something different . . . even if you don't exactly know what that is? Isn't there something better than the goals our culture declares worthy of your attention?

In fact, there is. But first you must discover what difference would actually make a difference. That difference is found, I believe, in the spiritual quality of true connection, a quality found only in God's design.

When Jesus was asked to identify the greatest commandment in the Torah, he gave a two-part answer: Love God, and love your neighbor (Matt. 22:35–40). It's really a matter of authenticity. Just as faith without works is dead (James 2:26), so the profession of love is hollow without corresponding behaviors. To say you love God and yet harbor ill will toward others is to deceive yourself (1 John 4:20–21).

It's true that even unbelievers can love one another. Charity to the less fortunate is considered a virtue even in a secular culture. Nevertheless, love's very existence depends on God's presence in the world. It's part of the divine image in humanity.

This brings us to one of the Bible's most puzzling statements. Before he sinned, Adam experienced complete, unhindered communion with God. And yet, the Lord said, "It is *not* good for the man to be alone" (Gen. 2:18, emphasis added). Why wasn't God enough for Adam?

I believe it's because Adam—who could never be self-sufficient, whose sociability was limited by a finite mind—needed interaction with someone similarly finite. We are created with the relational character of our Creator. And we can fellowship with God. But finite humans need something that an infinite God doesn't need. Unlike a triune God, who is whole within the intimacy of his own being, humans must find wholeness by connecting with others. Since God finds perfect completion within himself, he doesn't need us to complete him. We, however, need other finite humans to complete our sociability. Just as we must intimately connect with our Creator to fill our spiritual hunger, so we must also connect with fellow created beings to fill our social hunger.

Adam's loneliness was not due, therefore, to an insufficiency in God's companionship, but rather to the fact of his own limits as a created being. And so God created woman as the man's "helper," which is translated from the Hebrew *ezer*. Most often, the Bible uses this word to refer to doing God's work. It never implies inferiority, but rather elevates the woman's role to one of honoring God. So God created the woman to do godly work in meeting Adam's companionship needs at the finite level.

God meant intimacy between a man and a woman to serve as an earthly model for the relationship between God and his people. Human intimacy helped Adam understand the depth of relationship he also needed with God. That's why God constantly refers to his relationship with his people in terms of marriage. He refers to the New Testament church as his bride. Likewise, in the Old Testament, he describes Israel's sinful behavior as "harlotry" or "adultery," leading to a painful "divorce."

Here we see the creative genius of our God: Our desire for intimate relationship—part of the Creator's image in us—is ultimately responsible for the spiritual unrest that lures us back to our reason for being. We find meaning when we understand ourselves as we were intended to be.

The first sin blurred the original splendor of our design and left us in an unnatural state—spiritually dead and emotionally naked. Notice that Adam and Eve suddenly became aware of their physical nakedness *after* they sinned. They had lived in selflessness, absorbed in God's and each other's companionship. But sin, by nature, involves self-centered gratification—it refocused each person's attention on self. Their new awareness of their unclothed bodies symbolized the shame of their selfishness. They were "stripped" of their natural state—union of body and soul—and now hopelessly divided, bodies with spiritually dead souls. Since then, humanity's struggle in this broken world is, at its root, our ongoing grief over the loss of what could have been.

Now, if the first couple had become inclined toward evil, for what possible reason would God perpetuate the race, allowing the birth of children who would inherit corruption and multiply evil still further? It might seem like madness, but God's purpose was, once again, ingenious. He provided yet another relational picture to help us understand a renewed relationship with him. How better to understand God's forgiveness and grace than by raising and loving your own children? Don't you love your children regardless of their grievous misbehavior? If you're a good parent, of course you do.

Healthy parental love is, then, the best model for understanding God's love for his children, making sense of his actions and highlighting his grace as the natural overflow of a caring Father's heart. Reflecting this idea, my daughter once said to me: "Daddy, I know you love me no matter what I do—that's like Jesus isn't it?" Though still a child, she really got it. Of course, I scooped her up in my arms and showed my love for her even more!

CREATION: THE INTIMACY OF IMAGE MAKING

God's creation of humanity was itself a powerfully intimate act. He said, "Let us make mankind in *our* image" (Gen. 1:26, emphasis added). He made a personal investment in us—a spiritual and emotional likeness. Hebrew scholars draw attention to the profound implications of the grammar of Genesis 2:7. God did not *give* Adam a soul; he created him *as* a living soul, as a living personality interacting with his Creator. Your natural tendency to seek relationships in general, and intimacy with God in particular, is not simply an added human attribute—it's who you are! You were born for love, and nothing less can adequately define or justify your essence.

Most clients who walk into my office live in a world of relational pain. They talk about depression, loneliness, insecurity, never measuring up, resentments, and the like. But what they are invariably describing is a frustrated desire to be loved and to love someone in return. Ask a client if she is lonely, and she will often break down in a torrent of tears. Mention something about God's love, and he will comment on the lack of it in his relationships. One woman said to me: "All I crave is for someone to hold me and tell me I'm truly loved. I just want to feel special to someone. . . . Is that too much to ask?"

To capture the imagination and stimulate the hope of emotionally hungry people, we have to demonstrate that human-to-human love is an obtainable reality. This tangible demonstration has always been, and still is, the most powerful pathway to understanding the reality of God's love.

Time spent with, say, a Christian counselor or someone in a helping role may be a person's first true encounter with authenticity in a relationship. One of the goals of that relationship is the client's experience of God's loving presence. But, as important as that is, it's only the beginning.

Somehow, that person must also learn new ways of connecting this experience to relationships with the important people in his or her life — in ways that will eventually make counseling no longer necessary.

Confronting your hidden fears, dealing directly with your anger and guilt, admitting your feelings of shame — this work is not merely cathartic; it is transforming. It takes the energy you may have long used nonproductively and redirects it toward fulfilling relationships and meaningful interactions. But no one breaks old patterns easily. You would think the intense pain of such patterns would stimulate us to action. Sometimes it does. But we humans have a remarkable capacity for denial and, therefore, resist the change that would ultimately reduce our pain. Every time we ignore our natural warning signals, we are saying, in effect, "I know a better way."

The illusions of the fall die hard.

God's love has always been amazingly patient. He doesn't just endure rejection; he takes action. It was natural for him to lavish his sacrificial love upon us by sending his Son. He knew that it was the love we sorely needed (Rom. 5:6–8).

The gospel is the story of a sacred intimacy no other faith can duplicate. It moved the apostle Paul to claim that we become an entirely *new* creation when we accept our Lord's offer of redemption (2 Cor. 5:17). This offer of a new spiritual intimacy is utterly unique, which is why it has become the focal point of all of human history. Other religions focus on what humans can do for God; only Christianity looks at what God has already done for us. It is his grace, not our determination, that is responsible for the outcome.

It's reassuring that even Hollywood, in its moral vacuum, occasionally gets something right. The script for the film *Tuck Everlasting* (2002) was written around the theme that if we fear anything, it should be the unlived life—the stagnation of so many relationships that pass for intimacy. Our frantic lifestyles too often rob us of the time it takes for meaningful interaction. Many marriages, which somehow manage to avoid divorce, nonetheless exist in a state of living death. Isn't the indiscriminant self-medication of our culture evidence of this lifestyle's emptiness? Must we exist as mere caricatures of the divine image, always searching for momentary pleasure? Little wonder that depression is so prevalent.

Observe the woman displaying anger toward her husband but inwardly grieving over her loneliness—the loss of "the man she married." She turns away from him to church and friends as her only comfort. Or the husband, depressed about a marriage that's evaporating before his eyes, believing he can never please his wife. He retreats from her and into work as his only solace. Is this what intimacy was supposed to look like? The answer, of course, is obvious.

Often, both husband and wife are experiencing emotional crises. But what happens next depends on their choices. Will they listen to the signals and realize that their depression is pointing toward change? Or will they react defensively, resorting to blaming or stonewalling?

If they ignore the warnings of an impending relational meltdown, they will inevitably live a life of regret. I remember one woman said after her divorce, "My husband and I could never get past our accusations of one another—it just seemed like we were both so depressed that we were determined to make each other equally miserable. If only we could have realized what we were doing . . ."

We see, then, that depression not only serves as a warning, but it can also alter the relationship pattern itself. Emotional pain, like its physical counterpart, sharply narrows your focus. It turns you inward, creating a variety of communication problems. For instance, self-preoccupation can impede your ability to listen accurately to others and, as a result, to empathize with them. Without the ability to see life from the other person's perspective, you cannot connect intimately.

These effects are most profound when we fail to recognize depression in one another as potentially a sign of trouble in the relationship. It can be misused, instead, to justify retreat into silence or lashing out in defense. Some tend to talk about their depression as an overpowering "condition," as if it has a life of its own. If only they could have more understanding, more tolerance . . . and be held less responsible for their actions. Self-pity sets in as they sink still further into their "victim" mindset. One man who talked this way complained, "Why can't people see that I *can't* help myself . . . so why won't they accept that?" He failed to see that although God was in charge of creating the opportunity, *he* was responsible for changing his behavior.

Sometimes whole families—by their choices of words, decisions, and self-imposed limitations—are organized around a single member's depression. They are conditioned by the fear of triggering yet another wave of negative reaction. Mother will tell the kids, "Don't make any noise; your father is not feeling well, so we all need to be quiet." Or Father may say, "It's important to obey your mother—you know how bad she feels when you misbehave." Guilt manipulations are often part of the effort to avoid another meltdown.

These destructive relational outcomes result when you cannot see the purpose of depression. But when you understand it as the likely result of unprocessed problems, you have a better chance of discovering the core issues and resolving them. Sometimes, however, you are unable to reach this understanding on your own. That may be the consequence of judgment compromised by surrender to helplessness. You can better resist resignation if you view your depression not as personal defeat, but as a context for pursuing a different course of action. This requires, however, the willingness to do some hard emotional work— something that many people spend their lives avoiding.

You were created both for a purpose and with a purpose. God never leaves anything to chance. We see his purposeful actions throughout redemptive history. In the events leading up to the exodus, for example, God targeted each of the ten plagues at one of Egypt's false gods, demonstrating his superiority over each of them.

Though these were acts of judgment, they were also compassionate demonstrations (both to the Egyptians and the Hebrews) that God is the sole intervening power of the universe. Intimate connection is never far from his thinking.

We can see the design in God's every act of creation and in his every act in history—even in our lives. He is a relational God who loves all he has created. Given that initial investment, we are assured that all his actions in our lives are directed toward the goal of healing, protecting, and glorifying his image in us.

TAKING RESPONSIBILITY: A LESSON IN LOVE AND MEANING

Knowing what it means to be created in the image of God is essential for understanding the human experience. If you assume that everything is merely traceable to material causes, you will inevitably draw misleading conclusions and make false predictions. You must therefore look in a different direction to find the true blueprint for human behavior.

The average person, though, is not so much interested in the technical details as in the practical implications of human knowledge. He or she prefers to focus on what seems to make life more worthwhile, fulfilling, and meaningful. In the end, most people simply want to believe that their lives matter—that there's a point to living beyond just using up space and oxygen.

Ironically, centering the universe on ourselves can never achieve this goal. We cannot manufacture our own purpose, as humanists attempt to do. Rather, egocentrism has an ignoble way of leading us into an endless void.

Faith, however, leads us down a very different path. It prompts us to focus not so much on answering the questions the culture raises, but on questioning the answers the culture gives. We can only find meaning beyond the natural order by seeking truth with spiritual eyes. That's what makes the divine image so important. It's humbling to seek answers through God's revelation and not merely in ourselves. Then again, humility in the name of wisdom is always far better than ignorance in the name of vanity.

Following the path of wisdom is, of course, what reveals the importance of your creation. Yet those who are convinced they're unlovable inevitably look elsewhere for significance. In Andrew Lloyd Webber's musical *The Phantom of the Opera*, the disfigured phantom, caught up in his self-hatred, implores his young hostage to relieve his unbearable solitude and love him genuinely. But the maiden loves another, and the phantom lashes out in murderous rage. Tragically, the phantom's loneliness and "unworthiness" is self-imposed. He believes he is a victim, imprisoned by the ugliness of his burn-scarred face and spurned by a society that rejects anything short of beauty. But, in reality, he is his own jailor, thwarting his own yearning for a bond of intimacy. In the end, the strangely discordant opera he composed for his beloved, reflected a life out of tune with reality, inharmonious with the music of life he sought.

Here you see all the interacting elements of the divine image, intended to form loving connections but now distorted by rejection and humiliation. The phantom's misguided efforts ended in self-destruction. Few people seek answers by means of such monstrous behavior, but most of us have used some form of self-defeating behavior in our attempts to escape loneliness, rejection, and self-hatred.

In one way or another, every counterproductive attempt to find relief is a way of avoiding personal responsibility for your growth. Expressing outrage about your circumstances produces no long-term rewards. You may blame God, people, or fate—rarely, if ever, acknowledging your own poor choices—but to do so is to surrender to the deception of helplessness. Relinquishing self-control means giving up the idea of taking active steps toward a remedy.

FOLLOWING DEPRESSION'S LEAD

Louis Pasteur once noted, "In the fields of observation, chance only favors the mind which is prepared."[2] Everyone should understand the nature of depression, whether or not they're dealing with it now. It's never too early to learn what it really means, what to expect when this alarm system is triggered, and how to follow its path to growth.

Those who have gone through depression often experience, among other surprising benefits, a greater sensitivity to the suffering of others. Adversity strengthens not only your coping skills, but your empathy as well (2 Cor. 1:3–4). A client of mine who had struggled with depression was able to comfort his wife through a subsequent trauma of her own. With new understanding, he came alongside her as a healing companion in her despair. He was instrumental in helping her, in time, to successfully process her experience. After the worst had passed, she reflected on her husband's help: "He is so different now. I have never seen him as sensitive as he is now. Though it was awful when we went through it, his depression has changed him . . . and I mean for the good!" It was apparent that his personal struggle had produced an empathy that strengthened their marriage.

God never wastes an experience, even a painful one. Even if you don't understand what's happening in the moment, your anticipation of growth can help you endure and see it through.

The usefulness of this purpose-driven mind-set is captured in a humorous incident during a family vacation a few years ago. We were visiting extended family on a farm near the Ozarks. On a hot, humid afternoon, we noted that their dog, which appeared old and worn out, lay nearby breathing laboriously and moving as little as possible. My wife's cousin Ron grinned and told us the dog was his bird dog, capable of chasing down fallen birds with the best of them. He went into the house and soon reemerged, holding his favorite shotgun. Immediately, the slumbering dog leaped to his feet—ears erect, tail extended—and began running in circles and barking like a pup, ready for bird hunting. Ron broke into hearty laughter over our startled reaction and reminded us that "a dog with a purpose is a dog unleashed for action."

What a parable for the human scene! When you see a clear reason—for your depression in the short run or for your life in the long run—you find new energy, conviction, and longing to follow your deepest desire. It unleashes a revitalized motivation to pursue the blueprint of your creation!

When you fail to grasp the point of your existence, it is easy to slide into despair—even suicidal ideation. When depression becomes merely a part of life with no meaning beyond its symptoms, it takes on the color of resignation, washing your entire future in shades of gray. The resulting apathy cripples your ambition and fosters little more than some form of escapism.

This kind of acquiescence to the status quo is similar to the way so many rationalize sin as moral expediency. "That's just modern life" is the common refrain of relativism. They make a pact with culture: Cede moral authority to "them," and the anonymous "they" becomes the defense against acknowledging personal sin. Author John Eldredge laments, "Something awful has happened; something terrible. Something worse, even, than the fall of man. For in that greatest of all tragedies, we merely lost Paradise—and with it, everything that made life worth living. What has happened since is unthinkable: We've gotten used to it. We're broken in to the idea that this is just the way things are."[3]

In a similar fashion, when you adapt to depression, refusing to acknowledge its signal value, you slip into the abyss of lost hopes, dreams, and relationships—a continuous repetition of the same unproductive thinking and behavior that triggered the alarm in the first place. God has placed within us a desire for much more than that. But when we refuse to take the necessary risks in God's love, we fall back on the principle that nothing ventured is nothing lost. By then, *everything* has been lost already.

THE VIRTUE OF HOPE AND THE HOPE OF VIRTUE

It has been said even the remotest hope is far better than its absence. For with hope comes the determination to change. But its absence robs you of even the willingness to try. Remember, it's the precious moments of joy in your life that give you a glimpse of a future governed by hope.

A Samaritan woman came to the town well one fateful afternoon. She had hoped for a life of love, but her pursuit of tenuous marriages and promiscuous relationships had led only to disillusionment. Jesus met her there, knowing her soul's desperate thirst, and he offered her the living water of his transcendent peace. At last, her thirst was quenched and her hope for a life worth living fulfilled. With excitement, she exclaimed to her startled neighbors, "Come, I have found the Messiah!"

Today, Jesus calls you to something greater than you can ever imagine. But we humans are often blind to his mercy and deaf to his words of truth. A veil of emotional trauma obscures our view of God and distorts our view of self. We often have refashioned truth according to our own "wisdom," twisting it into something unrecognizable. God may choose to answer your pain with a compelling revelation of your irrational beliefs. Or maybe he will bring people into your life who point out these things for you. Or, in his wisdom, he may simply choose to wait and let life's consequences do their work of teaching.

God's actions or inactions may not always make sense to you. Indeed, you may become impatient, accusatory, even cynical. Yet, as remarkable as it may seem, God fully understands your response. He is not fragile! He knows full well that you will never completely comprehend his infinite wisdom. Nor can you begin to understand the sheer magnitude of his righteousness.

But trusting in his virtue is the choice that makes the difference between perceiving God as a righteous Father and viewing him as a petty dictator. It is your acceptance of God's goodness that gives you the confidence to disclose the troubled contents of your depressed mind and heart, knowing that it will provoke his compassion, not his wrath and judgment.

It's this sense of safety that's necessary to pry open the closed hearts of damaged people, to peel back the patches of lifeless bravado that have sealed their deep wounds. In relationship with God, a trusting heart is a healing heart. And a community of believers that speaks God's tender words of truth is a healing community.

With these loving connections, you may begin, at last, to reclaim and repair the character of your divine image.

FINDING HOPE

1. Emotional signals like depression are part of a warning system meant to guard the divine image. As such, they are vital for preventing further damage.

2. God's answer to humanity's dilemma? An incorruptible love brought to bear on a need to be loved that has been corrupted by sin.

3. You were created by love and for love. Understanding this concept is essential for appreciating your human identity and for providing personal meaning.

4. The best antidote to the temptation to withdraw into helplessness is to recognize that depression sets the stage for true change.

5. God never wastes an experience. When you believe he will grow you through your pain or disappointment, you are better prepared to endure it.

6. Trusting God's goodness is the first step in building the intimate connections that are healing to your divine image.

DEPRESSION AND
THE GRAND BLUEPRINT

Every one of us is given the gift of life, and what a strange gift
it is. If it is jealously preserved, it impoverishes and saddens,
but if it is spent for others it enriches and beautifies.

—Ignazio Silone, Italian politician and editor

When depression sounds its alarm, there is a clear reason you must take a closer look. But examining your core beliefs and the experiences that gave rise to them is an ordeal in which few of us find pleasure. Still, it can unearth the true basis for most of your problematic behavior. The trouble is that helpful information isn't all you turn up: pain, anger, guilt, and fear surface as well.

Yes, some core beliefs can arouse joy, excitement, and anticipation. But many of us dredge up old wounds and messages that formed what we believe to be the "real me" under our façade—the helpless, inadequate, unlovable, bad, worthless "me" that we believe in but try to deny. They also shape corollary beliefs about other people ("They're all malicious" or "No one can really be trusted"). Together, such notions grossly distort our view of the world as well as ourselves. And they blind us to the beauty of the divine image within.

Depression also signals the presence of that notorious companion of fear and guilt called *shame*, which tells you there's no reason to feel the way you do. False shame is a reaction of humiliation and self-criticism to pain and personal threat from the past—the origins of which are often cloaked in secret, selective, and often disturbing memories. Devastating abuse, parental neglect, or over-dominance by others early in life may have trained you to respond with destructive misdirection in the present. You may devise protective measures—parallel lives, illusions, denial—designed to keep others away from the door to your inner life. These self-defeating measures only cause, in the long run, worse pain than the truth. When your defenses begin to collapse, as they eventually do, depression is there, telling you to reconstruct your coping skills. Your injury once again takes center stage, insisting that the status quo is no longer acceptable.

Depression is a call to personal courage. Hard though it may be to accept, depression is designed to bring you back to the truth—to what you were originally intended to be. Shame and fear may tempt you to retreat, but depression challenges you to sift through the rotting garbage—the lies you tell yourself, learned from your parents or others, who themselves were in pain.

Courage doesn't mean fearlessness. Courage is doing what's right in spite of your fear. It means reversing the anxiety-driven, self-hypnotic trance of your internal monologues, confronting your secrets with the power of truth. But your self-deceptions will try to intimidate you, claiming the authority of people you used to trust. They survive as long as they keep you cowed—but the sooner you examine and oppose them, the sooner they will begin to crumble.

Whoever you are, at your foundation is the image of God, perfectly designed, conceived in love, and intended for nurture. You are forever God's handiwork, and no amount of emotional damage changes this fact. The people in your life who care and can help—therapists, pastors, or friends—are, in reality, servants of the soul, seeking to restore to visibility what God has already created in you.

A renewed life requires a revived blueprint, the original one that expresses God's goodness in you. The old family rules and experiences—the ones that crippled and distorted this blueprint—have made a mockery of the value God placed on you. In the process, they caused your identity in the divine image to fade from view. You must start, then, by reconstructing this identity. That means rediscovering the attributes of the divine image.

Together, these attributes help form the structure of human personality, making human beings utterly unique among the species.

THE COGNITIVE DIMENSION:
THINKING ABOUT OUR THINKING

I (Gary) was playing the game of peek-a-boo with our two-year-old grandson, Jacob, and I noticed he was doing something new. Before, he would giggle when he saw me suddenly appear from behind a wall—but now he would walk around the corner, looking for me. Peek-a-boo had now become hide-and-seek.

The former game is based on the element of surprise, the latter on the thrill of discovery. Our grandson had attained what developmental specialists call "object permanence." Early on, when objects or persons would disappear, in his mind they no longer existed. But now he understood that objects continued to exist even if he couldn't see them, and so he actively hunted for them. This and subsequent benchmarks of mental growth eventually lead to abstract thinking, which is what sets Jacob and all other humans apart from the rest of creation.

Perhaps foremost then among the attributes of God's image in us is this *cognitive dimension*. It gives us our self-reflective consciousness, enabling us to think about the human condition, to formulate a philosophy of life and to make free choices—including tragic ones—that determine our direction in life. It was once said that we are "the only part of creation that seeks to know *all* of creation."

This distinctly human thirst to know is also connected to our desire for control.

It's a pity, though, that we fail to better train our mental faculties for cultivating relationships. We learn to solve problems in order to adapt mentally and physically to the material world, but that's not enough. We must also learn to live with one another.

Our thinking cannot be separated from our freedom of will. Indeed, our thinking shapes our choices just as our choices shape our thinking. Choices like accepting God's imprint.

Our cognitive capacity allows us to discover significance in what we do, to plan a future with specific goals. It also informs our ability to see alternatives. Part of the reason for depression's clamor is to redirect our attention to the choices we've made to determine whether other options are better. Often, they are.

The Bible is by no means silent concerning the importance of our thought life. In Proverbs 23:7, we read, "As [a man] thinks within himself, so he is" (NASB). Our thinking habits form the people we eventually become, largely determining whether we become optimistic or pessimistic, rage-filled or peaceful, victimized or victorious. In Jeremiah 17:9–10, we're reminded that our thought life is naturally deceitful and self-serving, which is why we need the Holy Spirit's reality checks.

You put your thinking to the test by submitting it to the light of God's Word. This is a difficult personal discipline that requires a humble admission of weakness, ignorance, and sin.

But your thought life also represents the central avenue to your heart. In Philippians 4:6–9, the apostle Paul taught that right thinking can help you replace your anxiety with the peace of God. By monitoring the content of your thought life—meditating on whatever things are good and true, things that nurture truth and courage—you can remain centered in the reality of God's presence and avoid the paralyzing effects of obsessive negative rumination.

Paul was not a first-century Norman Vincent Peale, preaching the power of positive thinking, but rather a first-century proponent of the power of *godly* thinking. We're not talking about spiritualizing every problem and flinging verses in every direction at the slightest provocation. Those who do so may seem pious, but underneath they tend to be critical and insensitive to other people's needs. They're often insecure, attempting to live within an insulated, compulsive world they control. They hide behind their faith, intimidating others to prevent them from getting too close. This is clearly *not* what the apostle meant.

Paul's version of godly thinking focused on priorities such as reconciliation rather than destructive conflict; emotional freedom instead of burdensome restrictions; grace over legalism, progressing toward a clearer, sometimes uncomfortable reality, rather than regressing back to familiar but dysfunctional ways of thinking.

I know the effects of a legalistic thought life firsthand. I was raised in a church where playing cards was seen as corruptive, dancing of any sort—even square dancing—was seductive, and attending public school rather than private Christian school fell far short of the mark. (That is not to say that private Christian schools are not a good thing; they are. It's just that attending one was never meant to be the litmus test for proper spiritual standing.) These things were communicated not so much by formal teaching but by judgmental attitudes or behavioral codes. Thus, I became quite familiar with the experience of guilt and all the distorted thinking that comes with it. I also know, however, how freeing it is to be unburdened from false sanctions by having a truer understanding of genuine faith.

Fear of humiliation can cause you to seek advantage by engaging in a kind of intellectual subterfuge. You must be careful not to sacrifice truth by letting others do your thinking for you. But you also must not act out of vanity. When a husband and wife accuse each other of a "lack of submission" or "un-Christlike headship," they're often being intellectually dishonest, assuming a self-righteous position that is merely self-validating. Clinging stubbornly to their own version of "the truth," each spouse puts most or all of the blame on the other. At the same time, they avoid any reality testing for their own point of view. Their marriage usually suffers the consequences, with one or both spouses more than likely becoming depressed.

I saw a couple who were emotionally exhausted from being on trial all the time. "He never listens to me, but when he does, he dismisses everything I say," the wife said with exasperation. "She never gives my views the time of day," the husband countered. The two were locked into a perpetual battle for accuracy (and for control), completely unaware that their respective views were little more than subjective evaluations. More importantly, their arguments only reinforced the thinking that they really didn't matter.

The content of your thinking determines your feelings and behaviors in all of your relationships. Like modern cognitive therapy, the New Testament teaches that your thoughts influence the quality of your emotional life. But you can't make long-term positive changes by simply resolving to think well. Here's where the intellectual component of the divine image must lean heavily on the spiritual component. Without faith in God to guide and strengthen you, you have no moral compass to chart a new mental path. On your own, you can easily use your "beliefs" to justify a sinful lifestyle.

You've inherited your capacity for self-reflection from your Creator. It puts you in touch with your built-in desire to connect with someone beyond yourself. Above all, it gives you the ability to sift through the evidence of his love, to discover the purpose for living.

THE EMOTIONAL CONNECTION: THE DEPTH OF PASSION

Another attribute of the divine image in us is our capacity to emote. This *emotional dimension* makes sense only in relationships, where our feelings deepen our interactions and give communication its richness and complexity. It's also where we find most of the important alarm systems that warn us of relational trouble.

In the Gospels, we read that it was Jesus' emotional life that bridged his divine nature and his humanity (for example, Matt. 9:36; 15:32; 26:36–38; Mark 3:5; 11:12–17; Luke 7:13; 19:41; John 11:33–35). It's a major reason why we connect so deeply with him. Having been transformed by the power of the cross, we have unlimited access to his boundless compassion.

What's more, Jesus' free expression of emotion gives us the freedom to admit to our own. This is what allows us to blend our hearts with his. It is part of the "here and now" experience of redemption that complements and fills out our intellectual contemplation of it.

And it paves the way for the power of passion.

Passion is, of course, a two-edged sword. While it deeply enriches your experience of intimacy, if uncontrolled, it can be destructive. You can find both sides of passion in marriages where the spouses tend to have opposite traits (which are common). One partner may be more impulsive and expressive, the other more routine-driven and cautious. Each sees in the other some quality they intuitively know they need in order to experience a healthy balance—but that same quality can also be a source of significant irritation.

A socially gregarious, emotional woman may marry a quiet, introverted man because she is drawn to the fact that he seems to have his feet on the ground. But she will often find later that she is irritated by his "stick in the mud" attitudes about getting together with others. He, on the other hand, may become irritated by the sense that he is always being dragged to one social function after another, even though he was initially attracted to the way she seemed so active and "full of life."

One way a relationship can go wrong is when one or both partners try to change the other to be more like themselves. Usually, the extroverted person does this by means of overt aggression, and the introvert by means of passive aggression. This only puts the marriage under stress, often leading to depression in both spouses.

You most likely learned your more troublesome emotional reactions in your home of origin. If you grew up in an emotionally repressive family, you're likely to be much less spontaneous in your adult relationships, less emotionally open, and on guard against a closeness that feels unfamiliar and threatening.

This was the plight of a man who came into my office grieving the loss of his twenty-five-year marriage. He said he loved his wife but had found it nearly impossible, for some reason, to voice this love to her. Underneath, he yearned to be loved, but his wife felt deprived and eventually left him. The last thing she said to him was, "I can't take the silence anymore; I don't know how you can go day after day without showing any affection or demonstrating any interest in talking about our relationship. Apparently you'd just as soon be alone; but, for me, I want something more, a lot more." With that, she walked away.

Similar results have occurred in personal friendships and even work relationships that have suffered from a lack of emotional depth. Whether due to insufficient social skills or to controlling manipulation, or whether it is simply a smoke screen for anger, continual silence can be destructive. Even though silence may feel safe to some, too much of it tends to kill relationships. The crisis of depression in situations like these is likely telling you that your feelings are not as dangerous as they seem, and that you will find the fulfillment you seek when you set free the emotional characteristics of God's image in you.

Any practicing therapist will tell you that these are the kinds of issues that motivate people to seek help. It's rarely about intellectual differences. That's why it's the *process* of conflict rather than its content that usually arouses pain and anger. It's feeling invalidated—not experiencing disagreement—that destroys a relationship. In other words, believing your feelings, opinions, or preferences don't count.

It's not surprising then that the emotional dimension of the divine image, which is the source of many critical alarm systems, is so important in diagnosing and solving problems with relational intimacy. When people regain hope, they begin to see that these alarms, once activated, are urging them to take ownership of the solution.

While your thinking abilities help you develop your belief systems, your emotional capacities invest your beliefs with priority and intensity. Without the rich texture of emotional clarity, such beliefs lack the conviction to steer you in the right direction. The temptation of that indiscriminate glance or that risky indulgence only reveals the arid state of your emotional life. Terrible damage awaits you down this path— sometimes irrevocable damage. Paradoxically, the same passion that adds depth to your experience can also become the excuse for your most destructive impulses.

When you have abused your freedom by crossing the line, you have already lost the innocence of intimacy. Still, restoration is available. Jesus always stands ready to bring us back to the Father's image in us. It's his grace that frees us from the imprisonment of our past.

THE MORAL CONNECTION:
THE CHARACTER OF CONVICTION

Your intellect is necessary for understanding the significance of truth. Your emotional capacity is necessary for experiencing the significance of love. However, it's your moral character that's necessary for seeing the significance of sin and the beauty of righteousness. Your moral sense allows you to be convicted by God's still small voice and cheered by the murmurs of his pleasure. This *moral dimension* of the divine image provides you with the awareness of what is holy, just, and virtuous. It's the source of your ability to discern right from wrong, to distinguish between good and evil.

In the beginning, humanity encountered only good in fellowship with the Father. But after the fall, men and women discovered the destructiveness of evil. That's why every human society has followed some code of ethics that reflects the collective conscience of its people.

Because of our cravings for sin, we experience healthy guilt to guide us back to our moral bearings and to the joy of honoring God. It's our compass in times of temptation, confusion, and compromise.

Perhaps more than any other aspect of the divine image, we're apt to neutralize or neglect the moral dimension. We silence the voice of integrity, the claims of conscience within.

We underestimate the seduction of evil and minimize the dangers of vice. We ease our discomfort over ethical lapses with rationalizations like "Everybody does it" or "It doesn't harm anyone." Yet we often pay a price for such mental gymnastics—a type of depression that won't go away until we come to terms with our moral compromises.

Your self-defeating behavior demonstrates how easy it is to subvert the original intention of your alarm systems. Sometimes, the careless exercise of free will short-circuits God's design for your safekeeping. The truth is that you cannot think well, love well, or live well if you haven't chosen well. You can act with moral honor, or you can deceive yourself into accepting the unthinkable. Either way you're defining the self. As Andrew Solomon puts it, "We can never escape from choice itself. One's self lies in the choosing, every choice, every day."[1]

Without the morality of the divine image, you would be unable to appreciate God's view of your choices. Moral conviction may seem pitiless in its assessment of your foolishness, but it also affirms your godly intentions. That's the point of your heavenly Father's correction.

THE SPIRITUAL CONNECTION: CHANNEL OF DIVINE GRACE

Your moral sense interacts with and is activated by the *spiritual dimension* of God's image within you. This dimension makes you aware of a reality that exists beyond your temporal experience. Since the dawn of time, we humans have been aware of something or someone greater than ourselves. Although this awareness has often been expressed in idolatry and superstition, it follows from the unmistakable relevance of natural revelation.

Time and again missionaries have reported wholesale conversions of certain tribes in remote regions—conversions that occurred immediately upon first presentation of the gospel message. Long before any missionary arrived, these people acknowledged a divine power behind nature and sought a greater revelation. When they heard the gospel, they rejoiced that God had answered their petitions.

A missionary friend of mine once shared that he had had such an experience in the remote mountains of Mexico. From the first day he arrived, in one village after another, the tribespeople fell down and worshiped Jesus, exclaiming with tears streaming down their faces, "Our God has not failed us . . . at last, we have his name!"

Long ago the writer of Ecclesiastes taught that God has placed eternity in the human's heart (Eccl. 3:11). The seventeenth-century philosopher Blaise Pascal called it a "God-shaped vacuum." Yet, despite our consciousness of the supernatural, we still resist turning our hearts to the God of creation (Rom. 1:20–23). We invent our own gods or worship the created order itself. We worship ourselves.

If you recall from the last chapter, I argued that, in one way or another, every religion *except* Christianity makes good works the source of our salvation. In other words, people define their importance chiefly by the authority they assume for themselves—not by the grace God extended to them through the cross. This self-focus closes their eyes to God's eternal power in creation and leaves them vulnerable to their own finite thinking.

Much of human philosophy is a rational attempt to explain away our mysterious spiritual impulses. Most modern intellectuals refuse to accept the idea that spirituality is even an aspect of the self—let alone that it responds to God's voice. In psychology, this antipathy toward God began with Sigmund Freud, who struggled most of his life to come to terms with the "irrationality" of the spiritual worldview. His brilliant colleagues, part of a faith-sensitive intellectual community of the time, tended to dismiss his reasoning about God by raising questions he couldn't adequately answer.

Harvard psychiatrist Armand Nicholi, Jr., contrasts Freud's thinking with that of Oxford professor C. S. Lewis. Nicholi points out that Freud's private ambivalence fueled his public determination to prove his case for atheism. Lewis converted from atheism to Christianity because of the faith's inherent logic, but Freud never acknowledged the historicity or consistency of the Scriptures. Instead, Freud constructed a model that explained away human spirituality with such terms as "universal obsessional neurosis," "projected wish fulfillment," "ignorance," and "superstition."

Freud himself was raised in an Orthodox Jewish home. Yet his rejection of his father's faith led him not to "enlightenment," but to a lifelong bout with depression. He could have heeded this warning signal and acknowledged the emptiness of his atheism. But instead he tried to numb his despair through a variety of sedatives, leading eventually to a cocaine addiction.

Throughout history, we have seen cultural upheavals spawned by the denial of the spiritual, which led to degradation, violence, and downfall. The French Revolution, springing out of the distinctly antireligious bias of the Enlightenment, led to one of the most brutal and bloody periods of French history. It didn't help that the corruption of church leadership left the people with an insufficient cultivation of their spiritual character. So without spiritual guidance, there was nothing to moderate or redirect the rage unleashed by the revolution. What began as a noble effort to give voice to the peasant ended in the chaos of naked revenge.

The mayhem of the Bolshevik Revolution—and the ensuing nine decades of "national depression" in the Soviet Union—is but another tale of disaster that arose out of a spiritual void. It was sparked by the atheistic writings of Karl Marx, who inspired such despots as Vladimir Lenin and Joseph Stalin. Much the same can be said of the influence of Friedrich Nietzsche's godless thinking on Adolf Hitler's brutal Third Reich. As history shows, where divine revelation is denied, where God becomes merely an asterisk of a former culture, life disintegrates into human tragedy.

"The fool has said in his heart, 'There is no God,' they are corrupt, and have committed abominable injustice" (Ps. 53:1 NASB). Evidently, a spiritual worldview is important for building a meaningful society where goodwill is honored and the individual is valued.

It's interesting that those who most oppose spiritual things often come from strong religious backgrounds. They also tend to show clear signs of angry depression. When I was a psychology student in the late 1960s and 1970s, I learned that one of my professors who was hostile to Christianity had a strong, albeit legalistic, evangelical background. At the college where I taught, I discovered the same about colleagues who enjoyed dismantling a student's biblical arguments. I've concluded that many, like Freud, who are hostile to issues of faith may be trying to silence the underlying voice of their own spirituality.

Over the years, I have counseled depressed clients who have had a long history of struggling with the idea of God. Typically, they were annoyed by Christians who seemed confident in their faith. Depressed as they were, they could never bring themselves to believe that a Christian's spirituality was, in fact, real. They were convinced that it must be some sort of false front. Only when these clients became Christians did they understand why faith had appeared to be so disingenuous to them.

In a different way, this is what happened to Saul (who became the apostle Paul) after he witnessed Stephen's martyrdom. Saul didn't deny the reality of the spiritual realm, but he had spent his young-adult life attempting to force it into a legalistic framework rather than the true model of God's grace. Saul's doubts about Pharisaical Judaism were probably raised by Stephen's great defense of the gospel, his heroic death, his peaceful confidence, and his incomprehensible forgiveness of those who stoned him. At some level, Saul must have known Stephen had experienced something the rabbinical teachers had failed to discover. He embarked on a violent crusade to wipe out the Christian community. But God brought him to a point of crisis in which he submitted and allowed God to speak and work through him the way God had always intended.

Despite the continuous assault on the spiritual worldview—by governments and individuals—God refuses to abandon humanity to our own misgivings about things spiritual. Many who encounter depression are, in reality, being urged by their emotional pain to take another look at the divine image they've suppressed. Depression may even be the last wake-up call to our God-ward impulse.

THE SOCIAL CONNECTION: INVITATION TO INTIMACY

The *social dimension* of the image of God is what gives you the desire to connect with other people, to belong to a community of others. You were conceived in the mind of God, who in his essence is relational.

Is it surprising, then, that your primary purpose in life is to taste the fullness of companionship? Adam's greatest loss was his unbroken connection with God. His greatest gift was God's plan to restore it.

Studies have shown that the chronic recluse eventually experiences debilitating emotions, including prolonged periods of depression and sometimes even psychotic behavior. After spending most of a winter alone in Antarctica, Admiral Byrd realized the effects of prolonged isolation: "I find, too, that absence of conversation makes it harder for me to think in words. Sometimes, while walking, I talk to myself and listen to the words, but they sound hollow and unfamiliar."[2]

As the memory of ordinary conversation fades, so too does the brain's ability to process something even as simple as a loving touch.

As babies, we start life seeking caring, intimate touch, attaching ourselves to our parents for love and affection. This attachment provides us with the ability to later trust and feel secure in our relationships with others. Babies deprived of these bonding experiences suffer emotionally long term and even have higher mortality rates.

One of the goals of therapy is to clarify the importance of intimacy and how its absence has hurt you. Otherwise, the conditioned fear of rejection will continue to drive you into debilitating solitude.

Hebrews 10:24–26 warns us against failing to gather with other believers, precisely because our faith requires the nurture of a loving community. When you miss out on Christian fellowship, your faith becomes vulnerable and you become weaker in your beliefs. You're wired to spend time with people—it's absolutely necessary to preserve your spiritual as well as your emotional health. This is what James described as a living faith (James 1:26–27).

It's interesting to note that people who leave their churches seldom do so because of theological differences. They leave because they're lonely. They didn't meaningfully connect with other people and so became restless. Their sense of isolation and sometimes chronic depression reminds us about the importance of bonding. We are born to be in relationship, and our deep longing to be in community only highlights that unchanging truth. One woman told me, "The church has become, for me, the loneliest place on earth. Church members walk past you as if you are invisible; they seem to talk only to their friends, and, to be their friend, you must have to pass some kind of litmus test. . . . I guess, one I obviously failed."

What's true in the church is also true in marriage. In fact, the more intimate the setting, the more intensely you feel its significance. That's why there's nothing more wrenching than loneliness within a marriage.

Randy and Becky entered my office in a state of depression. Each felt let down by the other. Their conflicts fed a growing alienation. Randy escaped to his workshop, and Becky spent hours watching TV. They misunderstood each other's response as rejection, though in reality they were merely protecting themselves from further pain.

Randy moaned, "I just can't compete with that stupid TV—I think she's married to that thing!" Frustrated, she replied, "The only reason I watch so much TV is because you abandoned me to your work ages ago. Do you really think I would just sit on the couch in the dark waiting for you to talk with me?" Ironically, they both longed to restore the friendship they once loved. Eventually they did just that, but not before they suffered many needless wounds.

Our deepest longing is for a shared love, though many have found it sadly elusive. Perhaps you think such experience is little more than the idealism of movies and novels.

But I assure you—we've witnessed it as clinicians and experienced it in our private lives. It's achievable, but unlike Hollywood's portrayal, it takes time and effort.

In an age of instant gratification, where the quick fix is the remedy of choice, the necessity of working at relationships seems oddly foreign. What's more, we tend to define love by what's in it for us. But relationships are fundamentally about others and, ultimately, about God. Only when we accept this reality will we discover what love has to offer.

One of the greatest enemies to this freeing truth is the self-preoccupation of low self-esteem. Because depression is a common result of this divide, we will now turn our attention to this pivotal struggle.

FINDING HOPE

1. You are forever God's handiwork, and no amount of emotional damage changes this fact. What starts with his affirmation will end with it.

2. Your inherited capacity for self-reflective thought gives you the ability to consider a purpose beyond yourself. It also provides you with the ability to recognize the importance of intimacy.

3. Jesus' free expression of emotion is a model for admitting freely to your own. Stoicism is not a part of the godly life, but passion is.

4. You love well when you choose well. It's your moral sense that allows you to appreciate God's view of your choices.

5. Your spiritual longings make clear the unmistakable character of natural revelation and confirm your need for a Redeemer who gives you a purpose for living.

6. As a social being, you find fulfillment in relationships and discover belongingness in community. Depression highlights your need of these things.

PART 2

HOW WE MATTER TO GOD AND WHY IT MATTERS TO US

THE STRUGGLE WITH SELF-WORTH

Self-rejection is the greatest enemy of the spiritual life because
it contradicts the sacred voice that calls us the "Beloved."
Being the Beloved expresses the core truth of our existence.

—Henri J. M. Nouwen

Several years ago, Denise walked into my (Gary) office troubled about the emptiness of her life and her sense of failure as a Christian. Her feelings of worthlessness, inadequacy, and helplessness poured out in sobs. "I'm the biggest disappointment to God on the planet," she cried. "I've tried everything I thought a Christian is supposed to do, but I still feel hopeless and depressed. I can barely get out of bed each day. It's pathetic, isn't it?" She buried her face in her hands for a long moment before again looking at me. "All my life, I've been told that Christians are supposed to ignore themselves, that it was wrong to care about your own needs, even if it means despair." Denise's legalistic understanding of her faith had encouraged her to believe that self-reproach was essential to pleasing God. "I'm worthless; I don't matter," she said softly. "Why don't I just accept that?" Denise was exhausted from trying to alleviate her suffering. At her point of deepest depression, she had sought out her pastor, who had prayed with her and given her some Bible verses to comfort her. She continued her tailspin, so the church elders laid hands on her and prayed for her recovery.

When her depression persisted, an older woman was assigned to mentor her and give her reassurance from God's Word. Meanwhile, some of her friends in her home Bible study group suggested that she might be oppressed by an evil spirit. So they anointed her with oil and prayed for release.

Nothing seemed to bring relief. Denise began to believe she was beyond help and that God had abandoned her. She thought her depression must be due to some hidden sin—sin that, like quicksand, would drag her deeper down if left concealed. So she repented of any sin she could think of, searched the Scriptures, and prayed.

Still, depression kept its grip. In fact, by now, she was even depressed about being depressed. She believed that Christians, at least ones in good standing, were never supposed to suffer through these kinds of dark periods. This belief, of course, only made matters worse.

Finally, a coworker recommended a therapist. At first, she resisted this suggestion because she believed psychology somehow corrupted God's truth. But, eventually, her searing pain convinced her to give therapy a try. "Besides," she thought, "he's a Christian therapist—so he can't be entirely a tool of the Devil!"

So there Denise sat, trembling, certain she had failed God and her friends. Because she had no clue to the nature of her problem, or how to solve it, she was looking for a miracle that would transform her into the "right kind of Christian," happy and content. What she didn't realize was how much her mistaken beliefs, born of earlier emotional wounds, had laid the groundwork for self-rejection.

THE QUESTION OF SELF-WORTH

Some people might brand Denise's agonizing search as "spiritually misguided"—if for no other reason than because she had begun to question God's interest in her. God had seemed just like everyone else in her life. "If he's really unconditionally loving," she reasoned, "shouldn't even a reprehensible soul like me receive a little mercy?"

She just wanted to feel that she was worth something—that she somehow mattered to others—a desire she had been told by a friend was the work of vanity. The legalism she embraced, which focused on repaying God with good works, considered self-reproach almost a virtue. After all, wasn't that part of proper submission to him? She had accepted (but not without some ambivalence) the idea that valuing yourself was part of a worldly, feel-good philosophy that ignored humanity's sinful nature.

This belief is common among Christians. It's well intentioned, but flawed. It equates self-worth or self-esteem with conceit and self-worship, the offspring of a narcissistic culture, and the opposite of biblical humility. It describes self-esteem as "self-importance," an attitude encouraged by seductive pop psychology.

I've counseled some Christian leaders who believed this way. But, in the midst of their own personal crises, they came to realize just how much these ideas had sabotaged their walk with God. One of them put it this way: "It took me awhile, and not without a lot of pain and anguish, but I finally understand now that God actually *wants* us to feel good about who we are. I only wish that I had understood this for all those years I served the church."

So what does healthy self-esteem mean? Is it, as opponents argue, just a rationalization for a selfish lifestyle? Is it really the enemy of humility?

Certainly no one would deny that humility is a hallmark of Christian teaching. But at the heart of the self-esteem controversy is a question: Can a believer live in true humility without a genuine sense of personal worth?

HUMILITY VS. HISTORY

The question of self-esteem's validity is central to our understanding of depression. Virtually everyone with depression experiences low self-esteem. There is no question that self-focus is the greatest obstacle to serving others in a healthy way. Likewise, low self-esteem, which demands pre-occupation with every personal failure, naturally inhibits attention to the needs of others. That's why it cannot coexist with humility.

Let me explain. The Bible defines humility as giving ourselves to one another in love. It is an attitude of service. A humble person is one who reaches out to others, not for praise, but out of gratitude for what

God has already done for him or her. However, people who are hurting tend to withdraw from others (or else prevail upon them for sympathy). This self-preserving strategy is meant to salvage what is left of their sense of worth by protecting them from further rejection or other injury. It's a strategy that avoids taking personal responsibility in a relationship by seeking relief *in isolation*. But withdrawal is rarely a useful solution. It certainly doesn't help them to feel better about themselves. But that doesn't stop those who are motivated almost solely by the avoidance of pain from resorting to isolation.

As Christ-followers, we seek a lifestyle that is honoring to God. To that end, we want to remove every barrier to effective Christian living. It may seem a paradox, but depression serves precisely such a purpose, mainly because it signals that something must change. Low self-esteem often causes us to emotionally walk away from others rather than to walk selflessly toward them. But depression itself is telling us there's something wrong with this picture. It's telling us that we must, instead, experiment with new behaviors to find a remedy.

Sometimes your suffering is the result of sin, a sign that you've drifted from God. More often, though, such suffering is the collateral damage of life in a sinful world, which leaves its mark on virtually every human relationship. Depression results, for instance, from experiences of betrayal or abuse, particularly by someone close to you.

So, indeed, depression is commonly related to sin—at times, your own, but more likely the sin of others who have wounded you. Yet it's equally true that depression is not sinful—nor should it be seen as the central problem. Rather, it's a symptom of something else, alerting you to take a closer look at the real problem.

Sometimes examining your history leads you back to your family of origin and uncovers the sin of the people who were entrusted with your safety. You can begin to see with adult eyes the warped perspectives you developed in response to your parents' damaging behaviors.

You may start to recognize how your childhood grid still interprets the behavior of others—inaccurately—as threatening or demeaning, thus sending you into a nosedive. Although childhood experiences and environmental stressors are not the only factors in depression, they are perhaps the most important ones in identifying core issues.

Regardless of its source, however, one thing is certain: depression is a reliable indicator of emotional injury. It's a helpful diagnostic tool. Indeed, it is a gift, an important guide toward healing the wounds of your past.

LOVE AND SELF-WORTH

When Jesus was asked about the greatest of God's commandments, he offered a comprehensive assessment of Old Testament law: "You shall love the LORD your God with all your heart, and with all your soul, and with all your mind. . . . [And] you shall love your neighbor as yourself. On these two commandments depend the *whole Law* and the Prophets" (Matt. 22:37, 39–40 NASB, emphasis added). In other words, you are obedient to God's commandments whenever you love God and love others. You are to love God with passion (with all your heart), with conviction (with all your soul), and with clarity (with all your mind). And you are to love others in the same way *you* would want to be loved. This is what authenticity really means.

Together, these commandments flesh out in real-life terms the law of love—the law that Jesus came to fulfill both in the life he lived and the death he endured. The Pharisees believed the law of Moses to be a standard of outward conduct, but Jesus showed them that it was so much more. The law is the template for imitating God's love.

Christians read these commandments but often miss their wider meaning. They have difficulty, for example, understanding how loving God's way requires self-acceptance. You are not to use the law to beat yourself over the head. Instead, you are asked to understand that the righteousness of his love applies to everyone. It is this principle that reminds you that you are God's special creation in whom he delights.

This is what we mean when we say that a servant's attitude is the focus of the humble heart. It is an attitude founded on a sense of personal worth affirmed in Christ and a sense of adequacy empowered by the

Holy Spirit. Remember, it may be possible to give without loving, but it's impossible to love without giving. That's the humility of godly love.

As Paul wrote to Timothy (see 2 Tim. 1:7), God has not given you the spirit of fear (which characterizes low self-esteem), but rather the spirit of love, power, and a sound mind (which characterizes high self-esteem). The spirit of fear—that underlying anxiety that frequently accompanies depression—is what undermines your self-esteem and cripples your ambition. It's also what crushes your ability to give.

This is what happened to a young pastor named John. He came to me, paralyzed by a fear so disabling that he was no longer able to carry out his normal preaching responsibilities. He had always doubted that he had the right gifts, even though his friends and congregation routinely confirmed them. He was convinced he was a fraud and considered resigning from the pastorate.

John had struggled with low self-esteem all his life, pressing on only because he didn't want to let people down. Now he felt it was only a matter of time before everyone else recognized him as a failure. He'd grown up with a father who criticized him mercilessly. What's more, he was told daily that he was stupid and would never amount to anything.

Believing he was worthless, he joined other disaffected young people experimenting with drugs and alcohol, an addiction that almost killed him before age twenty. He finally gave up this self-destructive lifestyle when a Christian college professor helped him rediscover his roots in the faith. Turning his energies to serving God, he became a protégé of his pastor, who recognized John's people skills and preaching gifts. But underneath it all, the low self-esteem from a rejecting father never let up. When he took his own pastorate, John expected from the start that he would eventually fall apart and disappoint everyone around him.

But in counseling, John learned to challenge these beliefs and discovered that God had engineered his life as a pastor because he loved him and had gifted him for it. In time, John was "re-fathered" in a new kind of intimacy, a spiritual one. The voice of the critical parent was replaced with the kinder, gentler voice of his heavenly Father, building his confidence and joy.

John realized that he had perpetuated his own victimization. He had chosen to allow the echoes of his father's criticism to control his adult life. John thought he was emancipated, but in reality he continued to believe the messages of his father's earlier abuse. This was the message his depression was signaling, but he hadn't been able to see it until then.

CHOOSING INTIMACY

While your inherent strengths and early life experiences help shape the possible directions you might take, who you ultimately become is determined by the choices you make. These choices can be destructive or they can be growth producing. Your choice of friends, for instance, is important, because friends either encourage you to pursue selfish ends or they inspire you to give of yourself to others. When you make the choice of Jesus Christ as your *best* friend, it will do more than that: he will transform you entirely from the inside out. We have said that your heart's deepest longing is for intimacy. Nothing better is found than in your fellowship with your Lord. "Take delight in the LORD," invited the psalmist, "and he will give you the desires of your heart" (Ps. 37:4).

A client asked me, "Does that mean we get everything we want?" Knowing she meant even our momentary wishes, I answered her by emphasizing that we were created with a natural appetite for uncorrupted love and that only an inclination toward God can satisfy that hunger. She leaned back in her chair, acknowledging her own desire for that kind of love.

Intimacy with God requires a courageous investment. As the psalmist explained, "Commit your way to the LORD; trust in him and he will [satisfy your desires]" (Ps. 37:5). Commitment and trust are the essential pillars of any healthy, loving connection. But, unfortunately, these twin pillars are the first to be abandoned as too dangerous when you have a history of unhealthy, painful family interactions.

That's why people who've been hurt a lot rarely seek true intimacy. Even though they've heard about it, they don't honestly know what the genuine article looks like. Just ask their spouses. You will discover how empty they are, how resigned they've become to despair and loneliness.

That's the reason depression is a critically important signpost urging them to interrupt this pattern, to revitalize the life that's dying inside. Depression gives you the opportunity to listen to your heart's longing for relationship—including a relationship with God.

SELF-ACCEPTANCE AND HUMILITY

From the beginning, lovability has been linked to being created in the image of God. To deny your own lovability is to deny this truth. That doesn't mean your behavior is always lovable. Far from it. But to repudiate your own person is to reject the nature of his. You see, a God who is love cannot create anything in his image that is not lovable. That would be an act against his own character. When you insist on believing yourself to be unlovable, you have been seduced by a lie. Caught in this trap, you reject even logic, because personal experience has convinced you that nothing outside your own subjective reality can be trusted.

Persuasion alone can't change a person's view of him- or herself. A new, more charitable concept of self emerges only from the ability to distinguish who you are from what you do. The value God puts on you, as his creation, is far more accurate than the value you put on yourself as a product of your performance. Only when God's view of your worth becomes your own self-view are you able to experience unconditional love. It's this godly self-acceptance that finds its expression in humble acts of selfless giving—giving that is prompted by the joy of God's grace rather than by the expectation of something in return.

One of the reasons some Christian leaders devalue the concept of self-worth is that they're unable to understand this connection between self-attitude and a servant's heart. They confuse self-worth with arrogant, presumptuous self-importance apart from God. They cannot accept the paradox of grace. Being created in God's image, we're infinitely valuable by divine estimation. Yet, as a result of the first couple's disobedience in the garden, we inherited a corrupted and mortal nature due to our sinful state of independence from God (the original sin), which renders each of us naturally prone to think and act sinfully. But when we've become justified by faith, we are enabled to be obedient because of the work of the Holy Spirit indwelling us—this why, when we are being sanctified, we no longer need to naturally sin. We are intimately connected to the supernatural.

Nevertheless, there is the reality especially early in the spiritual maturation process that we can fall back into relying upon our own means and flesh, rather than God's Spirit—and therein slip back into our old dead nature and sin. These two conflicting natures (the self-willed "carnal flesh" and the Holy Spirit), though in conflict, can coexist within believers. This is why we can encounter so much confusion over explanations of Christian behavior.

To accept and respect your own person is to submit to the glory of God's creative power. This is no excuse for conceit—life is not merely about you. But you can be inspired by your intimacy with God to view yourself more through his eyes and less through your own distorted lenses.

Only when the old evaluation has been replaced can your eyes be opened to the wonder of his redemptive work in you. Only then can you understand self-worth as recognition of God's goodness poured out in your person.

Love changes everything: "I could never really understand when people talked about feeling God's love," said a client of mine recently. "All I ever really felt was fear—fear that he would come down on me if I made the slightest mistake. When I would blow it, I would then cringe, waiting to be struck down with a sickness of some kind or be involved in a car crash or something. But now I see that God isn't like that after all, that he actually wants good things for me. I can't begin to tell you how mind-blowing these ideas are to me!" This is the freedom that comes from knowing who you are in Christ and realizing that if you humble yourself before him, he will raise you up in his warm embrace, not push you away because he thinks your response is too long overdue.

It's important to remember that self-esteem is unknowable apart from its most important characteristic: humility. In fact, self-esteem and humility are so intertwined that the true expression of one cannot occur without the other.

It's only when these two are separated that attitudes toward self become a problem. Highly favorable self-evaluation without humility is indeed what many Christians suspect it to be—another expression of arrogance. But the opposite error, a "servant's attitude" without self-acceptance, is problematic as well; for it is an unrelenting search for social approval. It's a lifestyle of placating others out of fear of rejection, out of an insatiable hunger for affirmation. It's nearly impossible for such people to believe they're God's *beloved* children. A. W. Tozer insisted that "God never thinks any bad thoughts about anybody, and he never had any bad thoughts about anybody."[1] Tozer was talking, of course, about God's thoughts about your person, not your sinful behavior. Nevertheless, many Christians cannot imagine that God doesn't feel negatively about them. They're convinced that even if God's benevolence is true in principle, they are the exception.

In contrast to this pessimism, those who are humble accept not only God's loving attitude toward them, but also the fact that they are "fearfully and wonderfully made" (Ps. 139:14). Among other things, that means they're endowed by him with strengths and abilities to be exercised for his glory.

To experience personal worth, then, you don't have to advertise yourself to get others to notice you. Nor must you devalue yourself before others to get them to compliment you. Instead, a sense of personal worth means that you accept who you are as evidence of God's handiwork, and therefore honor his invitation to enjoy the strengths he's given you.

For that matter, when you as a believer do sin, it means you're free to acknowledge your true failing, which always comes down to not being in right relationship with God's holy, indwelling Spirit. God created us at the core of our nature to be in loving relationship with him—it's the most important aspect of how God created us in his likeness.

This is why sin in the life of a believer is such a contradiction of what God means for our natures to be. All sin is brought about by trusting in one's own human weakness, while God's work of sanctification is about restoring us to what we were created to be. This is why honest, godly humility is *not* destroyed by self-esteem; on the contrary, it's activated by it. Godly humility is not about deserving or knowing one's place—it's about choosing to value another's interest (ultimately, God's interests) above one's own, which is exactly how God himself is humble. When our esteem is about being in God's likeness (rather than being like gods), arrogance is impossible.

When asked why he ran competitive racing events instead of immediately leaving for the mission field, the lead character in the film *Chariots of Fire*, Olympic runner Eric Liddell, shared this memorable line: "I feel God's pleasure when I run because God made me to run fast."[2] Now that's divinely inspired insight into the purpose for God's gifting! Never did Liddell languish in self-reproach for his passion. He understood that God enjoys our triumphs, much as an inventor enjoys the success of what he creates. In time, Liddell went on to other victories, laboring and dying on the mission field in China.

The close connection between self-acceptance and humility is at the core of God's desire for you. You will find no greater statement of your personal worth than in the sacrifice of God's only Son. To God, you are worth that ultimate sacrifice. So when Jesus quoted the law as commanding you to love your neighbor *as yourself*, he was assuming that any acceptance and respect toward others had to be undergirded by your divinely determined self-worth. He taught this almost two thousand years before psychologists recognized the connection between self-attitudes and attitudes toward others and incorporated it into the canon of clinical principles.

Every novice therapist now understands that self-acceptance—not self-centeredness or self-repudiation—is a necessary precondition to open, natural, and nonmanipulative relationships with others. When we are truly self-accepting, we are liberated from preoccupation with how others see us. As one writer put it, "Instead of thinking less of ourselves, we simply think of ourselves less."[3] This frees us to reach out to our neighbors, not self-consciously, as if to impress them, but humbly, so as to serve them.

ARTISTS AND THEIR CREATIONS

In many places in the Bible, God is likened to a potter, crafting what he has willed in his incomprehensibly creative mind. When clients talk of their self-hatred and expressly lament their deep feelings of worthlessness, I often recall this description of God. In fact, I often share with them an experience I once had that forever cemented this potter analogy in my mind.

Years ago, my wife and I traveled down to Laguna Beach, California, to attend an art festival called the "Pageant of the Masters." We'd arrived early, so we decided to visit the downtown area, well-known for its reputation as a haven for artists of every stripe. Browsing through a variety of art stores, I ducked into a pottery shop (an interest of mine) while my wife wandered into the store next door. I admired the beautiful work of this particular potter, while he labored quietly at his potter's wheel in the back of the store. In due time, however, he got up and came over to me and asked if he could help. I told him I didn't have the money to buy any of his pottery, but I really loved and admired his work. I then proceeded to point out some of my favorite pieces. In response, he leaned back and, smiling, said, "Let me give you a glimpse into the soul of the artist."

Taken aback by his unexpected invitation, but also fascinated by the contemplative nature of it, I asked him to please continue. He then proceeded to tell me that the art community of Laguna Beach was a very tightly knit group and that though they differed on many issues, they all agreed on what prompted them to do their work. He said that while he must sell his pottery to make a living, he was not in it to make a lot of money. Instead, what really inspired him (and the other artists) to do what he did was the full pleasure he derived from knowing that his creative handiwork brought pleasure to art-loving people, such as me. "Consequently, my friend," he said, his face glowing, "you made my day . . . in fact, you made my week!" Not knowing what artists thought on this matter, I was grateful that this young man in his tattered overalls had enlightened me about the sensitive inner life of the artistic mind.

I thanked him for his explanation—and his hospitality—and departed. When I got outside, I suddenly remembered (by divine provocation, no doubt) the words of Isaiah 64:8, where we are told that God is the potter and we are his clay. It was as though God had tapped me on the shoulder and said to me, "My son, did you hear what that potter said in there? He spoke for me. You see, I am the potter, and you are the clay from which I crafted something beautiful; all I ask is that you enjoy it. Remember, as the artist, I take great joy when you take genuine pleasure in my creative handiwork, which includes what I crafted in you" (Gen. 1).

In one eye-opening moment, I received confirmation of my worth as inherent in who God created me to be. For you—just as it was for me—it is validated in the strengths with which he has gifted you. When you denigrate yourself and ignore or diminish the value of your strengths (and we all have them), you miss a wonderful opportunity to thankfully acknowledge God's handiwork in you . . . and, likewise, fail to give him the pleasure he desires. That's why genuine, high self-esteem is *not* self-adulation or self-worship, as some mistakenly believe. It's about respecting God's creative hand. It is esteeming what God has produced as the artist.

If you make it all about yourself, you have missed the point entirely. As Isaiah put it, "Does the clay say to the potter, 'What are you making'? Does your work say, 'The potter has no handle?'" (Isa. 45:9). By no means! Such criticism is out of place. The Potter who shaped you is in command of everything. He, not you or anyone else, is the one who determines your value, as well as the value of everything you see and experience. Whether you boast in yourself or, conversely, ruminate on how useless you feel, you make yourself the center of your attention. But the apostle Paul asked us, "For who makes you different from anyone else? *What do you have that you did not receive?*" (1 Cor. 4:7, emphasis added).

So, you see, it is far better that you enjoy your strengths and thank God for giving them to you than to turn it upside down and backward and fail to see his glory. Applying his Word on the matter of your essential worth settles a lot of questions; indeed, it can restore your soul and heal your wounds!

FREEDOM IN THE CROSSHAIRS

Your faith in Christ creates a tension between the forces of good and evil. The struggle between the new nature and the old is always a turbulent battle. But you have the assurance that such inner conflict comes with the territory of redemption and is, in fact, evidence of it.

The apostle Paul expressed honestly the real threat of this struggle. He affirmed the only resolution to it as well: resting in the hope of salvation (Rom. 7:15–25). He affirmed that any compulsive misbehavior only underscored God's mercy, which is why he broke out in a song of praise rather than descending into a spiral of despair. He was saying that a person's struggle with sin should be a reminder of the magnitude of God's forgiveness and an incentive to trust the Holy Spirit to do his work of transformation, not merely perform better or struggle harder.

The purpose of redemption is to reconnect you with the Source of all intimacy. Redemption accomplishes this purpose when you've allowed it to sweep away the debris of your sin and the sins committed against you. In this way, you fine-tune your soul to the same frequency as God's voice.

Free will gives people the unhindered ability to choose evil; that's what makes the choice to love meaningful. That's why, too, we can have among us both an Adolf Hitler and a Florence Nightingale. Eliminating freedom would eliminate any possibility of a truly loving relationship, even though it would also remove the risk of terrifying evil.

As long as believers keep on sinning, there will be corruption in the church. Church splits, religious wars, and the presence of hypocrisy have done untold damage to the cause of Christ. We've all heard non-Christians argue that religion in general (and Christianity in particular) is responsible for more wars and unnecessary deaths than any other single cause in history. This over-generalization paints a false picture of faithful believers. It also ignores a central belief of Christianity—that redemption from sin is an invitation to peace, not a free ticket to sin even more. The apostle Paul said it best: "What shall we say, then? Shall we go on sinning so that grace may increase? By no means!"

(Rom. 6:1–2). So, we can never excuse our sin against others as somehow serving a higher purpose.

Nonetheless, our freedom can seem like a dark force tinkering with the dials of our souls. Sometimes, as wounded believers, we initiate one conflict after another to distract us from the emotional emptiness inside. At other times, we may simply drown ourselves in a sea of self-pity. Either way, we can't seem to silence the boisterous lie of worthlessness within, nor can we solve the riddle of an unwelcome world outside.

To cope, many of us cloak ourselves in a superficial piety, unhesitant to judge others for their sin. Having become brothers and sisters of intolerance, we destroy freedom and creativity, joy and productivity. Even when we become a cause for outside criticism of the church, we dismiss it as evidence of the world's spiritual ignorance. We need to rein in this judgmental attitude, recognizing its harm to our witness, as well as its damage to our own spiritual lives. You cannot dishonor others without also dishonoring yourself . . . and dishonoring God as well.

If behavior alone determined our destiny, divine justice (meaning, punishment) could never be averted. If being right with God were about nothing more than what one deserves, then that's all we'd ever get. But God's infinite grace has nothing to do with deserving: it is always seen beyond the outward behavior to the person—his handcrafted creation. And after all, love never is about deserving or earning; it's always an unconditional gift.

Not even we fallen and failing humans believe it is right for any of us to stop loving our children because they misbehave. Why should we think God, who defines love, could stop loving us because we sin?

His compassion is greater, and so is your value to him.

SELF-DENIAL VS. DENIAL OF SELF

During your early years, you come to believe self-messages from your friends and family. In adulthood, these messages speak so loudly that you may have difficulty hearing, let alone accepting, the new messages of faith. This is particularly true in cases of childhood abuse or neglect. As children, you can't tell the difference between truth and lies, dysfunction and health. But even in adulthood, when these capacities for discernment are in place, few revisit their distorted belief systems. Consequently, old falsehoods continue to damage your self-esteem. That's why the call of your faith is, in part, to do the healing, worldview-changing work of reevaluating your assumptions.

Replacing the messages you give yourself isn't easy, but it can be done. You must learn how these early messages had little to do with you and much to do with the dysfunction of those around you. You must try to understand, too, how these old rules of engagement now sabotage your current relationships, so you can begin to experiment with new ways of engaging others. You'll definitely go outside your comfort zone for a while. But how else can divine grace do its healing work in your wounded soul?

My client Denise was one of these wounded souls, raised in a rigid, perfectionistic home under an autocratic, emotionally cold father. Her dad's unrealistic expectations left her with the enduring belief that she failed constantly and deserved little. With this belief, she ended up in the same kind of relationship in her marriage. She had never understood grace, nor did she question her role as a whipping post for those who were important in her life. Frequently during the course of therapy, Denise returned the conversation to matters of faith: "I'm so afraid I'm going to be guilty of heresy if I start thinking that feeling better about myself is what God wants." She couldn't begin to fathom God's assessment of her worth to him or believe he was interested in her. The best she could hope for was that she could slide quietly under heaven's door—maybe no one would notice she wasn't supposed to be there.

Like Denise, many people suffer under legalism, striving for acceptability by substituting imagined merit for God's standing offer of divine grace. The result is reliably the same: an enduring sense of insecurity before God.

Denise insisted on equating self-rejection with humility. She quoted Jesus: "If anyone wishes to come after Me, he must deny himself and take up his cross and follow Me" (Matt. 16:24 NASB). However, Jesus wasn't saying we should deny our identity or our worth and dignity before God, but to deny selfish desire and self-centeredness. He pictured the Pharisees' displays of righteous posturing, motivated by self-promotion in the eyes of people.

There is a crucial difference between *denial of self*—the humility Jesus taught—and *self-denial*—an emotional and physical deprivation of the kind promoted in Eastern religions. It's the difference between divine grace and human works. Denial of self, by grace, defeats selfish desire—but self-denial is little more than a ritualized system of deprivation, including the rejection of various personal comforts in the pursuit of some kind of mystical spirituality. The importance of works has been the bedrock of Eastern philosophy for more than three thousand years. In fact, in many Buddhist and Hindu sects, you don't even need a concept of God to reach spiritual freedom—a person is capable of attaining spiritual perfection entirely independently. What a contrast to the kind of humility to which Jesus invites us!

Of course, Denise had no idea of this distinction between grace in the denial of self and works in the practice of self-denial. Instead, her self-hatred had entirely blocked her understanding of God's grace toward her. So she had replaced the freedom of the Christian ideal with the deprivation of the abstinence ideal. She attributed her pain to God's silence rather than to her misguided thinking about herself and her faith. Ignoring the warning signal of her depression, she ran aground on the shoals of self-inflicted rejection. That's the tragedy of a faith so distorted by legalism that it no longer serves the emotional needs of the wounded believer.

We need to dispel the notion that self-rejection is the price of discipleship. The true challenge of faith is to regard the suffering in our personal histories as *human* grace denied, not as divine judgment delivered. If the truth really sets us free, then we don't have to repeat these painful histories as adults. We're invited by divine grace to leave behind the baggage of our past—to release resentments, fears, and self-hatred—and to discover for the first time what freedom in Christ truly means—a satisfying life of unobstructed love. God provides the power, but it's up to you and me to make different choices with what we're given in life.

It takes courage to accept God's offer. We can gain strength from the display of Jesus' mercy when he intervened with the woman caught in adultery (John 8:1–11). The Pharisees insisted she deserved stoning according to the law. But Jesus challenged her accusers, inviting anyone who had not sinned to step forward and throw the first stone. The crowd quietly, reluctantly dispersed. Jesus then turned to the woman and declared, "I do not condemn you, either. Go. From now on, sin no more."

Jesus speaks those words to each of us who are caught in the web of our own delusions. He's telling us, in effect, that others can't condemn us because they're sinners, too. And he won't condemn us. He then bids us to live our lives differently.

What an incredible promise—freedom from condemnation and, consequently, freedom from a life of perpetual victimization—in short, the prospect of a new life unburdened by an endless cycle of the same sin and by constant ruminations about the past!

I often give my clients the analogy of a cross-country runner, running while looking backward. What would happen? The runner would crash into signposts and trees, trip over curbs and potholes, doing him- or herself untold damage because he or she wasn't looking forward.

That's what you do to yourself emotionally when you review your past without looking ahead to deal with the present and change the future. You doom yourself to a world of self-condemning rumination or endless self-pity, a world bereft of any option to do something different to bring about a better tomorrow.

This doesn't mean you take a Pollyanna approach to life. Neither does it mean you're supposed to ignore your pain and redefine evil. It means you aspire to the kind of change that recognizes and rejects evil altogether. How can you deny yourself and others what God has so freely given to us all? Nonetheless, if you try, depression will be there telling you that self-rejection is a delusion, one that sentences you to the same emotional imprisonment Jesus saw in the adulteress.

Faith in God was never intended to be religious ritual; it was meant to embrace all you are and all you do. That includes your choices in life. And you do have a choice: Either you rally your resources to alter your course and restructure how you live, or you submit to the lure of resignation and give up. Your decisions can make your faith powerfully relevant or ineffectually irrelevant. It all depends on what kind of life you choose to pursue and what kind of faith you choose to embrace.

FINDING HOPE

1. Depression is neither sinful nor the central problem. Instead it is a signal, often pointing to a longstanding issue that is solvable if given appropriate attention.

2. Putting the emphasis on loving others is the engine of self-esteem and the antidote to personal fear.

3. Personal growth is the direct result of our choices, and healthy choices are the direct result of exercising humility.

4. To fully experience your worth, recognize God's invitation to take pleasure in the strengths he has given you.

5. Self-denial leads to emotional imprisonment, but denial of self leads to emotional and spiritual freedom.

6. Our past does not condemn us, because our future is determined by God's grace through the presence of our faith.

THE LEGACY OF SELF-REJECTION

*The courage to be is rooted in the God who appears when
God has disappeared in the anxiety of doubt.*

—Paul Tillich

Your body is subject to attack by countless viruses, bacteria, and toxins. That's why your physical immune system needs to be strengthened by good nutrition, rest, and exercise—to fight off these invaders. Your spirit, too, needs to be strengthened to resist dangers like hopelessness and self-victimization. For you need to be adequately prepared for injustice, misfortune, and that common pitfall for believers, the perception of unanswered prayer.

Nothing energizes a person for these tests of courage like love does—especially the presence of God's selfless, unfailing love. Love is central to all healing. It enables you to examine your inner self and accept what you see. That's why the most powerful conduit of restoration has always been the warmth and safety of a caring relationship. Once you are secure in a place of acceptance—most secure of all in God's acceptance—you find the strength to keep going and not give up when life's troubles strike.

It's important you understand that your very being is a joy to God. And when there is a consensus of wills—yours and his—it becomes the cause for mutual enjoyment. As A. W. Tozer once observed, "Then when God created man in his own image, he looked and said, 'It was very good' [Gen. 1:31]. God rejoiced in his works. He was glad in what he had done. . . . . Enthusiasm is seen in creation."[1] You are part of his handiwork (see Eph. 2:10), which is why your creation (and your redemption) so perfectly fulfills his joy.

THE PIVOT PRINCIPLE

We often hear talk that *receiving* love is therapeutic—and, indeed, that's true. But the door swings both ways: You also heal and grow when you give love to others. This is the so-called "pivot principle." Just as the Lord unconditionally loved you even when you were rejecting him, so you find joy in passing on that love to others.

Michael Reagan, son of former president Ronald Reagan, revealed in a moving interview the power of this avenue of healing. As a Christian, he became convinced that his bitterness concerning his father's failure over the years to tell him that he loved him was preventing his full recovery from a sad and turbulent childhood. So, as a middle-aged man, he decided to tell his father that *he* loved him. It didn't matter whether his father reciprocated. Michael just knew he needed to do it for his own healing.

To his great surprise, his father returned his affection. And they continued to exchange hugs and expressions of love up to the end of his father's life. He recounted, "One time I had forgotten to hug my father before I started to leave. I quickly turned around to go back and, when I did, I looked up and saw my dad standing on the porch with his arms outstretched, waiting for my hug!" Michael's—and his father's—emotional healing came in the giving. It released the hidden, positive feelings that became the source of their reconciliation.

Self-preoccupation can be difficult to abandon, especially when it is compelled by the powerful force of self-rejection. That's when you know that in those hidden places of the heart you've lost contact with your soul's identity. This secret betrayal of the self is revealed in your toxic treatment of others, by the way you lash out in reaction to your enduring sense of alienation.

Though a person may be unaware of it, the "what's-in-it-for-me" mind-set needlessly strains every relationship. Only when you fully realize this are you ready to do something about it and find the freedom of giving. To do this, you must first know your limits and then look for ways to act beyond your own self-interest. You'll find a deep satisfaction reaching out to others who are struggling and doing so with a love that focuses on *their* needs, not merely on your own.

What better way to discover our Lord's promise of peace than by dissolving the heart-hardening bitterness we all can so easily harbor when we encounter life's unhappy setbacks.

Once liberated from the domination of self-interest, you can then discover a life of meaningful impact for God, something people say they want. The apostle Paul said, "Do nothing from selfishness or empty conceit, but with humility of mind regard one another as more important than yourselves; do not merely look out for your own personal interests, but also for the interests of others" (Phil. 2:3–4 NASB).

He wasn't telling us to consider ourselves unimportant or to ignore our own personal desires. Rather, he was saying we should consider the needs of those around us as worthy of our attention as well. This follows from the principle that recognizing our value in God's eyes enables us also to recognize the value God places on others. This is what frees us to get outside ourselves long enough to understand another's pain. Oddly enough, when we're able to do this, we will often discover that some of our own emotional needs are met in the process. It is marvelous that our Creator has designed us in such a way that we benefit the most when we look beyond ourselves.

While we know that such selflessness is central to a meaningful life, it's still very difficult for many of us to grasp. Nonetheless, how else do you come to fully understand the actions of God's grace? It is sad, is it not, when self-rejection—which is the principal enemy of love—is so pitiless in its efforts to sustain itself!

THE SEARCH FOR INTELLIGENT LOVE

One way self-rejection keeps you cut off from love is by your refusing to believe it's real, by dismissing the idea that there is a God who loves like that. Or, if he exists, that his grace could possibly be granted to those who are as unworthy as you are.

Since the dawn of Israel's history, God has repeatedly demonstrated that he does not qualify the exercise of his compassion and mercy. He repeatedly forgave Israel's persistent idolatry. He displayed grace toward a people who only turned to him in times of crisis (the book of Judges). To be honest, his grace is counterintuitive. His actions defy human analysis, mainly because they don't follow any of our models of predictability. History is filled with his surprises.

Most of us live by the principle that you don't get something for nothing. Yet grace is precisely that—receiving something we haven't earned. Author Paul Tournier once observed, "For the notion that everything has to be paid for is deep-seated and active within us. . . . So the very people who long most ardently for grace have the greatest difficulty in accepting it."[2] People automatically think that if it's free there must be a catch to it someplace. Pure grace is foreign to our relational vocabulary. So, too, is love that sets no conditions and understands no limits.

There are those who think that a God who so easily provides such grace and loves so completely must be the figment of someone's imagination or the product of an irrational, maybe even desperate, mind. But look for yourself. He's right there in the biblical record: the convicted adulteress Jesus refused to condemn (John 8:1–11); the promiscuous Samaritan woman at the well, who was offered living water for her thirsty soul (John 4:5–26); a hypocritical Pharisee given an opportunity to explore his disbelief (John 3:1–21), a known thief granted mercy in his final hour (Luke 23:39–43). They all defy the logic of human justice. But sooner or later, you must come to terms with the reality of God's unparalleled benevolence.

In human experience, authority and power are usually wielded for personal advantage. But when we encounter God, the ultimate authority with absolute power, we find it exercised toward merciful, even sacrificial, ends. An encounter with such astonishing selflessness is likely to so shift a person's thinking that spiritual change becomes inevitable.

This God offers you a place of true belonging in a family. He's a Father who seeks companionship with his children, providing the nurturance and protection of his care. You can now confidently anticipate judgment day as a family matter, for the Judge is our adopted Father and our defense attorney, Jesus Christ, is his Son (1 John 2:1–2). In spotless purity, you will enter heaven among those who are welcomed home amid great celebration (Luke 15:11–24).

So when you stand naked in the cold winter of your despair, you who belong to him must remember you're not alone, even if you feel that way. You're never without his attention. When self-doubt and bitterness sweep over you, God is still there. Like the father's tender response to his prodigal son, God never tires of retrieving his children from their own folly.

The New Testament beckons you to this new, healing family with love coursing through its members—brothers and sisters born from the same spiritual womb, drawing life from the same source of God's grace. In the very place where you have been hurt so much in the past, God provides the meaningful connections for which you have so long yearned.

Because Jesus endured extraordinary loneliness and rejection on the cross, we are offered this new life. He suffered that agony during history's darkest moment, that epic moment at Calvary in which he bore our sin. We were lost, with no chance of finding our way back on our own. But he experienced abandonment so that we might experience inclusion in his Father's love. He chose death that we might choose life. By his sacrifice, Jesus told you that above all, you matter.

This message is your invitation to freedom. In the final analysis, it's the answer to the emotional baggage that has weighed you down and interfered with every meaningful relationship you've ever had. True personal change may not come in a day, a month, or even in a year. But it will come if you accept the invitation and work through the secrets and conflicts that have held you back. Abraham Lincoln, in the darkest days of his presidency, once observed that the most optimistic characteristic of the future is that it comes one day at a time. That's about the pace you can expect it will take to trade your old self-rejection for the growing experience of God's love.

The only other option is the secret life of compromise, the closet pursuit of careless indulgence. It can take many forms, but they all lead to a pattern of anxious compulsion and clinical depression. Whether the counterfeit emotional savior you seek is pornography or food or escapist fantasy or alcohol, the cycle of momentary comfort followed by still deeper emptiness and guilt will corrupt every attempt you make to find the true meaning of pleasure. Subtly it corrupts your ideals, your virtue, and your honesty. Yet you become blind to the price that such indulgence demands of you. Above all, it weakens your ambition for good, your desire for godly pleasure. C. S. Lewis recognized the trap we set for ourselves:

> We are told to deny ourselves and to take up our crosses in order that we may follow Christ; and nearly every description of what we shall ultimately find if we do so contains an appeal to desire. If there lurks in most modern minds the notion that to desire our own good and earnestly to hope for the enjoyment of it is a bad thing, I submit that this notion has crept in from Kant and the Stoics and is no part of the Christian faith. Indeed, if we consider the unblushing promises of reward and the staggering nature of the rewards promised in the Gospels it would seem that our Lord finds our desires not too strong, but too weak. We are half-hearted creatures, fooling about with drink and sex and ambition when infinite joy is offered us, like an ignorant child who wants to go on making mud pies in a slum because he cannot imagine what is meant by the offer of a holiday at the sea. We are far too easily pleased.[3]

When we separate healthy desire from its spiritual meaning, we neutralize the power of virtue in our lives. We settle for so little because we see unselfishness as deprivation. We see intimacy as a threat to our dishonesty. We run from the standard of God's law, where we would find the freedom to love. As the psalmist declares, "I shall run the way of Your commandments, for You will *enlarge my heart*. . . . So I will keep Your law continually, forever and ever. And I will walk at *liberty*, for I seek Your precepts" (Ps. 119:32, 44–45 NASB, emphasis added).

When God's desires and ours are indistinguishable, there will, at last, be complete fulfillment.

THE DEPENDENCY TRAP

Another situation in which self-rejection trumps love is when a person seeks validation in the wrong place—in an excessive dependency on other people. This is a common pattern for chronically depressed people. Many are terrified of being alone and will do almost anything to keep others aware of their pain and feeling obligated to meet their needs—sometimes even by threatening suicide. One of the family members of a client I (Gary) saw did this. Every time people told him they thought he was doing better and that their concerns about him had eased, he would do something dramatic, like making suicidal gestures, which often landed him in the hospital.

Just as the north and south poles of two magnets are drawn to each other, these people most often develop a mutual attraction with those who have strong rescuer tendencies. Rescuers seem driven to help depressed people find happier lives—an effort that is doomed to fail, leaving their emotional resources exhausted. The obvious futility of the effort persuades them to give up the struggle. But these self-appointed saviors want to feel needed and dread letting others down, so they remain trapped in relationships they no longer seek to change. When rescuers attempt to create some distance for their own sanity, the dependent person first panics and then feels victimized all over again. He cries foul and accuses the well-intentioned helper of apathy and hypocrisy. Everyone loses—no one wins.

Physicians (already seen as "saviors" to some of their patients) are often the first professionals to encounter those who are depressed. This is because of the patient's demand for attention to their "disease," not because of any conscious awareness of depression. With the repeated refrain, "There's nothing wrong with you," still ringing in their ears after visits to numerous "incompetent" doctors, such patients may seek alternative medicine, anything that will provide them the sympathy they're looking for (and the "correct" diagnosis for their symptoms). But in the end, they only forestall recognition of their depression and put off the day they come to actually realize their efforts to relabel it are wasted.

BEYOND COMPARE

You may have begun to notice a pattern by now. Each love-rejecting strategy underlying the struggle for emotional survival in some way paves the way for denying the real problems triggering the distress signal of depression. But keeping problems from awareness only sabotages any attempt to make the life changes necessary to solve them. True, you may find short-term relief from the anxiety those problems arouse; but in the long run you end up suffering far more and far longer. That's the paradox: These strategies tend to be only momentarily protective, not permanently constructive. Worse still, they result in a life of energy-sapping hypervigilance. Living in the grip of fear is indeed a sad thing.

We see this self-defeating characteristic in the mental habit of making unfavorable comparisons. When you compare yourself with others—your performance, appearance, or any other quality—you're trying to confirm the inferior self-assessment you already believe. It's not difficult to find someone who appears superior in some way—setting aside, of course, your own areas of special strength and skill. This justifies the illusion of inadequacy and removes any real responsibility for change (a perceived "impossibility" anyway). So, most likely, you will withdraw. As you sink into deeper despair, you become more certain than ever that you're worthless and deserving of rejection.

Too many people tell themselves that they always do the wrong thing at the wrong time. They're boring and stupid. They're certain to fail. The only point to life is mere existence—the only role they have in relationships is to be a bother to others.

Though Brad was, by all accounts, a successful engineer, he would emerge from regional business meetings with other engineers in a state of depression. He claimed that he met many engineers who were so much better than he: "When I go to those meetings, it's discouraging to see how much more effectively the other engineers solve the problems presented in the workshops. I may have the bosses fooled in my own company, but I'm telling you I'm nowhere near as good as they think. After these meetings, I feel like such a fraud. Sometimes, I feel I should save my company the money and resign. But then I wouldn't have a job." He just couldn't get past his own inferiority feelings to appreciate the strengths he brought to the table.

The comparison game is, of course, rigged from the start, designed to guarantee your isolation, maintain your perception of incompetence, and perpetuate your conviction that no one will abide you for long. It's an irrational mind game driven by self-fulfilling prophecies. It's irrational because it overlooks every basic reality check. For instance, each of us has strengths in some areas in which others are weak. But these are usually dismissed as irrelevant. Yet, if this one-sided self-evaluation is seen in the light of reality, we discover that the unique talents and positive traits God has given us are complemented, not devalued, by the talents and traits of others.

Once again, this reveals that the yardstick of your worth and adequacy is found not in your performance or any particular characteristic you have, but in the absolute, unchanging character and opinion of God. To him, we are on a level playing field. In spite of our sin nature—our common starting point—God sees us with the eyes of affection.

Just as God never intended you to use your strengths to lord it over everyone else, neither did he intend you to use your weaknesses as a battering ram against yourself. God has gifted you individually because you belong to him, and you serve a unique purpose. It is this very diversity that provides the basis for unity essential for healthy relationships. Between one person and the next, there's simply no comparison.

CONFRONTING THE FAIRNESS QUESTION

Perhaps the most debilitating way your self-rejection pushes away love is the tactic of playing victim to an unjust world. Of all the self-defeating strategies that sustain self-hatred, this is one of the hardest to recognize for what it is, because the world is indeed unfair.

Referring to the inevitable fate of death, the writer of Ecclesiastes intoned, "There is one fate for the righteous and for the wicked. . . . As the good man is, so is the sinner. . . . This is an evil in all that is done under the sun, that there is one fate for all men" (Eccl. 9:2–3 NASB). The writer was arguing that if justice were served, the righteous would live long and prosper, and the wicked would suffer and die. That, of course, is not how it happens. In fact, the beginnings can be just as unfair as the ends. Some people start life in destructive homes and others don't; and some start in poverty while others in wealth. What's more, misfortune strikes believers and unbelievers alike. The list of inequities seems endless. Is it unreasonable, then, to ask where God is in all of this?

Injustice is a part of life, a fact that makes faith difficult at times. King David, for instance, struggled to live with oppressive circumstances, especially when God seemed to be silent: "My God, my God, why have you forsaken me? Why are you so far from saving me, so far from my cries of anguish? My God, I cry out by day, but you do not answer, by night, but I find no rest" (Ps. 22:1–2).

As Christians, we grapple with the incompatibility of two worlds — one sin-poisoned, the other righteous. Our confusion is understandable. Experience leads some to conclude that God is either too disinterested or too distracted to help, or that they are not important enough to be on his radar at all. But to deny one's faith is to deny the one connection to meaning in life. It robs one of every motivation to think great thoughts and accomplish great things. Aspirations are reduced to mere momentary gratification. The desperation for happiness is the only goal. Any greater purpose seems like cruel fantasy. So dreams are abandoned as immaterial and "God's call" is dismissed as delusion.

But you didn't join the human race to sit it out. So how do you find the inspiration to run for the prize of his high calling (Phil. 3:14)? The answer is found in realizing that earthly life is meant to be a challenge, to stimulate the best you can give. Only if you take God at his word and accept the summons to experiment with change can you avoid the numbing resignation of fatalism.

C. S. Lewis pointed out that if we seek happiness before we seek our Creator, we will, in the end, be denied both. He recognized how easy it is to confuse our priorities. In his words, "Indeed, the best thing about happiness itself . . . is that it liberates you from thinking about happiness."[4] Happiness is an effect, not a cause. It's dependent on the situation and limited in duration. When we seek the answer to life in the fleeting state of happiness, our path leads only to emptiness, depression, and hatred of life itself.

In contrast, Jesus taught that meaning is found not in tenuous earthly pursuits but in seeking first the kingdom of God (Matt. 6:33). What he meant was nothing less than the quest to know God's heart. This is the real goal in the believer's life. Happiness, on the other hand, is better understood to be the result of a life well lived, rather than the reason for living. And so it is that, as C. S. Lewis concluded, the quality of our relationship to God only enlarges the quality of our earthly happiness.

So what do faithful believers do with the inequities of life? Do we just chalk them up to living in a fallen world? That's not very comforting in the midst of our pain. We need to believe our suffering has a greater purpose. That's why the growth that comes out of our hardships is so important. We need to understand God's promise "that in all things God works for the good of those who love him" (Rom. 8:28) as meaning that the eventual outcome will be beneficial in some way, even if not always what we expected.

Several years ago, I was involved in a serious bicycle accident in which I broke my hip and wrist, requiring surgery and extensive physical therapy. Initially, I asked God why. But soon I began asking God to use the experience to teach me more about him or about myself. He did both. Those months of recovery were among the richest of my spiritual life. I grew to know God far better. But there was more. The severity of my injuries prompted tests that revealed a silent hormonal condition that was slowly weakening my bones. Thankfully, the condition was treatable, but it would have remained hidden if not for the accident. True to his promise, God used this painful, confining experience for my physical and spiritual good.

Our response to injustice depends on our concept of God. If we believe God desires our good, then we know he can use even traumatizing events to further his purpose in us. Singer Michael Card affirms in his concerts that his painful childhood with a severely depressed father taught him how important it is to be an attentive father to his own children. He said, "I have a picture of me when I was a small child leaning down trying to speak to my father through the crack under the closed door of the den where he spent almost every waking hour when he was home. In large part, that was the extent of my relationship with my father." But Card chose to use that experience to define the difference in his own fathering.

Faith helps us put aside the contradiction of justice in a fallen world and shows us that the continuance of our sinful existence is unfair. If the impartiality of divine justice were to prevail, no one would survive. The corrupt world would be destroyed. We have the Old Testament account of the flood as evidence of that (Gen. 6–8). But God, in his mercy and forbearance, has forestalled the final day: "The Lord is not slow in keeping his promise, as some understand slowness. Instead, he is patient with you, not wanting anyone to perish, but everyone to come to repentance" (2 Pet. 3:9).

God has never stopped loving his creation. That's why his mercy calls us to endure the suffering of this world while he stays his hand of justice so that more people can respond to his grace and enter into the kingdom of heaven. So suffering *does* have meaning after all. But the day of judgment will most surely come—and when it does, it will end, once and for all, our opportunity to accept redemption.

Until Christ's return, we can rest in the promise that God will one day answer our cry for justice. Meanwhile, we find peace not in the fairness of earthly life but in our relationship with a patient, righteous God. Sometimes, though, after painful events in our lives, there is doubt that we'll ever be safe again or that life will ever return to normal. Indeed, life will never return to what *was* normal, but rather to a different, more adaptive life, a new normal, as it were, that can come only through hardship.

Contrary to your fears, putting the pieces of your life back together can be a creative learning experience. Poet Lindsay Lee Johnson likened this process to mending broken plates: "What you get is not an old mended plate trying to look the same as it was, but a whole new thing you never saw before. A fine new pretty thing. When things come apart, it's your chance to rearrange the pieces."[5]

Mending your life gives you the chance to begin something entirely new, something beautiful: the chance to craft a new mosaic of attitudes and behaviors, to more fully understand God and his will, to start trusting intimacy again, to discover yourself and the true fulfillment of your natural desires in God and his love.

THE SPIRITUAL BUSINESS OF LOVING

We've spoken of depression as signaling, among other things, a tenacious self-hatred. When much of a person's past experience of so-called love is associated with betrayal, abandonment, abuse, and a host of other wounds, there's not a lot to encourage a more charitable view. Self-rejection becomes both a conclusion from experience and a shield against further injury from the expected attacks of others.

The important thing to remember is that your healing starts at the spiritual level. Though human love may be limited and variable, God's is unlimited and constant. While ours is largely dependent on another's response, his is completely independent of it. That's why any stable intimacy must always be traced back to a spiritual beginning, whether or not those involved are Christians. It's God's presence in this world that makes the difference. Conversely, every broken relationship is related, in some way or another, to a lack of spiritual understanding.

In the beginning, God fellowshipped with Adam and Eve. And after time has ended, God will once again dwell among his people, enjoying eternal fellowship with them. It's no accident that we are reconciled to our heavenly Father by a personal relationship with his Son, not merely by obedience to a commandment. Intimacy is a central spiritual reality in life, now and for eternity. It's not hard to see why this is lost on an unbelieving world, which even has difficulty distinguishing between intimacy and sex.

This spiritual connection allows us to see below the surface of life's painful events. We discover there the triumph of redemption over sin, of life over death. Ultimately, everything will be determined by God's plan, even if we don't understand things now.

As King David concluded, "Surely your goodness and love will follow me all the days of my life" (Ps. 23:6). This cheerful expression of trust came from a man who knew long years of loneliness, rejection, and failure, and who lost three sons to violence. Perhaps we, too, can trust our Shepherd to lead us through those dark valleys of turmoil to the still waters of his peace.

Depression's alarm signal also awakens you from false assumptions about reality. Several years ago, I saw a client who had been adopted at birth. From her teen years onward, she developed a deep, resentful depression because of her "abandonment" by her biological mother. Only later did she discover that her mother, when she was an unwed teenager, had agonized over the decision to give her up, choosing to protect her from a life of poverty. It was one of the few selfless things her mother had done during that period of her life.

When my client learned that she had not, after all, been considered "excess baggage," she began to see the love of both her biological and adoptive mothers and was empowered to live a healthier life, one they had both wanted for her. She said, "I'll never forget the excitement in my mother's eyes when she saw me for the first time since I was a baby. I thought to myself, 'She *does* want to see me!' Then when she spoke about the pain of having to give me up for adoption, I saw the deep sadness flood into her eyes. I felt for the first time that she loved me all those years, even though she had no idea where I lived. It's been such a cleansing experience for both of us." This young woman had shifted perspective and was able to enjoy the experience of the love that had been there all along.

When God appears to be silent or even cruel, you may feel betrayed and may question his love. But when you come to know God intimately, you see things differently. You come to understand the experiences of pain that blindside you in the larger context of God's grief over sin. God is always there quietly providing you with new opportunities to heal.

Contrary to the mysterious and capricious gods of ancient idolatry, which only cultivated fear, our heavenly Father has made us privy to secrets that only an intimate would know (Ps. 25:14). Such free and open self-disclosure is itself powerful evidence of his trustworthiness. We open ourselves to others only when we trust them, don't we? But God did so even when we rejected him. Where else will we find that kind of love?

FINDING HOPE

1. When you give of yourself, not only do you discover the practical meaning of your faith, but also the purpose of life itself.

2. Where you have been hurt in the past, God has provided a new healing family. Though you may feel you didn't matter in your family of origin, you matter to your heavenly Father.

3. If you are prone to the comparison game, identify the strengths you have that the other person doesn't and then thank God for giving both of you strengths that each can enjoy.

4. Consider the difficulties you are experiencing in life as a path to new understanding. Ask God to teach you something about yourself or about him through this experience.

5. The presence of suffering in the world confirms that God has stayed his hand of justice to give us more time to respond to his grace and enter the kingdom of heaven. In this way, your suffering points to God's mercy.

6. The ultimate criterion for measuring life experience is God's goodness. Ask him to show you the good in the struggles you face.

PART 3

WHY WE GET STUCK

DISCOVERING OUR BLIND SPOTS

A PRIMER FOR REALITY DISTORTION

As strange as it may seem, hope has its roots in despair. . . . Indeed, if reality did not give us grounds for despair, it would never give us reason for hope.

—Robert Veninga

Jennifer and Steve were high-school sweethearts, but after nearly twenty relatively good years of marriage, their relationship was deteriorating. Jennifer had become irritable and fatigued. Steve had started working longer hours to avoid facing his wife's unpredictable moods. In their initial counseling session, both were depressed—he quiet and withdrawn, she puzzled and frightened by her chaotic emotional state. The couple felt the loss of the fulfillment they'd once found with each other, as well as the mounting frustration with the lack of change. Steve was confused: "I don't know what happened to the woman I married. Is it something I've done? I can't for the life of me figure out what's making her upset all the time. All I know is I don't want to be around anymore . . . but then again I do. I just don't know." Jennifer was equally adrift: "I don't know why I'm crying or why I'm mad so much, but Steve has made it a lot worse. He has no patience at all with me—he just walks away with a disgusted look and finds something else to do. . . . I'm so lonely!"

With a physician's help, we soon discovered that Jennifer suffered from severe hypoglycemia—a disorder of the body's ability to regulate blood sugar that, in turn, can affect emotional stability. Once she gained control of this disorder through dietary changes, we were able to identify additional factors that added to her depression.

For his own part, Steve began to see a pattern from his childhood. During his early years, he had learned to stay out of his depressed mother's way to "reduce her stress." That's why he withdrew from Jennifer. She, in response, felt abandoned, and so became critical of him. As a result, Steve felt inadequate as a husband.

Realizing what he was doing, Steve began to reengage Jennifer, erasing the isolation she had begun to feel. Both of them prepared for future challenges by developing better coping skills so the struggles of one did not have to destabilize the other. They learned that emotional pain and confusion could bring them together in a spirit of resolution rather than drive them apart and create anxiety about their future.

We see in this couple some of the many factors at work that contribute to the experience of depression. This dynamic is commonplace whenever we work with troubled relationships marked by depression. It can be a dissonant symphony of conditions within each person as well as their reactions to each other. Fortunately, these responses tend to follow fairly specific patterns.

The interplay of family of origin problems and physical conditions triggering the crossfire of marital conflict is but one of many such patterns that can give rise to depression. With the increasing number of broken or dysfunctional families, it's not surprising that as much as 12 to 13 percent of the entire US population is, at any given time, experiencing a depressive episode of one sort or another.

According to World Health Organization statistics, depression has become "the leading cause of disability worldwide in terms of total years lost due to disability."[1] It is increasing in frequency in every age group as well as every demographic group. Little wonder, then, that depression has sometimes been called the "common cold" of emotional struggles.[2]

In spite of the complexities that may underlie depression, we are able to identify and confront several basic thinking habits that increase its likelihood. Let's look at three of the most common: perfectionism, self-deception, and fear of rejection.

EXPECTING PERFECTION IN AN IMPERFECT WORLD

The first and perhaps most recognizable habit of the mind that sets the stage for depression is the one most familiar to the legalistic believer—perfectionism. We've seen this problem as a response to an emotionally repressive home where productivity was substituted for feelings. This pattern can be found any time someone insists on a faultless outcome—on a life essentially free of any significant setbacks or failures. Such people set their standards of performance unrealistically high and then attack themselves for failing to meet impossible criteria, virtually guaranteeing a sense of inadequacy. They're always anxious about life, even though by any objective measure they're doing well. In spite of their success, they can't shake the conviction that they're bound to fail.

Unremitting perfectionism soon leads to unrelenting depression. Preoccupation with perceived incompetence or fear of ruin crowds out any pleasure. You'd think the misery this produces would be enough to cause these individuals to reexamine and revise their distorted thinking habits. But people often remain stuck, unable to forgive their own mistakes and skeptical of their ability to correct them. The unavoidable reality of life's trial-and-error process promises a rough ride for the perfectionist.

For the Christian, this is compounded by perpetual guilt for not meeting God's standards. Because of their self-recrimination, many find it difficult to experience God's forgiveness. I (Gary) remember one woman in her late twenties who dated men who were abusive to her. This was her way of punishing herself for losing her virginity as a teenager. She asked me, "How can you reel back your teenage life?" And then added, "I must be dirt to God. . . . There are so many better people for God to choose from, so why would he bother with me?"

Of course, she neglected to mention at the beginning of her "confession" that she had been told by her father that she would go to hell if she failed to remain sexually pure. So she already feared the wrath of God over any indiscretion. She believed she didn't deserve a man who loved and cherished her, since she had committed the "unforgivable sin" and was now "damaged goods." Her graceless perfectionism led to only one conclusion: suffering was her inescapable fate.

Whether dealing with common mistakes or moral failures, perfectionists demand a no-win lifestyle that limits spontaneity and freedom. Consequently, they're reluctant to experiment with new life strategies. Yet without change, life remains one deadening routine after another.

Every day we have a choice either to be thankful for opportunities in life or be distraught by life's real or imagined liabilities. When we choose the latter, perfectionism is often the reason. It demands obsessive concern with uncovering evidence of failure in our careers, marriages, or friendships.

Life can be painful at times, even bewildering. But it becomes far worse when we interpret every struggle in terms of personal ruin.

Perfectionists add to their woes by typically employing black-and-white, all-or-nothing thinking, which inhibits them from effectively resolving conflict. They enslave themselves to a labyrinth of rules and unyielding demands, making it impossible to relax. They're desperately hungry for other people's acceptance ("What will others think?"), yet try to elevate themselves by defeating everyone around them. Inevitably, they react with bitter jealousy and judgmental attitudes toward those who seem to be doing better than they. To them, everyone else's accomplishments are either superior (and therefore unattainable) or inferior (and thus written off as unworthy of their attention).

It's easy to see why perfectionists are so vulnerable to depression. They simply can't adjust to life's unexpected setbacks. Self-reproach and criticism of others leaves no room for flexibility. While they may be able to cope when times are smooth, stress and adversity almost always send them into an emotional tailspin. They literally judge themselves into depression. Their fears and attitudes of condemnation create a looping mental tape that reinforces unchallenged myths that are toxic to a healthy concept of self.

My client Robert was like that. His first words to me were almost dictatorial: "I don't know why I'm here, doc. . . . No offense, but you can't fix me—nobody can. You see, I've been a screw-up from the get-go.

I can't help myself—it's who I am. I could entertain you for hours telling you all the messes I've created. But I'll save you some time by warning you that you are wasting your efforts on me."

In spite of this self-created defeatist "reality" in which many live, God never tires of reminding his children that his love turns away no one, even those others would call "train wrecks." No one is hopeless in God's eyes, but to the perfectionist that just seems too good to be true.

THE LAST WORD ON PERFECTIONISM

This discrepancy between the perfectionist's world and God's is starkly revealed in the Old Testament: God does not expect us to be perfect here on earth (Eccl. 7). Indeed, he warns us against being "over-righteous" and "overwise" (7:16). He tells us, instead, to seek him who is perfect. The goal is increased spiritual maturity, not puritanical zeal. The difference simply amounts to being directed by his Spirit rather than your self-reliance (that is, the "flesh" nature). Though difficult for those who are controlling, it means placing our confidence in the sufficiency of God's power, which is completely contrary to any legalistic fervor to accomplish by oneself a spiritual transformation (a self-contradiction if there ever was one).

In Ecclesiastes, the writer described life based on secular standards for success rather than on God's. He experienced everything the culture offered: enormous wealth, international fame, achievement, adulation, power, and sensual pleasure. He had enough wealth and power to realize all of his dreams, but in the end he was left disillusioned. Depressed and unable to dream anymore, he finally realized that what his culture offered was nothing more than fool's gold.

Real purpose, he concluded, was found only in a life of communion with God. So, life *is* worth living after all! The Teacher learned the hard way that life apart from divine wisdom makes little sense. Preacher Haddon Robinson has likened it to trying to complete a crossword puzzle with a limited vocabulary. He argues that while history can tell us what has happened since humanity's beginning, and science can tell us how it happened, neither can tell us *why* it happened.[3] Even Friedrich Nietzsche, the renowned German philosopher, admitted that we can live with almost any how, but only when we know the why. Nietzsche's atheism allowed him, however, only a humanistic why, a view destined to lead him to tragedy.

The church has the greatest opportunity ever given to humanity to teach a hope that fulfills its promise. But we endanger this opportunity when we let legalism—our own version of perfectionism—obscure God's message. Legalistic thinking encourages an endless list of dos and don'ts that reduce faith to mere religion. The result is a depressing array of "shoulds," which drains all joy from life.

When the Teacher observed that there is "no one on earth who is righteous, no one who does what is right and never sins" (Eccl. 7:20), he was making the *righteous* person the standard of imperfection. Not the average or disreputable person, but the spiritually mature person, the person after God's own heart. What this is telling us is that rather than pursuing perfection, pursue instead the perfect One. It is his perfection that compensates for our lack of it.

You might object, "But aren't good works important?" Yes. But we would respond with another question: Doesn't James 2:14–26 teach that we do good works as evidence of our justification, not as the basis for it? In John 15:1–10, Jesus said that the fruit of our lives—our righteous deeds—would flow out of an abiding relationship with him. We don't earn righteousness; we do good as a result of gratitude for his redemptive love. Sadly, perfectionism perverts this grace into an insatiable indebtedness.

Legalists may pay lip service to God's mercy but give little of it to themselves or each other. Faith becomes more the burden of obligation than the freedom from perpetual guilt. Little wonder this leads to depression.

Cristian Barbosu, a Romanian scholar, observed that decades of totalitarian rule and conformist thinking have infused the Romanian church with a legalism that persists even under the freedoms of democratic reform.[4] He found, as many others before him, that such institutional-ization of belief mutates grace into a set of rules. As John Piper writes, "This terrible moment is the birthplace of the 'debtors' ethic."[5]

A Christian client once told me he felt guilty as a child every time he wanted to watch the Wednesday night television program *The Wonder-ful World of Disney* because it conflicted with his church's prayer meeting. It's a toxic spirituality that raises uniformity to the level of worship. Unfortunately, legalistic measures do not strengthen, but only weaken, the importance of God's standards.

When my clients finally discover for themselves the bondage inherent in this tyrannical way of life and begin to let go of their overly regimented thinking, they find a freedom they never dared to hope existed. Their relief is a reward for accepting their heart's imperfect character and entrusting it to the power of God's grace.

It is clear that unchecked perfectionism is profoundly debilitating to a fulfilling life with God. But there is a second habit of the mind that similarly encourages depression: self-deception.

UNVEILING THE HARM OF SELF-DECEPTION

When I (Gary) was a child, an older playmate in the neighborhood used to play a trick on me that was terrifying. If I didn't do what she wanted, she threatened to take me to nearby "buggy alley" and abandon me to a bunch of deadly spiders. Compliance made a lot of sense to me. One day, however, she overplayed her hand and left me in that frightening alley. I panicked at first, but then I realized the place was harmless. Once I realized that she had been perpetrating a hoax, she lost her power over me.

That's what happens when deceptions are exposed. Only *believed* deceptions can frighten you. Many of the most powerful life-governing beliefs are nothing more than self-deceptions. They are hoaxes. But most people have proven they're experts at convincing themselves of untruths. Confronting your fears means confronting yourself. What are the "buggy alleys" you believe in, and how do you let them intimidate you into withdrawal or passivity?

Because self-deception is such a powerful habit of the mind, it affects many things you do. It's at the center of almost every painful lifestyle. Scripture issues more warnings against being deceived than against any other tactic of the Evil One. As the letter of James insists, unless we act in the clarity of the truth, we "deceive" ourselves (1:22) and end up "double-minded" and "unstable in all [we] do" (1:8).

Once truth is forsaken as the standard for behavior, the Christian walk is compromised. The resulting sense of meaninglessness then predisposes you to sin. Momentary feelings come to guide your reasoning. You stray from the mind of God, impairing your judgment.

So where does that leave you? First of all, it limits the criteria for success to merely feeling good, so that every adversity is automatically defined as a defeat. The predictability of suffering in this life then bodes ill for the future. But God's criteria for success are based more on *doing* good than on *feeling* good. In marriage, God commands you to respond to your spouse on the basis of principle (that is, doing what is right), rather than calibrating your response to how you feel at the moment about your spouse's behavior. "Always do right," Mark Twain once wryly commented. "This will gratify some people and astonish the rest."[6]

If you want to avoid self-deception, should you discount your feelings entirely? No. While feelings are not the measure of truth, they do perform a vital role. Remember, most negative feelings are alarms that alert you to take some kind of remedial action. Positive feelings, on the other hand, indicate that your needs and desires have been satisfied.

Feelings were never intended as ends in themselves. They are there as incentives for altering course. But they can't be relied upon to evaluate the outcome of your actions. Otherwise, your feelings would create the potential for a lot of misconceptions. Under these conditions, the experience of failure, for instance, would no longer have the ability to teach you what you need to learn. So, there would be no way to understand the true nature of success. It was once said, success can be found in experiencing failure without the loss of enthusiasm! Endurance of adversity often proves then to be the best teacher you have.

Emotional reasoning has another unintended result. Since feelings are often related to your relationships with others, you can, like the perfectionist, become vulnerable to constant worry about what others think. Evaluation apprehension will prompt you to become more concerned about the visibility of your work than the nature of your service.

Best-selling author Henri Nouwen was well aware of this problem. Though a great scholar who had opportunities to stay at several prestigious institutions, he chose to nurture severely impaired patients in a residential care facility. He was satisfied to serve God far from the spotlight of fame and fortune, though it took awhile for him to adapt to life outside the heady atmosphere of academia.

Likewise, long before the press made Mother Teresa a celebrity, she worked anonymously among the poorest of the poor in the slums of Calcutta. God enlists us, not for dramatic results, nor for accolades, but for our willingness to be channels of his grace, sometimes even in the unlikeliest of places.

If you feel God's good pleasure, it's likely because it involves your own pleasure as well. God's pleasure becomes yours, just as your pleasure becomes his. We see this in his "eternal pleasures" (Ps. 16:11)—the delights that truly satisfy the human heart. As author John Piper puts it, "The universal biblical mandate to believe is a radical and pervasive call to pursue our own happiness in God."[7]

When you are no longer deceiving yourself, you may be surprised to learn that desire begets desire, that you receive pleasure by giving it. Here you discover your true home. Like the client who said of the woman he loved, "I feel so at home when she's there, because there is nothing I can't disclose to her. With her, I have the overwhelming privilege just to be." No more self-sabotaging thought patterns that transform success into imagined failure, contentment into imagined deprivation. Only confidence in a more honest way of life.

One culprit responsible for the amnesia of a self-deceptive life is the cramping ritualization of Christian routine. Prayer rituals. Service rituals.

Liturgy rituals. Over time it can all become mindlessly habitual, religious without being spiritual. Like singing hymns without thinking about the words. Minds on autopilot, hearts disengaged. Losing your first love, resigned to the mediocrity of mere appearances—these are all sure paths to depression. Accepting a stifling, truncated view of God leaves you ripe for a life of terminal inertia, a life that sometimes makes even the shallow pleasures of culture appear better than the best offerings of faith.

Desire is not evil. God created it as a good thing. It was intended to be fulfilled by his eternal presence in your life. It's only when you seek to fulfill that desire elsewhere that you corrupt its true purpose.

Now let's take a look at the third habit of the mind: fear, specifically the fear of rejection, which is another common breeding ground for a lot of depression.

THE CASE AGAINST FEAR

Effective families and churches are characterized by unity, but that doesn't mean everyone is the same. In fact, God purposefully made us with an amazing variety of personalities, predispositions, talents, and other character-defining traits. God designed these differences to provide richness and texture within families and churches. But many of us find these differences threatening, irritating, or even unfair. As when the task-oriented Martha expressed resentment toward her more teachable sister, Mary, for preferring to sit at Jesus' feet, rather than help with the chores (Luke 10:38–42).

Personal insecurity may sometimes keep us from accepting the fact that others can tread paths unfamiliar to us—paths that may intimidate us not merely because they're different, but because we fear they might prove superior to our own. So we envy. We compare. And often we reject. Perhaps that's because earlier in life we were the ones rejected for expressing our uniqueness in the family. We learned that conformity is the ideal, and being different is threatening. When we have a history of such pain, our primary concern in life is to blend in. Our lives can become dominated by fear of rejection—a common precondition to depression.

Losing anything (or anyone) we consider important for our identity and security is a prominent theme in many emotional struggles.

Defense against rejection is understandable. But a constantly defensive lifestyle is destructive. It organizes life around a limited range of options, all focused on relieving anxiety and avoiding unpredictability. It encourages repression rather than the healthy expression that you need. Adversity, then, can literally frighten you into depression.

Sometimes other Christians, particularly those who regard any emotional battle as a sign of spiritual deficiency, will prompt you to hide your depression for fear that you'll be rejected for that too. This happened in the case of my client Denise. When she finally disclosed her despair, some fellow believers admonished her about her faith. Unfortunately, they succeeded only in intensifying her fear. It's hard to overstate how badly this damaged her spirit, contributing to her incessant anxiety about her eternal destiny and her increased withdrawal. Only with considerable help did she come to realize that acceptance by God was not dependent on the acceptance of others.

Though fear is one of our God-given alarm systems alerting us to true threats to our safety, its constant activation leads to emotional exhaustion. This can be seen in a variety of physical symptoms that will often develop. By this time, acute distress has already given way to chronic depression and hopelessness. The sufferer's spiritual life seldom remains unaffected.

Because believers with dysfunctional backgrounds rarely view God accurately anyway, their fear of rejection only distorts that view still further. They resign themselves, therefore, to an "inevitable"—even "God-ordained"—life of frustration. As with Denise, such deprivation is the expected punishment for past sins. Yet simmering resentment for this wears them down emotionally and spiritually, sometimes spilling over onto others—which only leads to more rejection, confirming their already pessimistic outlook on life.

Today, there are increasing opportunities for believers to confront these fears in groups (for example, Celebrate Recovery). Recently, I learned of a Sunday school group in a nearby church that formed specifically to study the biblical view of depression. This group began with a relatively small number, but grew steadily in the following weeks as others learned of its success. Eventually, it grew to be one of the largest Sunday school classes they ever had! Member after member remarked that, until the class, they had been afraid of being honest about their depression because they thought they were largely alone in it. They were surprised, relieved, and encouraged that there was a group of believers that was not fearful of discussing it openly.

Above all, they were comforted to learn that God had not rejected them. They learned, too, the importance of his tender counsel through the observations of those who themselves were suffering.

God provides a way of escape from the mental trap of unfounded fears. But the path is not an easy one. That's because years of self-destructive behavior can leave you cynical about anything different.

Confronting this cynicism requires you to trust God's revelation. There you find the real truth about yourself. Truth you may not be prepared to hear. It's humbling to admit that your lifelong conclusions may be wrong.

Sometimes it involves acknowledging your unflattering humanity, like a tendency to injure others. But personal growth requires it. We're not talking about self-punishing rumination, but rather a realistic review of where you've been and where you're going. Positive change is the goal. Without owning up to your offenses and doing something about them, you can make little progress toward the life you want. You might be tempted to wait for the "right time" to begin, but that usually means never pursuing it at all.

Remember, it starts with trusting God's declared interest in you. Jesus referred to this when he said that unless we become as little children, we cannot enter the kingdom of heaven (Matt. 18:1–4). He was describing in experiential terms the kind of faith it takes to enter God's presence. Children naturally trust the adults who care for them, for they know they can't escape danger without their protection and can't feel secure without their love.

Fear of rejection is not innate in humanity. It's learned. Young children don't initially hold back from adults, nor do they pull their punches when they're upset or want something. Often their transparency is charming, refreshing, and sometimes amusing. At other times, when it catches adults off guard, it can annoy them with its undisguised tone of demand. It's only when caregivers become abusive or neglectful that children *learn* to fear rejection; like Denise, who learned it while living with her cold, distant, and rigid father. This fear only later generalized to others, including her peers and even several of her close associates.

As a child's socialization continues, the increasing divide between the public and private self becomes more and more evident, especially in emotionally repressive homes. In the end, the degree of disparity between the two depends on the amount of rejection children have experienced and from whom they've received it.

Patty was an unexpected fourth child, coming ten years after her siblings were born. Her parents, who were active outdoors people, were disappointed that they would have to curtail their plans to go camping for a while. Actually, they resented having to start over with a new child. These attitudes had an enduring effect on Patty. As she recalled it, "I always felt like I was in the way, that I was some kind of burden to them. They left me in daycare for much of the time, and when I wasn't in daycare I often had babysitters. When I got older, they just left me alone. They came to few of my school activities and showed little interest in my accomplishments. To this day, I'm convinced no one is interested in me. That's why I rarely go out, and also why I almost never go to church. I'm lonely, but still I guess that's better than being ignored."

Fear of rejection can spill over into your relationship with God as well. For grace to do its work, you must first receive it. That's why Jesus compared the believer's attitude toward God with the natural transparency and trust of children. If you trust like that, you'll find that his love casts out your fear.

It takes courage to face your past with honesty. But it will awaken you, like nothing else will, to the possibility of redeeming your damaged relationships.

THE LANGUAGE OF DESPAIR

Language is the engine of your thoughts. It determines both the content and the process of your self-talk. It also determines the way you narrate your unfolding life story. This internal language determines the emotional nature of your thought habits. If you have been driven by unhealthy thought habits like perfectionism, self-deception, and fear of rejection, your internal language has probably been cultivated by emotionally conditioned responses to a painful beginning. So, it's necessary to intentionally cultivate a new inner language in order to shape new thought habits and a new worldview. Reforming your self-talk is one of the most important steps you can take in silencing depression's alarm signal.

Your perception of the world—whether distorted or not—is shaped by such internal language. When you rely heavily on "need language" (that is, language related to needs for physical survival), you're very likely to over-emotionalize your communication. This is what provokes irrational responses of guilt, fear, and anger, which, in turn, lead to depression. Your "need language" reflects the kind of intensity that normally is reserved for experiences involving a real threat to your physical existence. However, such threats are rarely genuine, which means that your words are more accurately "catastrophizing" normal life events.

You have few true needs in life: food, water, air, shelter, and the like. If, for example, you are even briefly deprived of air, you will panic and flail to regain your air supply. Anyone who has come close to drowning knows this kind of panic.

In contrast to true needs, however, most longings in life are best classed as *desires* or *preferences*. Where you live, whom you marry, what career path you follow, what friends you have, what car you drive, how many children you have, what church you attend, and so on, are all choices you make based on your preferences.

But what happens if you psychologically convert what is really a desire into a need (such as, a "counterfeit need"), and it appears increasingly possible that you'll be deprived of that "need"? You panic and flail in the emotional sense. For instance, if you convert your *desire* for someone's approval into a *need* for that approval, and when that person withholds it for some reason, you will either desperately attempt to get it (sometimes compromising your values to do so) or lapse into significant depression over its loss.

If this catastrophizing comes to dominate your thinking, you will end up in continual agitation, frustration, anxiety, and depression. Such need-language terms as "awful," "terrible," "horrible," "I should," "I have to," "I must," "I can't stand it," or "I could just die" take over your vocabulary.

This lexicon of need language creates an emotional volatility rarely justified by the circumstances. That's because catastrophes are rare. Your self-talk becomes a consuming liability, constantly prompting you to act upon a lie, an endless trail of worst-case scenarios.

Jesus said, "The truth will set you free" (John 8:32), by which he meant that the truth of the gospel will set you free from the bondage of sin. As it turns out, this axiom also serves as God's comprehensive litmus test for *all* truth. It's long been known that a nation's exposure to the truth is any dictator's greatest fear. Autocrats tightly control the press, radio and TV stations, private and public gatherings—any means by which truth might be disseminated, thereby undermining the falsehoods that have been presented as truth. The reality is that the truth will always argue for freedom.

When you become your own emotional dictator, you condemn yourself to imprisonment by your own lies. You must understand just how profoundly your self-talk determines your feelings, perceptions, and actions. If you tell yourself that it would be *horrible* if someone rejects you or that you *can't stand it* if some situation doesn't work out the way you want it to, you will find yourself in an endless state of emotional turmoil that will leave you exhausted—like road rage or bouts of anxiety that never seem to go away. Even simple things like traffic jams on the freeway can destroy your day. You tell yourself, "I can't stand this traffic; I've got to get to my appointment; it's terrible; I'm going to be late." As a result, you become upset, gripping the wheel and yelling at the other drivers. You're a wreck by the time you get to your destination. But is your survival at stake if you don't make it on time? Of course not! At worst, it's inconvenient, or you might be a little embarrassed. So, it would be far better (and easier on your emotional and physical health) if you used preference language; that is, if you told yourself something like, "While I don't like it, it's not the end of the world."

The apostle Paul spoke about how he and his companions avoided such turmoil by refusing to use the emotionally loaded "need language" to describe setbacks in their ministry. Life wasn't easy, but neither was it overwhelming: "We are hard pressed on every side, but *not* crushed; perplexed, but *not* in despair; persecuted, but *not* abandoned; struck down, but *not* destroyed" (2 Cor. 4:8–9, emphasis added). Paul described their struggles in realistic terms—they were pushed to the limit of their endurance. But he noted the inaccuracy of catastrophic terms such as "crushed," "in despair," "abandoned," and "destroyed."

Paul's inner commentary used more accurate and moderate self-talk—words like "hard pressed," "perplexed," "persecuted," and "struck down" (discouraged)—which we refer to as "preference language." It suggests outcomes we'd prefer to avoid, though the world won't end if they happen: "I'm disappointed, but I can handle it"; "It's inconvenient, but not the worst thing that can happen"; "I'd prefer it to be different, but I'll survive"; and so forth. Such self-talk leads to far fewer volatile emotional reactions and far more rational responses to adversity. Paul had the wisdom to describe his experiences as events he didn't like rather than as events he couldn't stand. God's mercy operated through this powerful principle, helping Paul weather ongoing persecution without paralyzing despair.

Each of these languages has its own distinct footprint, so you can identify which language you're using by tracking backward from your emotional experience. If you notice that you're upset to a degree that's out of proportion to the cause, chances are you're using need language for your self-talk. But if you're calm, you're likely describing the event to yourself in preference language.

Take a moment to listen in on your self-talk—you may be surprised how easily you can detect a lie, possibly the very need language that is the cause for much of your distress. Best of all, you'll find that changing this commentary is one of the quickest means to achieving relief. Your thinking habits are not dependent on what others do or say. To the contrary, *you* are fully in charge of your response to adversity.

FINDING HOPE

1. Examine your perfectionist tendencies, particularly the negative judgments you make about your mistakes. Remember, these mistakes are opportunities to learn, not failures to reject.

2. Emotional reasoning ("If it feels true, it must be true") is challenged by the fact that feelings are neither true nor false and that strongly negative feelings are most likely suggesting the importance of making positive change.

3. Whenever you feel guilty about things that don't involve actual moral compromise, remember, they can't serve as legitimate "shoulds." Picture instead the freedom you have in God, the freedom to live without constant guilt.

4. Because of your uniqueness in God's design, whenever you encounter the differences of others, remember that's their uniqueness too. This is what stimulates openness to new ideas.

5. Substitute "preference language" for "need language." Every time you catch yourself using the former, notice how this change alters your emotional reactions to things in a positive direction.

DEPRESSION AND THE TURBULENT TRIO

To be blind is bad, but worse it is to have eyes and not to see.
—Helen Keller

Julie, a forty-seven-year-old housewife, slumped in her chair in front of me (Gary), eyes rimmed with circles of fatigue. She avoided eye contact. Her fingers tapped the arm of the chair; her feet moved constantly. Her lips trembled as she whispered about the latest blow to her crumbling marriage.

She had learned of her husband's sixth affair during their eighteen years of marriage. Weary of the roller-coaster life with him, she was desperate for even a sliver of stability in her home. Her husband had promised, again, that he wouldn't wander anymore—and that he would somehow make it up to her. She knew, of course, that this latest version of the same empty promise was little more than a smoke screen for his denial: "I knew right then, of course, that this would happen again— but I'm stuck. Where am I going to go? Besides, my life is over anyway. I can't see any future worth living for."

You might ask why she hadn't left him long ago to live without worrying about the next nasty surprise. Why, after all, was Julie so tolerant of this compulsive philanderer? Because she was demoralized by the "turbulent trio" of guilt, rage, and abandonment. As a Christian, she was burdened by guilt for even thinking of leaving, for she had been convinced that it was her responsibility to stick it out, regardless of his endless lies and betrayals. She struggled, too, because she felt ashamed of her rage at the man who had brought her so much pain. Christians, she thought, should never feel that way about anyone, no matter what they've done. But most paralyzing of all were her powerful abandonment issues—her intense fear at the thought of living alone.

She came from a religiously conservative home where, to her shock, her father had left her mother for another woman when Julie was only six. She never saw her dad again until she was well into adulthood. Having been "daddy's little girl," she felt abandoned, punished by God for somehow failing him. She grew up adopting her mother's strong faith, but always fantasizing about a man who would never forsake her.

Ironically, however, she married a man not unlike her father—a man who destroyed her dream of a storybook marriage. Shattered, she felt trapped in a loveless relationship. Even though she had a scriptural basis for leaving her husband, she feared doing so would nonetheless violate her faith. She had even talked herself into believing she was "called" to patient endurance, sacrificing her happiness for her husband's compulsions in order to "rescue" him . . . and maybe herself as well.

It is, of course, essential to guard the sanctity of marriage. God asks no less of us. But this husband was making a mockery of it. He showed no signs of change. Until now, Julie's twisted logic had forced her to tolerate his pathological behavior. Meanwhile, an abiding rage grew inside her—secretly against God, but now openly against her husband. Her fury was tearing her body apart with intestinal disorders, headaches, and fatigue. She could no longer keep up her mild-mannered façade. Her anger triggered even more guilt. In fact, she felt guilty about almost everything. By the time she sought help, she showed intense anxiety, wanting to know just how a believer could feel the way she did and still go to heaven.

Like Julie, a surprising number of people wonder if their secret emotional life has sabotaged their chances with a righteous God. Even when they've repeatedly had their lights punched out, they believe God requires them to absorb the blows—if not with a smile, at least with a longsuffering attitude.

It doesn't seem to matter that their belief isn't taught in the Bible. They find it too hard to believe God understands their pain and the powerful feelings that spring from it—especially their anger. Their view of God is far too limited to see in him anything beyond the promise of judgment. They can't comprehend the fact that God cherishes them, not because they can offer something to him, but simply because he delights in his beloved children. They have missed the point that this was the reason for his Son's sacrifice.

God doesn't expect us to merely endure life or to live it riddled with false guilt. He rejoices in our joy, not in the pain of our poor choices.

CONTAINING FALSE GUILT: THE OVER-RESPONSIBILITY TRAP

Assertive living implies that we assume responsibility for our decisions and consequent behaviors. But as with so many things in life, there is wisdom in balance. It's no surprise that both under-responsibility and over-responsibility serve as poor blueprints for successful relationships. In the former, you blame everyone else when things go wrong. In the latter, you assume not merely your own but everyone else's responsibilities as well. It's easy to see why the tendency to assume fault provides fertile ground for false guilt. After all, when you shoulder the guilt that belongs to others, you become partners in a dance with manipulators who are all too glad to delude themselves and others about their "innocence." But you can't fool yourself out of your resentment for taking the blame.

Porous boundaries leave people incapable of distinguishing between their desires and those of others. People pleasers lose contact with what they want and mistake a placating strategy for humility.

Underneath, they are wallowing in self-pity and repressed anger. Despite their efforts to please others, placaters continue to be ignored, if not sometimes reviled. They endure the worst of both worlds—over-burdened with responsibility yet overlooked by others. No wonder they become confused and angry at the lack of "saviors" to come to their aid when *they* need it.

Why do they keep coming back for more? For starters, it gives them temporary relief from false guilt. It also provides for the reward of the occasional fleeting compliment that calms their fear of irrelevance. Sooner or later, though, depression sets in, as their efforts to stay afloat grind to a halt. When others fail to come to their rescue, they sink into an angry despair, yet with little insight into the futility of their placating lifestyle.

Hardcore people-pleasers lack the self-acceptance necessary to set adequate boundaries. Their fear of disappointing others is, in effect, their emotional Mount Everest. It's only when others finally recognize their depletion that boundaries are set *for* them. Christians only make matters worse when they spiritualize this dysfunction by redefining the placating lifestyle as "humble service" before God. They don't understand that boundary setting honors God—it prevents the sins of disrespect, manipulation, and exploitation from others. The alternative dishonors everyone.

Jesus actually lived this boundary-setting principle. After many exhausting days of teaching, he escaped the pressing throngs to find rest (Luke 8:1–4, 19, 22). Doubtlessly disappointing many, but recognizing his need for physical restoration, he set out to sea with his disciples. No apologies. No contorted explanations. Just a graceful exit. The wisdom of taking a break was clear when we find him sleeping through a storm the disciples feared would sink the boat (8:23–25). By his example, Jesus was teaching the disciples how to deal with the pressures of their own future ministries without becoming hobbled by guilt or over-exhausted by the demands of others.

Guilt-produced depression accounts for the convoluted thinking that never saying no shows deference to the Christian idea of sacrifice. False guilt strips us of the ability to acknowledge the longings of our hearts. We deny expression to our ideas, our preferences, and our opinions. As fatigue builds, we spiral down into a litany of self-condemnation, something we can't stop because we have lost touch with who we are. An exhausted Christian once told me, "Every time I am tempted to say no to somebody in the church who wants me to take on a new responsibility, something which I don't have time or the desire to do anyway, I feel guilty. Why can't I happily do things for the Lord? Is my spiritual life that messed up? Maybe I'm just tired of being on everybody's to-do list."

This man had practically abandoned his wife, forcing her to accept far too much alone time simply because he was too busy trying to fulfill everyone else's needs. His wife was rightfully resentful for being so low on his priority list, but felt guilty, too, since he was doing such a "noble" service. He, on the other hand, had grown weary of feeling like he pleased no one, least of all the endless line of sometimes ungrateful supplicants for his help. In short, he was burned out. This, together with his unceasing guilt, sent him into considerable depression, which only made things more difficult by driving a further wedge of emotional isolation between him and his wife. The result left everyone unhappy, except, perhaps, those who had urged him to take responsibilities they themselves wanted to avoid.

There are other times when we try to mask a vacuum in our identity—while covering our true sin—with a façade of false righteousness and religious legalism. We may even develop a certain false pride, convinced that we are, in some way, doing more for the kingdom than are others. But the truth is that, though we'd like to believe we are in the process of being sanctified by the Holy Spirit, sin must indicate otherwise. Sin is happening exactly for the reason that one is not trusting in and empowered by God's Spirit. As author John Piper puts it, "What does not come *from* satisfaction in God, and *through* the guidance of God, and *for* the glory of God, is God-less—it is sin."[1]

How much discomfort must depression's alarm signal inflict before we will choose to let go of these damaging ideas? When will we realize that where legalistic "shoulds" fail, grace wins? In psychiatrist Paul Tournier's words, "The obliteration of our guilt is free for us because God has paid the price."[2] The cross diverted the justice we deserve onto Jesus, so why do we think we need something more?

When you feel guilt, you must first determine its legitimacy, then consider whether restitution should be pursued. True guilt is, as we've seen, an emotional indicator of moral compromise—but false guilt is not. You address legitimate guilt by setting things right through repentance and contrition. You free yourself from false guilt by reviewing the mistaken beliefs that have spawned your self-defeating behavior. The following chart may help you to distinguish between these two types of guilt so you can take appropriate action:

TRUE GUILT	FALSE GUILT
is generated by healthy moral conviction.	is generated by unhealthy social expectations.
reflects disobedience of God's will.	reflects violation of internalized legalistic sanctions.
is measured by absolute divine standards revealed by God.	is measured by relative human standards taught in the home or church.
prods us to reach outward (and upward) to repair broken relationships.	promotes dysfunctional relationships and self-condemnation.
leads to a positive self-concept shaped by the truth.	leads to a distorted self-concept shaped by lies.
is based on the desirable connection between relationships and the experience of love.	is based on the destructive connection between relationships and loss of love.
signals the need for spiritual and emotional wholeness.	perpetuates spiritual and emotional deformity.
is intended to lead to true repentance and genuine healing.	leads to more failure and greater dishonesty.

With true guilt, the best antidepressant is a clear conscience. But with false guilt, the most effective antidote is a more charitable habit of thinking. Freedom from depression requires you to address both.

FINDING OUR LIMITS WITHOUT GUILT

False guilt ambushed Susan when one of her three children was stricken with a congenital disease that was fatal. The doctor said her son would begin deteriorating by age five and would die before his eighth birthday. As time wore on, Susan became obsessed with his care, being acutely aware of his every need or desire—so much so that she neglected her husband and her other children. As expected, the boy died, after which Susan suffered severe grief depression. What was unexpected was the fact that her depression seemed only to worsen with time. Finally, her husband brought her in for counseling, fearing she might become suicidal.

During the course of the interview, Susan shared her unrelenting grief. As she did, she was asked if she had any other feelings while caring for her son. She hesitated, then blurted out, "Once, when I was feeling tired and kind of lonely, I wished my son would go ahead and die so I could get back to normal life with my other children." Then she broke down and sobbed. Between sobs, she asked, "How can any mother worth the name feel that way toward her own son?" In truth, such thoughts are natural and common under these conditions, so her guilt was false. Nevertheless, she had tried to compensate for it by giving her son exaggerated attention, neglecting everyone else. What she was doing was trying to "prove" to herself that she wasn't such a terrible mother after all.

Susan's depression came from more than just the grief of her loss. She was also struggling with what she thought was her gross insensitivity. Once she understood that a normal, loving mother could have such human feelings and reactions, she began to heal. In a short time, her depression, having served its purpose, began to lift. She had taken too much responsibility for something she didn't understand and so had distorted her perception of her own character, assaulting her integrity as a mother.

False guilt often does this, which is why it often results in overcompensating behavior. The compulsion either to please everyone or to convince yourself you should be somehow above normal human shortcomings is your attempt to expiate your guilt over disappointing others (and yourself). But God doesn't want you to depend on acceptance from others for your personal legitimacy. Should you stop caring about others? No. But you must act on internal conviction, not on external approval. It's not easy, but it's the best thing for your mental and spiritual health.

If people-pleasing is your goal, you will find yourself in a constant state of stress. Just ask Moses. God asked him to be Israel's leader, not their slave—to bring them *out* of bondage, not to put himself *in* bondage. Nonetheless, he found himself overburdened with his people's demands.

If you want to avoid this error, you are best guided not by popular opinion but by the freedom of God's Spirit. For this is the way you prevent the chronic depression that comes with enslavement to others.

Sometimes people form unrealistic expectations and mistake them for God's direction. They respond to their fears by trying to create the conditions for these expectations to be fulfilled. But God often teaches us through the unexpected, sometimes even through disappointment, to release control. This can be more than disquieting, however, when we are part of the "safety first" crowd.

God wants you, of course, to take appropriate responsibility; but never mistake this desire for meaning that you must take his responsibility. Although you may not always see the pattern, he's weaving your experiences—even the painful ones—into a beautiful and unique design. Like everyone else, you're a work in progress. Nothing can happen to you that escapes his watchful eye. He even protects you from yourself, finding ways to rein you in when you take on more than your limits can handle. But you can join him in these efforts by learning to discern where your limits are.

Recognizing your boundaries enables you to serve God more effectively. You might resist this lesson if you think facing your limits questions your significance. But, strangely enough, facing them actually enhances it. How can this be? Because life is about God's strength displayed through your weakness. God's glory, not yours.

God doesn't accept your weakness as an excuse for failing to serve him. He takes you as you are and transforms you into what you can become. As someone once said, "What we are is our gift to God, but what we can become is God's gift to us." This gift is your high calling.

The unchurched are repulsed by the Christian's constant anxiety over incurring God's wrath or displeasure. Why would they be drawn to a life tortured by false guilt? When believers browbeat themselves—in keeping with their perception of an angry, autocratic God—it merely confirms the suspicions of a skeptical world. The picture of Christians dragging their "faith" around as a heavy burden does little other than show how depressing religion can become.

SWALLOWING ANGER:
THE CASE AGAINST MENTAL INDIGESTION

Closely related to the problem of false guilt is that of unresolved anger. We discussed earlier the way in which pain evokes anger, which, in turn, produces guilt for feeling such a "negative" emotion. This guilt may stay on the surface, but the anger often does not. Turning these strong emotions inward can trigger a depressive episode that baffles everyone, including your closest friends.

These hidden dynamics became evident in a young man who arrived at my office in a suicidal despair. Tim, a Christian, was distraught over a moral lapse he had promised himself would never happen. He and his fiancée, Elizabeth, had made a pact to avoid sexual involvement before marriage. But one night he stayed too late, and what was unthinkable to him happened. Consumed with guilt, Tim repeatedly asked Elizabeth to forgive him, to the point that she became concerned about his deepening depression. He could not forgive himself. He felt he'd failed God and Elizabeth and had decided to punish himself by forsaking his most meaningful aspiration—to enter the ministry. He grieved over the apparent death of his dream: "How could I let this happen? I've ruined everything. My dreams are gone. My virginity is gone. My relationship with Elizabeth is forever affected. And, to make things worse, I'm certain that God's done with me. In fact, I'm done with me."

The turning point came when he unearthed an emotion he'd denied to his own awareness in the aftermath of the sexual encounter: anger. He'd felt hurt and angry that Elizabeth hadn't stopped him, but instead accepted his amorous advances. He knew he was responsible for his misbehavior, but he also blamed her. Recognizing his anger spurred a new round of guilt for such an "inappropriate" emotion. But he sat down with Elizabeth and discussed his feelings with her, acknowledging that he was not trying to excuse his sin. He was relieved when she both understood and accepted his anger—she shared responsibility for that evening's events. This watershed moment enabled him at last to forgive himself, and thus to accept God's forgiveness. His depression lifted, and he once again began to live with hope and optimism.

Tim's depression had been related to guilt about the sexual incident itself. But it was only when he acknowledged and learned to accept the anger he harbored toward his fiancée that he was able to deal with his feelings appropriately.

Most of us don't manage our anger very well. Some lament their uncontrolled explosions, while others have trouble expressing their anger at all. Many are chronically depressed, unable to handle the reality of their angry feelings or to determine their source. Angry depressives struggle with inappropriate, hair-trigger rage, often aggravated by their gloomy pessimism about life itself. Or they may simply succumb to a stifling withdrawal that looks more like apathy. These are the extremes, between which people experience many variations. But neither extreme is helpful.

Some people—particularly Christians who view anger as a sin— refuse to acknowledge their anger for fear of exposing their unworthiness. Others suppress anger in order to avoid uncomfortable conflict. However, both are dishonest. When people limit their anger to nonverbal expression, they feel free to deny it altogether. Still worse, bottling up their anger denies them the only opportunity they have to use their feelings to discover the source of their emotional pain.

The healthy alternative is to talk through your anger with the person toward whom you feel it. Yes, it's possible to privately let go of some anger. But more often you'll harbor it; as a result, it grows into an emotional cancer, eating away at your relationships, eventually destroying your chances for a happy, meaningful life.

We're not advocating brutal disclosure without tact or kindness, or any kind of retaliatory accusation. It's just as dishonest as denial to verbally hammer someone to a pulp, claiming all the while that you're "just telling the truth." Instead, we're talking about revealing your insides while also acknowledging the other's right to believe and feel differently. When *both* parties' concerns are considered before reaching resolution, the relationship will only strengthen.

Confession and forgiveness should, of course, be the tactics of *first* resort whenever you've hurt someone and been hurt by them in return. But it's easy to resist admitting wrong when you think it weakens your position in the relationship and damages your credibility. The truth is that it makes you more believable, and, more importantly, it softens the other person's heart.

Like confession, forgiveness often seems difficult. Maybe you fear opening yourself up to repeated hurt and betrayal. Not wanting to be duped, you instead adopt the ultraconservative rule "nothing ventured, nothing lost" as your guiding principle. But don't forget that forgiveness and trust are two different things.

Or maybe you think forgiveness is letting the offender off the hook, as though he's free never to feel guilty or suffer consequences for his behavior. But forgiveness is not the same as absolution either. It doesn't excuse wrong behavior or shield the offender from consequences. Rather, it shifts the focus away from retribution, which only harms your integrity.

For others, forgiveness seems foolish, while "defending one's honor" feels like the more noble path. But the true ignobility of unforgiveness is revealed by its contrast to Christ's example (and Peter's call that we follow it): "While being reviled, He did not revile in return; while suffering, He uttered no threats, but kept entrusting Himself to Him who judges righteously" (1 Pet. 2:23 NASB). Impossible? Not with the healing, character-building power of Christ. Returning injury for injury demeans the self and sacrifices peace of mind—it's stooping to the same deficit of virtue as the other person. Like the aphorism "Bitterness is like taking poison and expecting the other person to die," a bitter heart is primarily a path to chronic depression.

When you become hardened by an unforgiving spirit, something life-sustaining dies within you. Your empathy and compassion fade, and you neglect intimacy in your relationships. You polarize your world into allies and enemies, most of them oblivious to the original injury. A resident defensiveness settles in, spelling a life of unhappiness, depression, and paranoia. Ironically, none of this has much, if any, effect on the original offender. Instead, the sin of bitterness wraps its poisonous fingers around your soul and squeezes out every drop of tenderness and kindness, leaving an empty shell of cynicism and cruelty.

When Jesus taught about turning the other cheek, he knew that contrary to our expectations, we would lose far more than we would ever gain if we remained secretly resentful or, conversely, if we lashed out in retaliation. Revenge plays on our natural self-centeredness but ends in self-destruction. It has killed many marriages and friendships. But humility is a hard sell to the overindulged and the terribly wronged, who mistakenly equate it with the philosophy of the doormat.

Forgiveness is difficult because it requires an act of grace—a commodity in short supply. Grace is an unconditional decision made in a definable moment, quite unlike trust, which develops with time and experience. Grace depends not on the recipient's merit but on the grantor's benevolence. Trust, on the other hand, is *earned* by the offender over time, not by words but by a discernable change in conduct.

As hard as forgiveness is, it's important for our spiritual character. It means acting with *assertive restraint* that exposes, by contrast, the offender's aggression. Equally important, it is likely to foster attitudinal change in both parties. How can we *not* forgive as God has forgiven us? "How can we speak of God's grace in our lives," a colleague once remarked, "and still bear so little resemblance in character to the one who gave it?" To "turn from evil and do good" (1 Pet. 3:11) is always challenging, even under the best of circumstances. But God offers his own presence as a source of strength to do what is foreign to our human nature.

How you conduct yourself determines your reputation among nonbelievers. It's God's desire to present to the world a body of believers who stand out by their acts of charity. An American pastor encountered a man in India who told him that he respected Christians because they were the only ones who compassionately tended to the poor (the so-called untouchables), who rescued women from their husbands' funeral pyres (in the Hindu practice of *suttee*), and who retrieved unwanted female babies thrown into the Ganges River. "How can someone," he asked, "consider such things as anything but noble and courageous in a society whose beliefs and customs have, for centuries, been so brutal and degrading?"

So far, so good. But the frequency of unforgiving attitudes (and resulting depression) we find among Christians in this country should serve as a wake-up call to revive the spirit of Christ in the church. We must change the ways we treat each other to provide hope to a world that promises what it cannot deliver.

DESERTING ABANDONMENT: REJECTION REVISITED

When I was twelve, my grandmother, who had been living with our family for a number of years, became ill and died. She had been close to my sister and me, so it was the first significant loss we experienced. I remember standing by her casket, overwhelmed by the grief that was tearing open a large hole inside me—a chasm that opened still wider when I saw my mother's tears.

This loss was painful, but I was fortunate that I still enjoyed parental nurture and a happy, connected home. Many have suffered losses far more traumatic than mine, including the loss or absence of a loving, intact home. Within them grows a deep and abiding sense of abandonment—the earlier the age at which this happens the more alarming the consequences.

Any traumatizing loss early in life can leave a person more vulnerable to subsequent loss—or even to the perceived threat of loss. Recently, I met with an unstable couple who were dating. The young man insisted on maintaining his friendship with his former fiancée, and his girlfriend was jealous. She had a long history of abandonment by the important men in her life, beginning with her father, and felt threatened by her boyfriend's continued association with this other woman. Her boyfriend's lack of empathy—in fact, outright annoyance over her insecurity—only aggravated the situation, casting serious doubt on the relationship's viability. "Why can't you understand how wrong your relationship with Sheri is? You'd hate it if I started seeing one of my old boyfriends. Why do you have to be like all the rest of the men I've known?" she asked. "You're so unreasonable. Do I have to give up all my friends just because you can't accept them?" he shot back.

Part of the reason a history of relational loss makes it difficult for many of us to trust is that it suggests that we are somehow unlovable and therefore incapable of holding on to any relationship. Depression is never far away. Some people, in fact, remain in unhealthy and abusive relationships, rationalizing that any relationship is better than none at all. When failure threatens a current relationship, the abandonment history surfaces and quickly leads to hopeless, sometimes angry despair, far deeper than someone without this history would experience.

The relationship, if it survives, becomes a lonely one, either because each is wary of any further commitment or because there were too many problems from the beginning. To those who question the sustainability of a relationship, emotional safety is always the chief goal, which is one reason why they become so possessive.

Among adults, twice as many women as men seek treatment for depression. That's partly because women tend to more openly admit to their feelings. It is the father—the first significant man in a woman's life—who is more likely to leave the home. Men, on the other hand, typically tend to treat problems as a challenge to their adequacy in handling things on their own, so they're more likely to "tough it out" in difficult circumstances. Or they bury their emotional distress altogether.

When anyone suffers childhood abandonment, it can result in considerable emotional insecurity. A young man might lack confidence in his male role, experience gender confusion, or feel intense attachment to his mother. Or he might display aggressive, even criminal, behavior that could land him in prison. He could become involved in gangs, in the heavy use of drugs, or in promiscuous relationships.

This is the typical profile of young felons who grow up without fathers—often because their fathers are in jail or are involved in criminal behavior of their own.

Women with abandonment histories may also take drugs and bear illegitimate children, but they're more likely to develop a helplessness that makes them vulnerable to abuse, to become targets for pathological men. They migrate from one transitory relationship to another. They must have a man in the house, but these men rarely stay for long, certainly not long after a baby is born—which, of course, starts the cycle all over again.

In Victor Hugo's *Les Misérables*, we meet a profoundly depressed young woman who worked in the factory owned by the main character, Jean Valjean, a woman whose illegitimate daughter Valjean sought to help. She spoke desperately of her grim circumstances and wretched life on the street. From a broken home, and abandoned by the man she had loved, this woman longed for relief, something she believed only death could give her. Representing so many abandoned women whose lives have been turned upside down, her emotional agony is distressingly palpable. In the musical version, the character sings haunting lyrics that portray her despair in terms of the shattered dream of her youth. They speak of her once high hopes of finding a life of love that would "never die," but that her dream dissolved into a hellish nightmare of abandonment and abject poverty. It so vividly depicts a young woman's complete disillusionment with a life that killed her dream.

Such may be the devastation of abandonment, the cruelty of misplaced hopes. Did you think your life would turn out differently than it did? Have you become resigned to feeling completely alone? You are the very one to whom Jesus came to minister. He didn't come for the comfortable people who see no need for spiritual rescue, not the "religious," self-sufficient people who see life going their way. He came to heal the sick of heart, those who reach out in despair to his healing hand.

God knows more than anyone that the common denominator among both men and women who experience extensive loss and trauma is usually depression. He also knows that by merely experiencing more of the same, they lose all hope for something different. Ultimately, if this hope is to return, they must look not *out* but *up* to find a new meaning to life. As C. S. Lewis put it, "Aim at Heaven and you will get earth 'thrown in': aim at earth and you will get neither."[3]

It turns out, then, that our hope for salvation becomes one with our hope for intimacy, both in this world and in the next. Conviction is the substance of courage, just as courage is the substance of vulnerability. Although intimacy depends on both, withdrawal is found in neither.

FINDING HOPE

1. Setting appropriate personal boundaries frees you from false guilt. It's the best antidote to the passive, placating lifestyle.

2. With true guilt, the best antidepressant is a clear conscience. But with false guilt, it is confronting your mistaken, legalistic, injury-inflicting beliefs with the truth.

3. When you are no longer guided by the evaluations of others but rather by the Holy Spirit, life becomes emancipating.

4. Consider anger as a valuable emotion that can expose the source of your emotional pain. Handled appropriately, hurtful issues can be resolved before they do further damage.

5. The willingness to forgive protects your tenderheartedness. Forgiveness keeps you from suffering the larger injury of bitterness and, later, the pain of depression.

6. If self-protection has been your chief goal in relationships, challenge yourself to take small incremental steps of interpersonal risk to discover for yourself that success is possible.

PART 4

THE GOD-CONCEPT

CONNECTING SPIRITUAL
AND EMOTIONAL WHOLENESS

STEREOTYPES OF DEPRESSION

A beautiful thing never gives so much pain
as does failing to hear and see it.
—Michelangelo

Diane tearfully approached her pastor after Sunday service and asked to speak with him for a few minutes. He agreed and led her to his office. For thirty minutes she poured out the story of her endless depression, pleading for help. He promised to connect her with a church counselor. In the meantime, he encouraged her to trust God for his peace.

A few days later he called to inform her that all the counselors were booked up, but one would call her when an opening became available. He reminded her to continue trusting God, even if she couldn't see his hand at work. He hung up after promising to keep in contact. Though three months went by before she got in to see a counselor, this pastor continued to contact and encourage her, even after she had been strung out on drugs and hospitalized.

While counseling helped her understand why she had become so self-destructive and what she could do to change it, it was her pastor's compassion and encouraging spiritual instruction that sustained her through her crisis. As she reflected, "My pastor spent more time with me than I could have asked for. He didn't pretend to have all the answers, but he seemed to care about me . . . and, when it was all said and done, that was probably the most healing thing of all, especially since I never got that from my father."

We naturally turn to our pastors, busy as they are, to find help for our depression, and we expect their wisdom and prayerful insight to lift our spirits and give us direction. And many times this is what happens. The simple hope of connection with someone who cares to alleviate our loneliness promises some measure of relief.

Christians who are unsure of their standing before God long to be affirmed by the church as obedient believers, approved and accepted by their leaders and God. The importance of this kind of social approval increases in direct proportion to the lack of self-acceptance. The less people feel validated by their own self-talk, the more they seek validation from others. But social validation doesn't always materialize, often because the hurting person's behavior pushes others away. That person soon comes to believe that he or she is not worth *anyone's* attention, even God's.

Despite the oft-repeated affirmations of God's Word, the harsh self-judgments of depressed people rob them of the means of properly understanding on their own what God has to say. Though empty and abandoned, still they turn to support from the Christian community. They come for caring and compassion, maybe even for some helpful advice. But, unlike Diane's experience, sometimes they encounter the coldness of certain stereotypes that find their way into the church. The caricatures of depressed people painted by these stereotypes darkly imply that it's always due to moral failure, which only depresses the seeker even further.

While it's true that moral lapses can trigger depression, most episodes of depression, as we've already seen, have other causes. In fact, many converging factors can come into play in such episodes. To broad-brush the experience as inevitably a moral problem often creates needless doubt and self-condemnation.

Bill and Sally sought counseling for a marriage that had become organized around Bill's depression. His struggles began a year earlier, shortly after he resigned from his church's deacon board and its heavy requirements. He took this action because he could no longer handle the demands of his job, the responsibilities of his home, and the heavy requirements of the deacon board's search for a new youth pastor. This commitment was sapping the time and energy he needed for his job and young family. He was spent, yet he felt guilty.

Despite the prudence of resigning from the board to preserve his health and his marriage, the chairman reproached him for reneging on his responsibility to the church: "I'm disappointed in you, Bill. I thought you understood that true discipleship required great sacrifice. It's God and his church you're letting down, so please reconsider what you are doing and get your priorities straight." With that shot across the bow, the chairman of the board, upset at the prospect of losing a good deacon, kept up the pressure on Bill to reverse his decision.

Bill was taken aback and began thinking that the chairman might be right. But his angry wife urged her husband to ignore the chairman's so-called advice. In fact, she wanted to leave the church altogether. Bill was caught between an important leader of his church and his wife, each demanding opposite courses of action. Bill had resisted the notion that church service is the measure of spiritual maturity, but now he spiraled into self-doubt and depression.

During the course of counseling, he began to realize that his vulnerability to self-doubt stemmed from his history with a mother who used guilt to manipulate her children. In time, this insight helped him reaffirm his family as his priority. He became a more confident husband and father and learned to combat his passivity and approval dependency. He began to respond with God-guided assertiveness, rather than with guilt-induced depression.

As this example suggests, it might be useful to take a closer look at some of the stereotypes that beleaguer the Christian community.

CARICATURES AND CORRECTIVES

To their credit, most Christian leaders *intend* to help believers follow a biblically based approach to depression. They have no wish to kick people when they're down. But the unintended consequences of many people's preconceptions are the same. For such stereotypes involve beliefs that end up oversimplifying the complexity of emotional behavior and often over-spiritualizing its root causes.

God never intended his Word to provide cookie-cutter approaches to psychological problems. In the New Testament, Jesus always tailored his teaching and responses to fit the characteristics of the group or individual. With the legal scholar Nicodemus, Jesus used a provocative doctrinal approach, yet with the condemned prostitute or the cohabiting Samaritan woman at the well, Jesus spoke in concrete, compassionate terms. He channeled his redemptive message through the spiritual, intellectual, and emotional needs he encountered.

Jesus' practical relevance was so effective that Jewish leaders formed an unlikely coalition of sects, normally hostile toward one another, to silence his message. Their imbalanced instruction of the Scriptures had replaced grace with works, and humility with religious pride. Clearly, they were determined at all costs to keep their unquestioned authority.

In one form or another, legalism has continued to survive through the centuries, and today such thinking is the source of many stereotypes Christians hold about emotional struggles, including depression. Religious platitudes have rarely been useful with the depressed. In fact, they cause many Christians to doubt themselves because they sound so spiritual. Our purpose in this chapter, then, is to replace misleading clichés with the truth so the believer's response to emotional upheaval is more appropriate and healing.

The two greatest barriers in the church to accurate thinking about depression are the rigidity of a closed mind and the misjudgment of an indiscriminately open mind. With the former, the helper's inflexible agenda presents a caricature of love. With the latter, the helper's naïveté can lead to a caricature of the truth. Neither, however, can offer much help to the hurting believer.

What we need from sound counsel is patience, insight, and, above all, wisdom to sort through all the factors responsible for triggering the alarm of depression. To the untrained ear, many of these factors will escape notice, which is why some well-intentioned Christians are puzzled (and maybe frustrated) when those whom they are trying to help are not improving.

Meanwhile, in church, depressed believers sit passively in the pews, halfheartedly singing the choruses and half listening to messages that seem irrelevant to the devastation they feel inside. Eventually, some abandon their faith altogether. Others play the game, inwardly dying while outwardly going through the motions of the Christian life.

The church is God's institution, yet it is comprised of imperfect people who can be misguided. What's more, hurting believers can, in turn, hurt others.

Conviction and good intentions don't make the stereotypes promoted any more right than did the zeal of medieval crusaders make their cause right. Misguided conviction is not a virtue.

To capture the power of this argument, we will limit ourselves to four of the many existing stereotypes of depression—the ones we've observed to have the widest influence on suffering believers.

THE STEREOTYPE OF DEPRESSION AS SIN

Perhaps the most harmful of all the stereotypes is the belief that it's sinful to be depressed—that all obedient Christians are happy ones. This implies that depression itself is invariably a problem worthy of rebuke. Now, it's true that ongoing, undisclosed sin can be a cause of depression. But even then, depression is not the sin, but rather the emotional consequence of a sin.

We see this illustrated throughout the Bible. For instance, Saul (later known as the apostle Paul) struggled internally to maintain his rejection of Jesus as the Messiah, despite all the evidence. He set off on a rampage against Christians to drown out his nagging conscience. When Christ confronted him in person on the road to Damascus, he pointed out the futility of Saul's attempts "to kick against the goads" (Acts 26:14), an idiom referring to pointless resistance against a superior power.

Immediately, Saul dropped to his knees and offered surrender, overwhelmed by the enormity of his sin. Indeed, in his subsequent depression, he refused to eat as he contemplated the evil he had committed against Christ and his followers (Acts 9:9).

So depression can be the result of personal sin. Moral culpability generates real guilt—and when depression is the result, it serves as a built-in signal directing us to confess and repent of our wrongdoing. But depression can come from many other causes that have nothing to do with the depressed person's sin.

This point often gets confused because the concept of sin can be considered on two different levels—the general sinfulness of the world in which we live, and the specific sinful acts for which we are responsible. In our fallen world, bad things are going to happen—diseases, accidents, natural disasters, suffering caused by the sin of others—that are beyond our personal control. But when we make sinful choices, we bear the burden of culpability.

The stereotype of depression as sin fails to make this crucial distinction—it places all causes of depression in the second category (personal sin), when many causes belong in the first (circumstances for which we're not responsible). As a consequence, we fail to appreciate depression as the invaluable signal system that it is. Instead, it's regarded as evidence of the work of the Enemy.

As if that weren't bad enough, many Christians become convinced that because of their depression, they're of no value to God and his kingdom—or worse still, that God sees them as a hindrance to the cause of Christ. When their faith becomes a reminder of their pain, its capacity to give comfort vanishes into the night of despair.

This thinking, of course, has tragic consequences. To believe God can no longer use us, we must ignore the fact that many prominent figures in the Bible wrestled with profound depression. Yet God's plan of redemption used every one of them as instruments for his glory (as we shall see in a later chapter). What a pity that our theology can so limit what God can do with our brokenness!

Nevertheless, defending the personal worth of the depressed believer is a battle worth fighting. Christians who equate depression with sin are likely to label themselves as hopeless degenerates, crippling their motivation to discover and solve the issues underneath. What's more, they are trapped in a prison of counterfeit "shoulds." Little wonder they learn to respond inappropriately to adversity and inflexibly to God.

They enslave themselves with rules of their own making and then become their own enforcers. Although "shoulds" are invariably tied in one way or another to the law, and are therefore limited to moral and ethical concerns, this fact is ignored. Instead, these are disengaged from their strictly moral base and applied to virtually everything we do.

How you interpret God's response to your depression often affects the strength of your faith. If you see him as judging you for it, as if it were willful disobedience, you're destined for deeper depression and weaker faith. But discerning the truth can rejuvenate you with a renewed sense of hope. To get there, you must understand that depression is a doorway to new understanding, not a wall trapping you in irresolvable conflict.

This means differentiating cause from effect. Depression is an emotional alarm system (an effect) indicating that something has injured you or that something needs resolution (the cause). The cause (which can involve your ability to choose) may or may not entail sin. But an effect never shares such responsibility, because it stands entirely separate from choice. For instance, how you respond during the course of your depression can be sinful or not. That's because your response is always a moral decision of your will. On the other hand, your emotional state is, as we stated earlier, always morally neutral. So, you can determine whether or not you've sinned by what you do with depression or by what choices you made that led to that depression. But sin can never be determined merely by the existence of depression itself.

Believing you're guilty because you're suffering is a false assumption, one that leads to fraudulent self-condemnation. Remember Job's cry: "My heart is broken. Depression haunts my days. My weary nights are filled with pain" (Job 30:16–17 TLB). Yet the Bible reports, "In all of this, Job did not sin" (1:22 TLB).

If depression were sin and happiness the only expression of true faith, then repentance would resolve the issue and produce happiness. But that's not what happens. Many depressed Christians fail to find any relief through "repentance." Instead, they see themselves as beyond redemption. As long as no one thinks to question this view of depression, the sufferer's faith will provide no consolation.

Even the father of the Reformation, Martin Luther, suffered most of his life from this vicious cycle. He experienced what he called "Devil sweats" over supposed "forgotten sins." These were, in reality, nighttime anxiety attacks. He even had nightmares of the Devil dragging him down into hell. These visions prompted him all the more to spend as much as six hours a day in confession. He was never persuaded that he had repented enough, so he never experienced security with God or stopped dreading the fires of hell.

To believe that depression is evidence of sin is to create a classic double bind for believers. Pretending that all is well in order to avoid public stigma only allows the problem to worsen. But openly admitting to depression and seeking help invites suspicion and condemnation. Bad news either way. And that's the problem with this stereotype: It interprets our alarm system as something sinister rather than something good and necessary for our emotional restoration.

THE STEREOTYPE OF DEPRESSION
AS LACK OF FAITH

The belief that depression represents inadequate faith and the failure to trust God is related to the stereotype of depression as sin. It argues that God is sufficient to meet every circumstance of life (true), but assumes that happiness is the *necessary* evidence of our faith (false). Therefore, the presence of depression means that we do not trust God enough. This view minimizes or ignores the emotional effects of the painful circumstances of life in a fallen world—circumstances such as interpersonal stress; childhood traumas like abuse, neglect, or significant loss; adult traumas like rape or divorce; and many other crises.

It also fails to account for "cluster stress"—several stressors taxing (and overwhelming) our coping systems at the same time, any one of which could push us to the breaking point. If you lose your job, encounter marital problems, and suffer the loss of a parent all within a short time, your coping skills can prove inadequate to the task, leaving you in a state of depression.

That doesn't mean, however, that a lack of faith in God's ability or desire to intervene in some way can't trigger depression. It can—if for no other reason than to add to the burden of helplessness. But to assume that depression is automatically an expression of faithlessness leads to a lot of false guilt about your emotional responses to traumas, many over which you have little or no control.

Yet, in spite of these considerations, someone who equates depression with weak faith sees no reason for a Christian with strong faith ever to be depressed. Belief in God's promises is assumed to be the sole source of power for strength and coping. The problem is that it reduces every human experience to spiritual explanations, a position that defies the multilayered nature of the divine image. I (Gary) call this position "Christian reductionism." It rarely does justice to the complicated character of depression, and, frankly, it's out of step with biblical teaching.

In Scripture, time after time, God responded to depression not by reproaching his servants for lack of faith but by bringing his compassion to bear on their struggles. He provided new perspectives and timely strategies for change that helped them resolve their dilemmas and encouraged them in their walk with him. That's because something other than their trust in God was the problem.

The prophet Samuel despaired because the Israelites wanted a king, and he interpreted their demand as a personal rebuke of his ministry. God reminded him not to take it personally. He wasn't confronting sin in Samuel, but correcting a misunderstanding. In the New Testament, we read that God eased the apostle Paul's distress in one of his darkest times: "For when we came into Macedonia, we had no rest, but we were harassed at every turn—conflicts on the outside, fears within. But God, who comforts the downcast, comforted us by the coming of Titus" (2 Cor. 7:5–6). The problem was one of insufficient respite from affliction, not of insufficient trust in God.

How many times has God sent a Titus to comfort you, someone who ministered to you in your darkest hour? God's gentle touch is perhaps most evident in our weakest moments—and that's especially true during our episodes of depression. What a contrast with our own tendency to become judgmental toward others and to shoot our wounded in the church!

Author Philip Yancey once described an elderly man who had spent his life pursuing godly character—reading the Bible, praying, devoting himself to his family and others. But when he lost his wife, whose faithful companionship had been life-giving, his behavior changed. Speaking of this change in his grandfather's state, his grandson observed: "Since the death of his wife, he has lived alone in a state of near-paranoia, anxious about heating bills and lights left on. When I look at him . . . I don't see a joyful saint in communion with God; I see a tired, lonely old man just sitting around waiting to go to heaven."[1]

This grandson's harsh judgment implied criticism that for all his grandfather's pursuit of godliness, there was little evidence of it in his final days. This grandson failed to acknowledge, however, that profound depression was his grandfather's grief reaction to his life's greatest loss. His apparent inability to cope with a loss of such magnitude had little bearing on the quality of his faith in God. More than anything, this man needed a Titus to comfort him and renew his sense of meaning.

Those of us who object to the stereotype of depression as a lack of faith are sometimes accused of psychologizing away the importance of the spiritual life. On the contrary, we do *not* dismiss spiritual problems in depression. But limiting causal explanations to matters of faith alone ignores what years of clinical experience and biblical study have taught us.

Scripture reveals a God whose response to our emotional conflicts—though sometimes paradoxical, sometimes confrontational—always provides, in some way, life-changing insights if we are attuned to them. That's when depression, as an alarm system, is working precisely according to its design.

Still, you might argue that the Bible teaches we should take joy in our trials and tribulations (for example, James 1:2–3), and that this is evidence of happiness as the criterion for the good Christian life. But if you look closely you'll notice James is speaking about our response to what God is doing to strengthen our ability to endure tough times, not about enjoying the circumstances themselves. We are not asked to become masochistic, cheering every occasion when adversity may occur. Instead, we are to take heart in the fact that God still can use our painful experiences to make us more like Christ.

If the church is to be a healing community, Christians must be honest with themselves and each other about their emotional experience. As Christians, we're not merely in the business of informing minds. We're in the business of changing hearts. Our preaching and the values we live out must be relevant to people's pain.

THE STEREOTYPE OF DEPRESSION
AS GOD'S PUNISHMENT

The third stereotype of depression is a grotesque example of the ability to turn truth into a lie. It's based on the idea that since God is our judge, our depression must represent his judgment. Our depression becomes the personal price we pay for displeasing God. This view differs from the others in that depression is not the display of sin or the proof of inadequate faith, but the penalty itself. This view fits with the concept of God as a feared dictator. It produces a Christian who is always looking over his or her shoulder for some visitation of divine wrath—perhaps a personal loss or physical illness. Repentance is accompanied by dread of retribution, not the freeing anticipation of forgiveness.

This view of depression breeds fear in people who are already pessimistic. With this twisted logic, any self-destructive act, including self-mutilation and suicide, could be justified in the sufferer's mind as carrying out God's judgment. One middle-aged woman who had been hospitalized over the years many times for self-inflicted injury revealed, "I only feel good when I am cutting myself. I'm not worth anything anyway. Besides, I deserve to be punished and God is pleased when I am. Why should he want me to go unchastised? All I've done is let him down a million times."

These thought patterns are difficult to break. A person's fear-based beliefs about God are similar to a child's expectations of an abusive parent. God becomes someone not to love, but to avoid or to placate.

Yet we read in 1 John 4:18 that "perfect love drives out fear, because fear has to do with punishment." By "punishment," John meant the eternal punishment of unbelievers, not the discipline of believers. Discipline involves fatherly lessons for our good.

In contrast, punishment is meted out as the consequences of the sin of one who refuses God's forgiveness. The Bible says God is teaching his children to love him, not to dread him. He sometimes teaches us through adversity, but then adversity is transformed into a good tool to a loving end. It's not a retributive end in itself.

Believers who already hate themselves readily accept this stereotype, understanding their depression not as an alarm system but as evidence of God's justice. They deflect the solace of others and the grace of God as carrots meant for the spiritually acceptable. They, however, should only get the stick. God becomes the avenger, not the protective Good Shepherd.

Author Henri Nouwen dared such believers to "change from living life as a painful task to *prove* that you deserve to be loved, to living it as an unceasing 'Yes' to the truth of that Belovedness."[2] He refers to God as "a Lover who wants to be loved."[3] We, too, are meant to be lovers in search of someone to love. This is the reason for our existence, the point of our creation.

Anger for feeling badly about yourself may also result in your punishment of others, especially those closest to you. You may even blame them. Most people, however, do not understand how despair drives this pattern, partly because it goes underground.

Years of profound depression were evident in Edith, a Christian, who sat limply in her chair. Her controlling husband, Dan, directed every activity in the home, punishing Edith with silence if she tried to help. She spent most of her time in bed, unable to take a shower or even get dressed. Dan had tried many times to get her out of the house but to no avail.

One day she came alone to her counseling appointment, smiling and energetic. I noted the remarkable change in her behavior and asked what happened. She replied, "My husband is sick and is flat on his back in bed. And he hardly ever gets sick. So, I had no choice—I had to get up and get going. By the way, I've got a thousand errands to do, so I need to leave a little early!" However, by the next session, a month later, Dan had recovered and Edith had relapsed. It turned out that, underneath, she was outraged at Dan's control but felt helpless to do anything about it. To a large extent, she retaliated by sabotaging his efforts to cheer her up and by using her depression to avoid sex with him. Only when he was down did she allow herself a normal life.

So punishment can cut both ways. When we mislabel depression as God's punishment, we open Pandora's box, and *every* relationship can become punitive—all because we're so good at punishing ourselves.

THE STEREOTYPE OF DEPRESSION AS DEMON POSSESSION

One of the most controversial stereotypes of depression is the notion that it's the result of demonic possession, or at least oppression. This stereotype assumes that satanic influence invades by way of weaknesses in our character, slowly and subtly destroying our spiritual health.

Like previous stereotypes, this one also views psychological issues as really spiritual issues. In this case, the problem is demonic activity, and the best treatment for depression is intercessory prayer and solemn rituals to cast it out.

In the Middle Ages, whole orders of Christian clergy were devoted to the task of exorcism. Treatments were sometimes harsh, even fatal, designed to make the body unfit for an evil spirit. Today, exorcism techniques are far more humane, tied to specific spiritual procedures. Studies have shown, nonetheless, that many such people have seen their depression return weeks or months later, sometimes with greater severity. Several Hollywood films have raised both fear and curiosity about the paranormal, spurring a fascination with demon activity.

Few Christians would deny that demon possession can occur, although the community is divided over whether it can happen to a Christian. Instances of demon possession are well documented in the Bible, throughout history, and today, especially in cultures where the practice of the occult arts is popular. While we're not sure how prevalent true demonism is in American culture, we see an alarming increase in evil practices in general, and the number of satanic cults and occult practices in particular.

So by challenging the demon-possession concept of depression, we're in no way questioning the reality of Satan and his sway over the world. He exerts a powerful influence, and we must guard against him. Even our Lord, before beginning his earthly ministry, had to defeat satanic power on the battleground of his own humanity. But his temptation experience makes one point clear: Satanic power at its pinnacle of strength is no match for Christ's power even at its weakest point.

When Jesus came into the world as the light of life, he faced accelerated demonic activity. We know, likewise, that the Christian message will not go supernaturally unopposed today. But we must be careful about labeling a specific emotional struggle as a case of demon possession. In a case widely reported several years ago, a woman was told by her therapist that her depression was the result of demonic activity and that her parents had, in all likelihood, subjected her to a satanic cult when she was a child. The result? She alienated her parents and divorced her husband. By the time she discovered that none of this was true, it was too late. She sued her counselor, though her courtroom victory could never recoup her relational losses.

It's risky business to brand an emotional alarm system, intended for a person's benefit, as the work of an evil spirit. At the very least, before making judgments of this sort, we must review pertinent Scripture passages. The New Testament, for instance, describes three major characteristics of demon-possessed behavior that are relevant to our discussion.

First, the behavior was violent and aggressive. Second, the evil spirits acknowledged Christ's divinity—they knew they were subordinate to his power (for example, Matt. 8:28; Mark 1:23–26; Luke 4:41). And third, demon possession incorporated common physical and psychological symptoms—like blindness, inability to speak, and convulsive attacks—

but these same symptoms were also documented in cases that did *not* involve demon possession (for example, Matt. 4:24). If the Gospels make these distinctions, then we should do so as well.

It is interesting to note that all these accounts in the New Testament occurred during a time of scientific awakening in the ancient world. The Jews had in fact become quite sophisticated in their thinking about mental illness as a result of their contacts with Babylon, Greece, and Rome. They cultivated philosophy, law, and medicine, accounting for the large number of physicians practicing among them (for example, Mark 5:26). Luke, one of the gospel writers, was himself a physician of note and would have been well aware of the recognized differences between demon possession and mental disorders.

While depression might accompany some genuine cases of demon possession, it does *not* follow that depression is itself an expression of demon possession. The biblical and psychological evidence speaks to the contrary. Those who stigmatize depression as demonic activity have caused much heartache among hurting people who can conceive of few things worse than falling prey to the forces of evil.

We are, by design, psychological as well as spiritual beings. One dimension can affect the other, but that doesn't allow us to interchange them willy-nilly in our causal explanations. Doing that only blurs the differences critical to understanding and effectively treating depression.

FINDING HOPE

1. While religious platitudes create a caricature of love and truth, addressing one another's emotional struggles without the prejudice of an artificial religious formula reflects both biblical principle and sound psychological practice.

2. Depression is not sin but can be the emotional consequence of sin. Yet it can also come from many other causes that have nothing to do with a depressed person's sin.

3. In Scripture, we read that God responded to depression not with rebuke for lack of faith, but with compassion, instruction, and grace-filled intervention.

4. Good things, like encountering a "Titus" in your life, can come from difficult events. It is in this context that your pain can be an occasion for lasting gratitude.

5. God is in the business of teaching us to love him, not to dread or resent him. God is a lover who forever delights in your love.

6. Satanic power, at its pinnacle of strength, is still far weaker than God's power in its most minimal demonstration.

THE GOD WHO DEFIES
STEREOTYPING

When can I go and meet with God? My tears have been my food day and night. . . .
Put your hope in God, for I will yet praise him, my Savior and my God.

—Psalm 42:2-3, 5

Over the course of history, many religious movements have aimed to control our natural appetite for evil. Through the centuries, the monastic movement has attempted to curb excesses in mind and body by exercises in "purity," the practice of meditation, and engagement in self-restraint. But discipline alone has never been successful in conquering these appetites. At best, we deceive ourselves into *thinking* we've achieved righteousness, much as the rich young ruler's legalistic zeal concealed, even from himself, his secret love of wealth (Matt. 19:16–22).

Even among those who have rejected religion altogether, there is the belief that goodness can be achieved by human effort. I (Gary) met a young man a couple of years ago who proudly admitted that he was an atheist ("I gave up my parents' 'fantasies' a long time ago"). At the same time, he argued with great passion that the solution to the world's ills was to foster cultural change that brought out humanity's "better nature."

Sound familiar?

Most people simply do not want to hear that they are, by nature, imprisoned by their own sin. They want to believe that people are essentially good, and that peace—personal and global—can be achieved through collective determination. They falsely blame their repeated failure to accomplish these things on certain systems of government or on wrongheaded religious dogma. Yet they cannot deny the existence of evil.

The fact is that God has a better way—the way we have through his grace, a grace that allows us to acknowledge our sin without feeling hopeless. This life of humility is the most effective antidote to the impoverishment of virtue so characteristic of the utopian ideas of secular culture.

Changing belief systems always creates a crisis—whether at the level of the culture or in the life of the individual. As troubling as this crisis might seem, in God's hands it can be the doorway to a revelation that liberates our thinking. Personal healing and growth can involve many such crises, opening many such doors.

You'll never attain complete understanding this side of heaven. But spiritual maturity is measured not by knowledge alone but by the strength of your faith. God desires your wholeness rather than demanding your perfection. And it is the quality of your connection with him and with one another that determines that wholeness.

AUTHENTICITY: A GIFT BELIEVERS RESIST

"Know thyself" is one of the oldest admonitions in life. It is also part of God's plan. We can see it in our natural curiosity to discover why we do what we do. Yet scientific interest and personal insight are two different things. While the former is always stimulating, the latter can sometimes be threatening, which is one reason we tend to live in denial. But this way of living can carry a heavy price—including the inability to learn from our mistakes and our insensitivity to others. It even hinders our ability to know why we injure them. Failing to understand these things can damage our view of God, our world, and ourselves, which often leads to loneliness and depression.

The healthy alternative—*authenticity* in our relationships—will change our thinking about the past, our experience of the present, and our expectations for the future. Authenticity involves honest self-examination. It becomes godly when it means examining our pain through our Lord's redemptive lens and revealing ways to avoid compounding our pain. Authenticity invites good theology to drive our experience rather than allowing bad experience to drive our theology. Whenever we let denial distort either, the likelihood of depression increases.

In a recent book, author Alane Pearce describes the importance of this point in her own life:

> You don't need to pretend that everything is okay. You don't need to put on a smiling mask at church. You don't have to be happy all the time because you're a Christian. Life is hard and there are many twists and turns that we don't expect. I think God wants us to acknowledge our pain, but instead of bathing in it, I think he wants us to bring it to him; that's what I did. For many months, I brought my doubts, fear, frustrations and anger right to God's feet. You'll be amazed at what he did with them.[1]

Honest self-disclosure was the beginning of her healing journey with God. At no time does God suggest you should disown what you feel. Instead, he invites you into a trustworthy relationship, first with him and then with those who are significant in your life. There is a kind of emotional cleansing and spiritual recalibration that comes from having that sort of transparent intimacy with our Lord (Matt. 5:8). Your confessions before him become the raw material from which he fashions new ways for you to see your world. The challenge is to stop limiting your life to behaving according to what others think and start living according to what God thinks!

We Christians often continue to have our own "sanctified" forms of dishonesty. When we attempt to help the despairing with well-intended but pointless spiritual platitudes, we only make things worse. The blinders of our denial keep us uncomfortable around those who are struggling, so we try our best to spiritualize their depression away (notice how it becomes more about *our* discomfort than about *their* pain). Little wonder we aren't helpful. Here's one pastor's testimony from his experience with depression: "I'll never forget the well-meaning but exquisitely painful platitudes offered by uninformed friends during those gloomiest days of depression. . . . But those 'platitudes' always hurt much more than they helped. In fact, they *never* helped! So I apologize to anyone who is shaken by the assertion that God might want to use things as painful as depression to do good, or that depression could be a 'companion' that enriches or helps us in any way."[2]

This pastor possessed a forceful personality that intimidated some people, but he became softer, more humble, and more approachable after his depression. He identified this newfound empathy as God's gift to him and to his church. "And I can *definitely* say that depression has often been the only thing," he said, "that could pin my nose to the carpet in search of the Lord's feet."[3]

The tipping point for almost every imbalance is found in how you see yourself. Inside you may feel worthless and inadequate—a weakling who can't resist temptation. Damaged goods. A failure God could never use.

Publicly you wear a protective disguise of joviality. You may even convince yourself that your false face is necessary for Christian appearances. But your lack of authenticity will lead you not to healing, but to a confusion of your identity. What's more, your misconceptions of God and your stereotypes of depression will keep both you and others in the Christian community from discovering what is healing.

In the previous chapter, we looked at a few of the misperceptions some Christians have of the way God deals with depression. They all involved denial and dishonesty in some form or another. We've examined the counterfeits. Now let's take a good look at the real thing. Once we understand God's perspective, we can devise better strategies for changing our own.

In order to get a better picture of how God works in our down times, it's useful to examine the conditions under which his servants in the Bible walked through episodes of depression. Prophets, judges, kings, and commoners—all of them served God in extraordinary ways, sometimes changing the course of history to enact God's redemptive purpose. Yet they did these things in spite of—sometimes *because of*—their depression. Some suffered turmoil because of self-injury through sin; others suffered despite their righteousness. Still, the common theme was the important role their depression played in highlighting something God wanted to teach them or the people they served.

When we stare into the mirror of Scripture, we find a familiar face. But we're also startled to find a radically different outcome, one that forces us to rethink our choices, to realize that there's a different way to live.

WHEN DISOBEDIENCE GETS YOU DOWN

You may think you're too broken to find your way back or too lost to ever serve God again. Likewise, you may read the Bible and tell yourself you are too destitute, that you sin far too much to ever aspire to do great things for our Lord. As a result, you may give up and withdraw into mediocrity.

But what made the Bible heroes heroic? Did they have unusual strength to resist temptation and sin? Let's examine the record and see.

First, we might look at the father of the Israelites, the enigmatic Abraham. Twice he lied about his marriage to his wife, Sarah, so that pagan leaders wouldn't kill him in their lust for her (Gen. 12:10–20, 20). It was God, not Abraham, who protected Sarah from these men. How do you think wives today would feel if their husbands shoved them out in front to protect themselves from a potential assailant? "Here, take her. She's not my wife!" I don't think any wife would feel very safe with that kind of husband. Most likely she'd be outraged.

So Abraham didn't exactly burnish his image with that gambit. Later we find him discouraged by the infighting in his own home. Not wanting to hear any more complaints, nor do anything about it himself, he gave Sarah carte blanche to do what she wanted to defend herself against the attacks of Hagar, his proxy wife. Anything to quiet her. Of course, that only made things worse, compounding Abraham's problems.

Then there was his son Isaac, who, like his father, lied about his marriage to protect his own skin in fear of the Philistine king Abimelech (Gen. 26:1–11). The apple did not fall far from the tree. And because of his dysfunctional parenting, Isaac encountered the depressing reality that his beloved son Esau was cheated not once but twice out of the family inheritance by his other son, Jacob (Gen. 25:29–34; 27:1–40). Not surprisingly, Jacob incurred the wrath of his brother, who threatened to kill him, forcing him to flee the family (Gen. 27:41–45). Sadly, everyone lost. It's ironic that Jacob, later in his life, suffered the loss of his own son Joseph when his jealous brothers sold the young boy to traders (Gen. 37). The sins of our fathers do indeed reach across generations.

Centuries later, despite the privileges of the royal court, Moses became a murderer and an exile (Ex. 2:11–15). When God commanded him to deliver his people from slavery in Egypt, Moses used every possible excuse to avoid obedience (Ex. 3–4). And as Israel's leader, he became overextended and, in moments of despair, accused God of retribution against him (Num. 11).

Then there was Samson, a judge of Israel with his own checkered history. He made special vows of separation unto God and then proceeded to violate every stipulation of these vows (Judg. 13–16). He violated God's prohibition against marrying women from the idolatrous nations neighboring Israel. He was promiscuous, even taking up with at least one prostitute. It was with Delilah that his sin finally caught up with him, landing him in the depressing confines of a Philistine prison (Judg. 16:1–22). Yet despite the fact that Samson sinned often, God used his gift of unusual strength to protect his people from the oppressive Philistines (Judg. 16:23–31). And, of course, there was Rahab, who was even granted a privileged role in the lineage of Christ and yet she was a prostitute, which was regarded then, as well as now, as an occupation of disgrace (Josh. 2; 6:25).

Perhaps most famous of all was King David's sexual encounter with Bathsheba, a married woman (2 Sam. 11). He proceeded to compound his sin by having her husband, Uriah, killed in an attempt to cover up his adultery. These were terrible actions that David had to live with for the rest of his life. Indeed, this reflected later in his readiness to accept another's cursing as a sign of God's judgment (2 Sam. 16:5–12).

The cracks in David's character were also seen in his responsibilities as a father, raising sons so out of control that they committed rape, murder, and treason (2 Sam. 13–15). Still, God's inspired Word describes David as "a man *after his* [God's] *own heart*" (1 Sam. 13:14, emphasis added). In fact, God established the Davidic throne forever among his people and designated David's ancestral line to produce the coming Messiah (2 Sam. 7:11–16; Luke 20:41–44).

Though this isn't a complete list, we have a sufficient sample of flawed, sinful men and women whom God nevertheless loved and used to accomplish great things for the kingdom. The Bible even says of these and others who subsequently served him that "*the world was not worthy of them*" (Heb. 11:38, emphasis added; see also vv. 17–40). Imagine that! These servants of God did things most of us would regard as reprehensible. It's doubtful that, given their backgrounds, any of them would have even qualified to become an elder or deacon in our churches today. Yet God didn't consider them beyond his forgiveness and restoration. Rather, he gave them the highest accolades, and we call them heroes of the faith!

If they were considered as such by God, then perhaps you can see that despite your own frailties and flaws, you are also honored by God if you have faith in him. Notice that even in their greatest despair, the highly imperfect "heroes" of the Bible listened to his voice. You are also invited to become a hero of the faith. God presented the major players in redemptive history so you might understand that it is not your sin that defines you; it is God's love and power, alive through your faith.

DOWN EVEN WHEN DOING RIGHT

Just as we find encouragement from those whose battle with sin has been overcome by faith, we also find an uplifting message in those who struggled with circumstances not of their own making. Let's look at some of these.

We all know that life can be cruel at times. And no circumstances seem more cruel than what happened to Naomi, as recorded in the book of Ruth. Due to a drought in Judah, Naomi and her family moved to the land of Moab. There she endured the tragic deaths of her husband and both her sons. In her deep grief, she wept as she said good-bye to her daughters-in-law, telling them, "Return home, my daughters; I am too old to have another husband" (Ruth 1:12). Her crushing losses had left her alone. But God, in his mercy, placed in Ruth's heart the desire to go back to Judah with Naomi so that she might serve Naomi and lessen her loneliness.

In another narrative, we find the story of Hannah, who, like Sarah before her, could not bear a child, which was humiliating for a woman in that day (1 Sam. 1). For a long time, Hannah wept and even refused to eat. But in the midst of her depression, she cried out to God, vowing that if she were given a child, she would dedicate him to God's service. God granted her petition through the word of Eli the priest, after which her depression lifted: "Then the woman went to her quarters, ate and drank with her husband, and her countenance was sad no longer" (1 Sam. 1:18 NRSV). That child's name was Samuel.

We know of Samuel in his later years. Though faithful in his mission, he was devastated by his people's rejection of God's rule (1 Sam. 8:5). But such rejection was recorded as well in the New Testament, where we read that the apostle Paul also struggled against opposition. "We were under great pressure," he said, "*far beyond our ability to endure, so that we despaired of life itself*" (2 Cor. 1:8, emphasis added). Whatever these hardships were at the time, he appears to have suffered physically and psychologically. But God, the Father of compassion, greatly comforted him in his depression (1 Cor. 1:3).

Most of the Old Testament prophets suffered similar episodes of depression. They felt the weight of their messages of condemnation, even as their fellow countrymen continued to resist God's call to repentance. Men like Amos, a shepherd from Tekoa, and Ezekiel and Jeremiah, both of whom were priests, were called away from their own vocations to address the crisis of their nation's sin. Though they did so with heavy hearts, God never failed to console them with the truth of his righteousness. They kept preaching with the knowledge of God's good purpose on their side.

Again there was David—icon, warrior, musician, and composer. His poetic descriptions of depression are exquisite in their detail (for example Pss. 22, 42, 130). His episodic despair was most often prompted by his weariness of fighting a never-ending parade of enemies. "For dogs are all around me," he cried, "a company of evildoers encircles me" (22:16 NRSV). Yet he spoke of God's faithfulness: "For he did not despise or abhor the affliction of the afflicted—he did not hide his face from me, but heard when I cried to him" (22:24 NRSV).

We cannot conclude this discussion without mentioning Job, whose experience of depression we will discuss in greater detail in the next chapter. For now, it's enough to point out that here was a man who had, by all accounts, lived a laudable life. Yet when adversity struck, he disintegrated to the point of wishing death. Was that because he was a spiritual fraud? No. Rather, he was a follower of God caught up in the disastrous events that can happen in a person's life. He was also a man who was open to learning new things, and indeed, with God's help, he did.

Though this is but a small sample, we can see that Scripture provides ample evidence of God's understanding that even when we are doing things right, we cannot avoid the occasional struggle with depression. Knowing this gives us courage to confront the issues that may have paralyzed us. By encouraging others to do the same, we make our victories contagious to the body of believers. This is, in its deepest sense, what it means to love one another.

To know God's heart, we must allow him to transform our cheerless expectations into joyful anticipation of his goodness. Never does he condemn or scold us for being depressed. In every instance, we see him as wise and gentle, what we would expect of the Wonderful Counselor he is (Isa. 9:6).

CHANGED LIVES CHANGE MINDS

Skilled counselors will always respect their clients' faith. It's their professional and ethical responsibility. But Christian counselors can take it one step further. As fellow believers, they integrate their therapeutic work with matters of faith so clients can better understand how their spiritual lives are connected to their emotional lives. Far from "leading them astray," Christian counselors are interested in helping clients value even more the relevancy of faith to everyday life.

It's with sadness, then, that counselors sometimes encounter opposition in the church. Many assume that the humanistic arguments of some outspoken secular psychologists speak for the entire field of psychotherapy—and that Christian clinicians draw from the same well of metaphysical ideas. The real losers in this tug-of-war are our hurting brothers and sisters—God's own children—who need the help Christian therapists can provide.

A surprising number of our clients are pastors, some of whom once believed and taught that psychology was a tool of the Devil. The actual experience of deep depression often changes these opinions. When a pastor finds relief after receiving psychotherapy or medication (or both), he or she discovers that God has worked through a trained fellow believer to help strengthen his or her faith. Review the comments of one pastor:

> Some pastors struggle with the appropriateness of receiving help that isn't exclusively theological or specifically scriptural in approach. Others are so used to being the ones giving help that they find it difficult to receive any. And, of course, some question the ministry of Christian therapy altogether. I was a member of the second and third groups, especially the third. "The Scriptures are my therapist," I would say, "and they don't charge me $100 per hour for the service."
>
> Certainly the Bible contributed much to my recovery. Its comforts were amazing; its instructions and insights incredible. But being forced by my circumstances to ask for help from an able counselor changed my entire outlook. Without that wonderful man's prayer, honest questioning, and practical help, I don't know how long it would have taken me to heal or if I ever *would* have. I continue to find strength and guidance from the Word of God. But in it I read about the importance of Christian community in discerning the deep things of the Spirit. In my experience with depression, the Bible was good, even excellent. But it was the

Bible in partnership with a gifted, discerning therapist that God used to loose me from the hands of this unrelenting monster called "depression."[4]

Since God created the emotional as well as the spiritual dimension in humanity, it's no surprise that he speaks to us through both. God's tenderness toward us when we're in pain teaches us this principle.

Some years ago, a pastor experienced depression that rendered him unable to get out of bed and preach on Sunday mornings. The congregation was simply told he was "sick." One Sunday morning, several months after receiving emergency professional treatment for his deep depression, the pastor revealed the nature of his problems and apologized for his misguided preaching against psychotherapy and his depression-as-sin dogma. He acknowledged that he may have discouraged some from seeking professional help, causing needless suffering. Shortly following that revelation, several congregation members came to him and thanked him for his honesty. They shared with him just how much it had liberated them to seek help for their own depression, help that unexpectedly brought a renewal of joy to their faith.

The Christian community is called to lead dying hearts to living intimacy with God. That means that we must be honest about our pain and willing to engage in open dialogue that can bring healing to the church. This is what happened with these pastors who began remarkable healing ministries that rapidly spread the message of God's restorative power to their communities at large. The Bible's honesty about the struggles of God's servants testifies to his high regard for authenticity. As we have seen, he can accomplish great things through our weaknesses as easily as he can through our strengths. From the wellsprings of his love, God transforms broken lives into whole people eager to serve him.

ADVERSITY: A NEW OPPORTUNITY

By now you know that depression is not a monopoly of the unfaithful or disobedient. But even though many of life's hardships don't stem from spiritual causes, we know nonetheless that God can still use them for spiritual purposes. You may remember Corrie ten Boom's cruel imprisonment in a Nazi concentration camp. She saw it as an opportunity to see God at work and as an occasion for her to serve God by ministering to others. Because of her confidence that a purpose was being served in her suffering, her life remained meaningful and she experienced a quiet inner contentment that seemed strange to those around her. Yes, she walked the valleys of depression—the inevitable human response to such horrific circumstances—but she didn't give up. Instead, she developed new coping skills and continued to make a difference among her fellow death-camp inmates.

Many believers find such joy and contentment elusive. But that doesn't mean it's not available. Life may deal its depressing blows, but we lose sight of our destiny because of all the added emotional baggage we bring into every situation. We are too busy questioning God's plan—maybe even questioning our salvation—to enjoy what he has given us. Instead of asking what we can learn on the journey, we react with the disillusionment of a cheated tourist.

In Ecclesiastes 3:1–11, we read that the bad times, like the good, are seasons that will pass. They may seem endless, but with purpose and God's provision, we can endure them to their conclusion. The writer of Ecclesiastes revealed a worldview that sees beyond our horizon, through lenses of hope and wisdom. As Ecclesiastes puts it, those who follow God are in his hands (Eccl. 9:1). What better place to be, when earthly life seems so cruel and unfair! No matter how bleak things may look, the end game remains the same: God's goodness and justice will prevail.

When depression strikes, you may not find answers to all of your questions. But wisdom gives you the advantage of living more comfortably with paradox and mystery. Life can be so complex that you can't understand every circumstance or avoid every pitfall. But this need not distract you from the reality that God is in charge. Strengthening your confidence in him means establishing a secure beachhead against emotional paralysis. For this reason it's important to have the wisdom to know the difference between what you can change and what you must accept.

God offers this wisdom to every believer for the asking (James 1:5). But wisdom means a change in the way you think and in the way you act, which at first may be difficult. This difficulty can be eased, however, if a therapist works in collaboration with a pastor and together they provide an effective combination of strengths to help burdened people heal. But both the pastor and the psychologist must value the collaborative effort.

A client asked her pastor to work with me to help her through her depression. To her surprise, he declined. He doubted such consultation would be of much value. He told her he didn't feel it was his strength. Disappointed at first, she knew she needed counseling, so she pressed on. She achieved success in therapy, in part by recognizing how her rigid ideas about spiritual things were getting in the way of identifying the issues causing her depression. It's a pity that her pastor, who had been such a wonderful influence in her life, felt uncomfortable joining us. He missed out on the joy of seeing how her unfolding freedom contributed to the reemergence of optimism in her faith. I have no doubt he would have added a valuable dimension to her recovery.

THE WISDOM OF LOVE

Several years ago, I spoke with a friend who had taken his nine-year-old son deep-sea fishing. A violent storm developed on the open sea. Huge whitecaps crashed over the bow of the boat, rocking it viciously. When the father saw his boy throwing up and then reduced to dry heaves, he implored the captain to turn back. Once in port, the man helped his son out of the boat and onto the dock, where the boy lay down, unable to walk. The father bent down and began stroking his stricken son. Then the young boy looked up, managed a weak grin, and blurted out, "Wasn't that a great trip?"

Later the boy recounted his experience to his family as a stirring, memorable adventure, not a miserable disaster to be forgotten. Why? Because he prized every moment he spent with his father. And no mere circumstance could blur this reality. He even talked enthusiastically about going again!

When we experience the fulfillment of our deepest desires, it consumes us and sustains our focus in spite of painful distractions. This is the kind of fulfillment the Bible intends when it speaks of the abundant life. It's the uninterrupted time spent with our heavenly Father. Here we find wisdom, the secret of hope, and peace in the midst of suffering.

The book of James speaks of this wisdom—not just knowledge, but a transformation that the world can't explain (James 1:2–5; 2:14–18; 3:13, 18; 4:4–6; 5:17–18). It means accepting difficulties that the Holy Spirit can use to shape our character, finding purpose in the synergy of faith and adversity, and working out our faith in service to others who need our help. But this involves a personal investment in our belief. Although it's possible to believe in something you don't have much commitment to, it's not possible to be committed to something you don't really believe in. That's why James speaks of serving widows and orphans as the natural and necessary outworking of true faith.

So we come full circle. Responding to the alarm system of depression, you seek professional help and pastoral care. You experience psychological and spiritual growth. You discover wisdom and richness in intimacy with God. And your deepening intimacy with him stirs you to share hope and vision with others who are depressed—one desert survivor showing another where to find the life-sustaining oasis. It's in this way that you authenticate your transformation.

At last, we've established a virtuous cycle to replace the vicious cycles— an elegant, pragmatic pattern of Christian witness and multiplication— freely offered to a world helpless to provide its own meaning to pain.

James invites us to be *doers* of the Word and not merely hearers (James 1:22–25). Intimacy with God is active, not passive. Real faith is demonstrated in real works (James 2:18). We have a choice: to be hearers only, who forget and do not act, or to be doers who enact the unforgettable.

Healing from depression is the destiny of doers. What's more, "They will be blessed in their doing" (James 1:25 NRSV).

AN ABNORMAL LOVE

Few of us connect love and suffering because few of us experience loving feelings while we are suffering. Yet implicit in genuine love is the risk of suffering. God made himself vulnerable to this risk when he created humanity.

Jesus' love and mercy for us led him to the cross. Our invitation to his eternal wedding banquet is printed in his blood. What other evidence do we need to know that his goodness and compassion are real?

So why do people resist this invitation to love? Inside, they believe something is wrong with who they are — their shame prevents the vulnerability of self-revelation.

In the Sermon on the Mount, Jesus invited us to place our trust in a love that prompts behavior that runs counter to everything we've learned. Who in his right mind would turn his cheek for a second slap? Or respond to coercion by walking with an assailant twice as far as he demanded? Or give everything to someone taking him to court? Or loan money without promise of repayment? Or, most bizarre of all, lay down his life for someone who hates him (Matt. 5:38–48)? Picture today's fanatical, genocidal terrorists who would murder someone you love. Would you love them in return? Yet these are the things our Lord did (Matt. 26:36—27:56). He stood on the Mount of Olives on that Sunday before his crucifixion, looking across the Kidron Valley to Mount Zion, on which stood Jerusalem and the magnificent temple complex glinting in the sun, a city filled with scribes and Pharisees who hated him and were plotting to kill him. And what did he do? He wept for the lost souls of his beloved Jerusalem!

He did what we find impossible. He fulfilled every admonition he gave in that memorable sermon, the ones that seemed absurd to his audience. He was beaten but didn't fight back. He was accused in court without defending himself. He carried the cross that was forced upon him. He allowed his clothes to be taken and distributed among the soldiers, even when he could have stepped down off the cross to reclaim them. And he died because he loved his persecutors (1 Pet. 2:23–24).

Crazy, right? Only from our human perspective. On our own, we could never imagine loving like that. But because God *does* love that way, we can receive healing for our wounds. But we must trust him enough to open our wounds to his inspection. And we must allow his appointed doctors of the soul to nurture us back to spiritual and emotional health.

Jesus came to heal the sick, not to congratulate the self-righteous. He responds to those who know they need him, not to those who want him to need them. What better Counselor do we have to entrust with our pain, with whom we can welcome into our lives the healers of the mind he has commissioned for his service?

FINDING HOPE

1. Depression can help you become gentler, humbler, and more empathic, which, in turn, can make you more approachable to others.

2. In biblical history, God did great things through his servants, sometimes in spite of and sometimes because of their depression.

3. The fact that God uses flawed people to accomplish his purposes demonstrates how you are defined not by your sin but by his love and power, through your faith.

4. Because depression occurred among God's most trusted servants, you can know that depression is no respecter of persons. Indeed, it is in periods of depression that God sometimes most powerfully manifests his wisdom.

5. The advantage of living with God is to more comfortably live with paradox and mystery. It is characteristic of the abundant life.

6. We have a choice: to be hearers only, who forget and do not act, or to be doers who enact the unforgettable.

11

UNFINISHED VIEWS OF GOD

No nation, no people has ever risen above its religion,
and no religion has ever risen above its concept of God.

—A. W. Tozer

I feel all alone in the universe," she read from her journal, reflecting on our last session. "If only I could just lie down on the wind and let it bear me up and away just to let go and stop trying to understand the mind of God. How do people find belief when nothing makes sense?" Her words were tense and her mood anxious. She paused as if to study my (Gary) face for some kind of reaction. She continued. "I feel like a kid with my nose pressed against the glass. The people I see on the other side struggle over the details, but they always have their faith as a firm foundation in the darkest time." Tears were beginning to fill the pages now. With tight pen strokes she wrote, "I seem to be spinning through space unable to hold on to a sense of meaning and purpose and yet I do believe that there is someone in charge." And then after another, still more pensive reflection, she added, "Maybe my longing for faith is the reason for the depression I'm experiencing; maybe then I'd feel significant."

This lovely divorced woman wanted nothing more than to be important to someone else. She couldn't let go of her belief that God was out there someplace giving comfort and meaning, at least to others. But she couldn't apply this truth to her life. In the midst of her agonizing conflict, she ached for someone to see her pain, to respond with a little nurture. Her despair had not only driven her to the emotional edge, but also to a crisis of faith.

We might wonder that God would allow a person whose longings for intimacy could be so frustrated. A person whose soul is crafted for love, but whose life seems so bereft of it. We find the answer to this question in God's response to Adam and Eve when they squandered their opportunity for companionship with him. He did not revile them. Nor did he condemn them to their own endless futility. Instead, he wasted no time inaugurating a plan to redeem his most precious creation.

So, rather than wondering whether he cares, it might be better to ask, who is this God who would give humanity freedom and then pursue their hearts after they had turned against him? Why would he purposely create human life with the capacity to reject him and then enter the brutal world of human brokenness and suffering to set things right again?

This is the story of God's response to fallen humanity's struggle with unrighteous character. There is a momentous beginning, a tragic middle, and a glorious end to this story. While it has captured the imaginations of people around the globe, it has also been reviled by many as threatening to their way of life, as a dangerous tale that prompts reactionary thinking.

In truth, it is a simple love story. It reveals the force of God's grace and the final triumph of his love.

We are still in the middle part of this story, though we are drawing ever closer to its conclusion. In the meantime, though, we must deal with life in the trenches. That's where faith always has its greatest impact.

We see this impact in the gripping accounts of people whose crises served as a backdrop for God's great lessons of living. We have alluded to some of them earlier, but now we turn to them in more detail to see what more we can learn.

SAUL: A LESSON FOR ALL SEASONS

While Saul was no hero of the faith, he was nevertheless Israel's first king who, by a predicament of his own making, fulfilled God's purpose. It came about because the Israelite people demanded to have a warrior king "like all the other nations," a dramatic moment in their capitulation to pagan values (1 Sam. 8:4–5).

In a surprising move, God then instructed his servant Samuel to grant the people what they wanted. Saul was tall, muscular, and a courageous warrior. In short, he was the popular image of the perfect king to protect them from their enemies. Like their pagan neighbors, they were persuaded by external appearances, something not unfamiliar to our society today. But Saul was flawed as a king. His feelings of inadequacy clouded his judgment and perverted his behavior as he swung from intensely frantic activity to depressed mood states in which he was incapable of any intelligent action (1 Sam. 16–18). It is likely that he suffered from what today we would call bipolar disorder. About the only relief he found came from the music of the young man David, who played a harp for him to soothe his darkened spirit.

Driven by unrestrained jealousy over David's growing popularity, Saul turned against him. In his delusions of persecution, he saw David as a self-styled pretender to the throne and was convinced David was trying to usurp his authority and take over the reins of power. As we have sometimes seen in ourselves, Saul personified in his behavior that moral contradiction in which people are drawn to a course of action that, in their more sober thinking, they would otherwise recognize as self-destructive.

In the end, Saul's distraction compromised his military judgment and led him into a suicidal engagement with the Philistines that ended his life and left Israel once again helpless against its enemies. While the judges who preceded Saul had only to perform a single feat of military glory to fulfill the promise of leadership, as king, Saul was required to perform such feats continuously. He was always onstage. It was too much for his fragile state and forced him to exhibit the darkest element of his personality.

Why then did God provide a king who was so long on appearances but so short on stability? The biblical story underlines God's intention: He gave the Israelites what they wanted in order to teach them what they needed. They had wanted a warrior king like all the pagan nations of their day because they believed that such a figure would save them from their enemies. But they were rejecting God's leadership in favor of a physically tangible ruler. And how did that change of allegiance work out for them? It led to a national disaster.

Have you ever gained something you really wanted only to discover that something else would have been much better for you? This is an important way God teaches us his wisdom. This would be useful to think about the next time you are upset that God doesn't seem to be answering your prayers.

JONAH: WHAT WOULD OTHERS THINK?

Anger was no stranger to Jonah. God asked him to take the message of forgiveness to the people of the Assyrian capital of Nineveh. He refused the mission and tried to escape by boarding a ship sailing in the opposite direction. But God had other ideas. Through his unusual use of a large fish, God brought the unwilling Jonah to Nineveh to do his bidding. When Jonah began to preach, there was an awakening among the Ninevites such as had never been seen. With great remorse, they repented of their sin and covered themselves with sackcloth and ashes. As a consequence, God withdrew the calamity that was about to befall them as judgment for their sin.

This outcome was what Jonah had feared all along, and it angered him. Why? Because the Assyrians were Israel's mortal enemy, and nothing would have pleased Jonah more than to see them destroyed. But, alas, that was not going to happen, at least not anytime soon.

Jonah became depressed because *he* had played a pivotal part in these events. He was convinced this news would not play well back home. It appears that Jonah cared too much about what his fellow Israelites thought. Of course, he also wanted to indulge his own hatred of the Assyrian people. As a consequence, Jonah was willing to disobey God's command.

It might surprise you that God responded to Jonah's anger and depression with tolerance, not rebuke. Twice he asked Jonah if he had good reason to be angry, and Jonah replied that he had. He then proceeded to win Jonah's heart by giving him the reason for his compassion and forgiveness of the Ninevites, whom he described as blind to their sinful ways. Contrary to Jonah's heart, it was God's desire to forgive every contrite heart, whether Jew or Gentile, friend or foe. To withhold his mercy from a repentant sinner would have violated his loving character.

It's hard to confront our own pettiness. But that was what Jonah had to do. If God had allowed Jonah to circumvent the chance for the Assyrians to repent, God would have proven himself to be unworthy of worship. Even Jonah himself would have had a diminished view of God.

Jonah demonstrated what happens when we compromise our virtue for the sake of the crowd. He showed us, too, how remorseless revenge can be. These are important lessons to learn if we wish to avoid traps that trigger depression.

JOB: THE ABUNDANT LIFE REVISITED

We bestow honor on those who serve as models of inspiration. But let them fall from their pedestal of success and we can be merciless in our criticism. This is what happened to Job. He had everything: wealth, social status, great family, strong faith, and the good health to enjoy it all. His friends agreed that Job was blessed by God for living righteously before him. All this changed when Job lost everything, including his health. When even his friends challenged the purity of his faith and the righteous character of his life, his spirit sank into the hopeless anguish of a broken heart.

It was in this depressed state that God met Job with an awe-inspiring revelation. He challenged him, enlarged his vision, and restored his soul. Above all, he opened Job's eyes with such astounding self-disclosure that he was moved to declare God's goodness as never before. In his concluding conversation, God had proceeded to reveal his majesty and power through a series of penetrating questions. Unable to answer God's questions, Job then replied to the Lord: "Surely, I spoke of things I did not understand, things too wonderful for me to know. . . . My ears had heard of you but now my eyes have seen you" (Job 42:3, 5).

God challenged Job to reexamine his anger. He knew that if Job bottled up his anger and failed to understand what it was telling him, he would never learn anything from it. Instead, he would only languish in depression. Then God taught Job about his eternal power and purpose by pointing to what could be seen in all of creation. That God would consider Job important enough to disclose his glory revealed his desire for Job to know the meaning and purpose of creation. Think about that. Would you disclose more about yourself right after you'd been subjected to someone's anger and frustration? Not likely. But that's precisely what God did . . . and all for the sake of his love for Job!

Everything else paled in comparison to the revelation of the God of the universe. How could Job remain depressed when exposed to such grandeur? Listen again to Job's response to all he had seen and heard — but this time, I will state it in contemporary terms and interpret it in the first person:

> God has shown that he cared enough to uplift my troubled spirit and clouded mind with teaching too astonishing for words. Although I was instructed in the faith of my fathers, as every Jew has been, I know now that I only knew the words and the actions of justice but didn't grasp the full meaning. Oh, I knew God was righteous all right, but now I really know his grace. Before, it was more of an intellectual and ethical understanding, though my zeal was always there; but now it's experiential. I had never understood how love and power could be displayed together like that. I learned, too, that my circumstances are not an adequate criterion of his caring. I will never question him again.

Job was never the same after that experience. Because he had been told by his friends that the cruelty of his circumstances was the result of God's judgment, he had momentarily lost his ability to trust. He saw God as harsh, as one who would inflict deep wounds, even for sins Job wasn't aware of. Now, however, Job's fear was erased by the perfect love of God, who desired to have a relationship with him. Above all,

Job learned God had blessed him by an act of his own free grace, not as a benediction for a meritorious life. For Job, on that day, any semblance of legalism died.

Though he was mistaken, even presumptuous, in his accusations, Job remained true to the way he was feeling as he questioned God. He was able to ask the hard questions, even though he admitted he was fearful of God's power. Instead of cutting off Job or punishing him because of his challenging questions, God used those questions to confront him about his misconceptions, especially those concerning his right to cross-examine God's righteous purpose. Most importantly, though, God took the opportunity to teach Job new things about the majesty of his person, to enlarge Job's vision concerning the limitless scope of his eternal nature.

The problem with us today is that we rarely ask the difficult questions. Too often we back away from examining the tough dilemmas, the ones that open up uncomfortable issues that are not easily resolved. We are often left without any answers that are credible to the crowds of young skeptics who are looking for something to believe in. Nonetheless, as with his servant Job, God invites us to question him, so that we too might be strengthened in our faith.

AHITHOPHEL: THE GAMBLER WHO LOST

The desire for social approval characterizes almost every human relationship. It is the driving force behind our constant search for something we can offer others. When approval is denied, the consequences can be severe. Anyone, great or small, can fall to the frustration of this powerful social impulse.

In the Old Testament, Ahithophel gave clear testimony to this truth. He sat on the inner council of Absalom after Absalom had ousted his father, King David, from the throne. This coup had forced David and the troops loyal to him to flee to the east side of the Jordan in order to regroup and prepare for the battle to take back his throne. Meanwhile, Absalom was soliciting counsel from his closest advisors about what to do next.

Ahithophel had been a counselor of David, one whose wisdom was heralded throughout the kingdom. It was once said that "the advice of Ahithophel, which he gave in those days, was as if one inquired of the word of God" (2 Sam. 16:23 NASB). Not only did he enjoy great prestige, but he also was related to the royal court through the marriage of his granddaughter Bathsheba to David.

Though Ahithophel was a man of great reputation, as well as a man who had far-reaching family connections, it turns out that he had placed all of his personal worth in his accomplishments. As long as the events in his life were going well and his advice was esteemed, this did not appear to pose much of a problem. But when those events took a sudden downturn, as they did when Absalom rejected Ahithophel's advice to pursue David, then it was a different story.

Ahithophel was devastated that his advice was overruled in such an important matter of state. To him it was the supreme humiliation, something that meant a fall from grace. He knew, too, that Absalom's foolish decision to allow a veteran warrior like King David time to regroup with his men spelled disaster, and that he, Ahithophel, would be executed or exiled as a traitor once David returned to power. Any way he looked at it, the prospects for his future seemed grim. As he saw it, the best he could hope for was a life of obscurity, one that forever carried with it the stigma of betrayal.

The result of these conclusions was a reactive depression so severe that it prompted a suicidal course of action. Ahithophel, driven by the shame of public rejection, did not have the emotional stamina to withstand such a major blow to his social and political position.

His advice was his stock-in-trade. Since it was now no longer accepted, he felt he had nothing left for which he could lay claim to respect and honor. He knew his career was over, figuring that David, whom he had betrayed, would see it the same way.

With hopelessness having run its course, Ahithophel took his life: "When Ahithophel saw that his advice had not been followed, he saddled his donkey and set out for his house in his hometown. He put his house in order and then hanged himself. So he died and was buried in his father's tomb" (2 Sam. 17:23). When his life's work was gone, so was his desire to live. That's the danger of emotionally investing everything in your career.

Thinking himself wise, Ahithophel became a fool. He had taken the ultimate gamble, expecting to come out on top. But his choice left him linked as a conspirator to the fate of the rebel Absalom. As a consequence, Ahithophel became as disgraceful in death as he had been acclaimed in life. That was the price he paid for turning his strength into a weakness and assuming his reputation represented his personal worth.

MOSES: OVERWORKED AND UNDERAPPRECIATED

For Moses, answering God's call was no easy matter. That's because it required him to return to the land from which he had escaped as a fugitive. Moses feared the dangers posed by the mission, but he also worried that his own people would reject him as their leader. After all, he reasoned he had neither the poise nor the courage to be their leader, nor was he good with words: "Pardon your servant, Lord. I have never been eloquent, neither in the past nor since you have spoken to your servant. I am slow of speech and tongue" (Ex. 4:10).

Understanding that Moses' fear was greater than his desire to obey, God nevertheless pressed Moses into service because he knew the enterprise rested on his own sovereign power, not on Moses' confidence to do the job. Yet he was compassionate in responding to Moses' needs, providing him with the support of Aaron, a proven leader.

Despite the success of the exodus, however, Moses struggled with his people-pleasing tendencies. While he tried to accommodate the people's many demands on his time, he failed to protect himself from the exhaustion that comes from trying to be the jack-of-all-trades. Even his father-in-law, Jethro, recognized this problem. And so Jethro advised Moses to delegate some of his responsibilities (Ex. 18). In reality, this was God's timely guidance through the words of a concerned family member — guidance that was as merciful as it was sensible.

Unfortunately, Moses didn't follow this helpful advice for long. Later we find him again assuming responsibility for solving every problem and, consequently, becoming exhausted (Num. 11).

Moses routinely ignored his own limits until it was too late. Worse still, the people complained to Moses about almost everything. So Moses was not only exhausted, but frustrated as well. No matter how hard he tried to satisfy them, his leadership never seemed to be appreciated. It was a nightmare scenario for a people-pleaser like Moses. In the throes of his depression, he took his frustration out on God, not on the people who were always whining. Moses accused God of "punishing" him, because he had burdened him with such people (Num. 11:10–15). But of course it was Moses, not God, who had abdicated his responsibility to protect his boundaries.

Instead of taking Moses to the woodshed for his unfounded charges, however, God instructed him a second time to delegate his responsibilities to lighten the load. Once more, God intervened on behalf of his beleaguered servant. Moses' depression lifted, and he returned to his post, having learned that listening to God instead of placating others was the best way to manage his stress.

ELIJAH: THE DISCONNECT OF OVER-RESPONSIBILITY

Unlike Moses, Elijah had a problem knowing when his responsibility ended and God's began. After he defeated the prophets of Baal, he expected a great awakening among his people—but instead he saw little change in their behavior. With the Israelites still loyal to the false gods of Ahab and Jezebel, Elijah became depressed. Jezebel herself, having pledged to kill Elijah before the day was out, compounded his troubles. He was now convinced he had failed in his mission as a prophet of God.

By assuming blame for the results, he had concluded that *he* was the failure: "It is enough; now, O LORD, take away my life, for I am no better than my ancestors" (1 Kings 19:4 NRSV). In other words, he had failed just like those who had gone before him. It was his job to bring them to repentance, he believed, and that didn't happen. Now he was a fugitive with a bounty on his head.

God was moved with compassion at the sight of his wounded but obedient servant sitting there, fearful for his life and in despair over what he believed had been a useless mission. Instead of rebuking him for wanting to quit, God challenged Elijah to rethink his response. He did this by using a demonstration of his power as a means of teaching Elijah that it was the small quiet voice of the Spirit that calls people to repentance (1 Kings 19:11–13).

While great displays of supernatural force are impressive, the real work of renewal comes from God's gentle but persuasive "whisper." Elijah's error had been to attribute his people's resistance to the ineffectiveness of the messenger rather than to their insensitivity to the quiet presence of God.

To prepare Elijah for this teaching, God knew that Elijah first needed to regain his physical strength. It had, after all, been a long ordeal. Once he had gotten some rest, God fed him not once, but twice, to give him the energy necessary to complete the journey to Mount Horeb. No one who is exhausted and hungry is going to be ready to rethink his response to anything.

Once Elijah understood the work of the Spirit, he had a better grasp of how God works in the souls of men and whose responsibility that is. And with that understanding, he was ready to serve God again, but this time with a more humane perspective.

In the book of James, we read that Elijah had been an ordinary man doing extraordinary things: "Elijah was a human being, even as we are. He prayed earnestly that it would not rain, and it did not rain on the land for three and a half years. Again he prayed, and the heavens gave rain, and the earth produced its crops" (James 5:17–18).

Just like us? That doesn't sound like most of us. What could James have meant? What he seems to have been saying here is that Elijah had suffered adversity like everyone else. But what stood out about him was that "he prayed earnestly" about big things, not halfheartedly about small things. He *believed* in what he prayed for. A great deal is said about the power of prayer, but much less about the power of conviction behind it. Most of us are such timid souls, asking for so little, always afraid to dream big dreams. "You do not have because you do not ask God," James observed (4:2).

God has called us to have a vision, one that's irresistible to others. Unregenerate people need to see something in our lives that they don't see in their own. Otherwise they will no longer be interested in what we have. This "something" could be seen in Elijah, and great things happened.

PICKING UP THE MISSING PIECES

Many of the biblical stories recounted in this chapter have been about people with damaged concepts of self and unfinished concepts of God. Like believers of old, many today see God as an *accountant* who "audits" their performance to determine their worthiness for the kingdom. Every behavior is entered on a sort of divine ledger as a credit or a debit, depending on its moral character. The prevailing "balance" of their "spiritual bank account" then determines the position they have before God.

In this legalistic system, suffering is seen as borrowing from God's judgment to cover the deficit left by sin. On the other hand, blessings are viewed as the interest paid on the investment in good works. They spend much of their time in this debtor's ethic, plagued by guilt, most of it false guilt. And when they aren't feeling guilty, they're often feeling anxious—afraid they won't measure up.

Others see God more like a *dictator*, a kind of celestial policeman, who is ever mindful of the believer's shortcomings and always alert to pounce on that spiritual miscue. In effect, they believe God is driven more by retribution than by love. This idea is similar to the unpredictable bully who prefers to intimidate people and dole out punishment at the drop of a hat. These people live in constant fear of God's punishment.

Still others view God's actions as those of someone who is *detached*. God is seen as aloof and disengaged, his attention difficult to capture.

This view does not so much question God's sovereign power in the world as it does his basic interest in our person. With a detached God, it is up to us to run our lives as best we can rather than wasting time with appeals for divine intervention. Underlying this thinking is the idea that if God cared, he wouldn't let things happen the way they do.

Then there is the *peer* concept of God. With this approach, God is viewed more as a friend who is obligated by the relationship to use his divine power to ease a person around the rough spots of life. In effect, the relationship is a reciprocal one wherein most of the expectations flow to God on the one hand, and most of the benefits flow to us on the other. There is no sense of awe and little sensitivity to his transcendence. It is almost as if God, as their friend, must sacrifice his very righteousness in order to make their lives more comfortable. It is in this sense that personal comfort is elevated to the level of the highest good.

Finally, there is the *rescuer* concept. People who think of God as a rescuer usually marginalize him in their daily lives. They only cry out to God for help when adversity strikes, promising renewed dedication if he does. Essentially, God becomes the fireman who is needed only when there is a fire to extinguish. Once the crisis passes, the promises are forgotten and God recedes into the background again. The Israelites were notorious for this. And so, too, are many of us.

Each of these concepts denies some important attribute of God. The *accountant* concept denies the grace of God, so that he is someone to impress. The *dictator* concept denies the mercy of God, so that he is someone to fear. The *detached* concept denies the love of God, so that he is someone to convince. The *peer* concept denies the holiness of God, so that he is someone to manipulate. And the *rescuer* concept denies the sovereign purposefulness of God, so that he is someone to ignore outside of crises.

The result of these denials is a truncated image of who God is, which breeds unrealistic expectations, anxiety, and a lack of attachment.

Come to think of it, that sounds a lot like grounds for depression.

PETER: FINDING THE WHOLE GOD

To find the remedy, we must visit the apostle Peter, that fiery disciple of Jesus who, in his darkest hour, discovered the freedom of God's love. Though he was a bit rough around the edges, Peter felt deeply about things. Right after he declared that he would never betray his Messiah, he denied knowing him at all. He did this not once, but three times to a crowd gathered to watch the proceedings of Jesus' trial. Each denial became more emphatic than the last, until Peter swore that he had nothing to do with Jesus. At that moment, the rooster crowed, and the crushing reality of what he had just done sank in. Peter left quickly, walking out of the city in despair, weeping uncontrollably over having done the unthinkable. He was bewildered, too, that he had so easily caved in to the pressure of the crowd. He had underestimated the power of fear to silence even his firmest conviction.

Nothing had prepared Peter to handle the mob mentality with its narrow focus on conformity to the group. Still, at that moment, he hated himself for betraying the one Person who had given him meaning and purpose. Indeed, so disconsolate was Peter that after the crucifixion it seems he separated himself from the company of the other disciples. For when the angel at the tomb told Mary Magdalene and her companions to go tell the disciples Jesus had risen, he mentioned Peter by name (using the phrase "and Peter") as though he was not with the other disciples (Mark 16:7).

Jesus yearned for Peter to know that he wanted him there with the others, that he still saw Peter as his trustworthy disciple. And later, at the Sea of Galilee, he made a point to ask Peter to "feed my sheep." Think of that. He was entrusting Peter with the task of teaching others how liberating it is to embrace the gospel message. It's like the boss who gives you a promotion after you screwed up on the job, costing the company dearly. Jesus was saying, in effect, "I love you and forgive you, and now I want you to do something great, something with eternal consequences for the kingdom." What a welcome message from someone whom Peter had betrayed in his greatest hour of travail!

We can now understand, perhaps, why Peter spoke with such power and conviction on the day of Pentecost. He had been relieved of his despair and burden of guilt by the Messiah himself. Unlike many, Peter understood grace. He knew firsthand what it meant to serve a master who never stopped loving or ceased forgiving. He knew the whole God, the one who was at once just and merciful, sovereign and benevolent. He wanted to shout this message of hope from the rooftops.

And, indeed, he did.

FINDING HOPE

1. The Bible is a love story that reveals the unstoppable force of God's redemptive purpose.

2. God sometimes gives you what you want in order to teach you what you need. The goal? To understand the superiority of his wisdom.

3. No matter how momentarily satisfying revenge can be, mercy and forgiveness yield better outcomes.

4. Asking the tough questions not only strengthens your own faith, but it also gives honest skeptics something to think about.

5. Investing everything in your career carries with it the danger of emptiness when it's over. Better to invest in intimate relationships for the long term.

6. God understands your limits even better than you do. That's why he encourages healthy boundaries.

7. You are called to believe in what you pray for. God bids us to pray earnestly about big things, not halfheartedly about small things.

8. While you may be limited by an unfinished concept of God, you are more likely to challenge your fears when you understand God in his wholeness.

PART 5

HOW CAN I GET MY LIFE BACK?

EXPERIENCING THE POWER OF CHANGE

12

THE BIOLOGY OF DEPRESSION

A BODY OF EVIDENCE

*So in my brain my body comes together,
every part knows that it is not alone.*

—Dr. Paul Brand

That Christians and non-Christians alike would trust a family physician to share the sacred space of the intimate issues regarding their persons and their bodies is always humbling to a professional. Let me (Greg) share an experience I had with one of my patients.

As I glanced over the list of people I was to see one afternoon, I recognized a familiar name of someone who is a marriage and family counselor in the community. I assumed that I would be seeing him for some type of medical problem like back pain, sore neck, or indigestion. As I entered the room, John and I exchanged a warm greeting before I opened his chart to begin the office visit. To my surprise, John began describing a long history lasting multiple years of severe mood swings. Recently they had become so bad that he was having thoughts of suicide. He expressed frustration in the fact that in his role as counselor, he had helped innumerable people in similar situations achieve relief from their sense of hopelessness. "I know all the right answers and have studied all the books, yet I find myself incapable of experiencing relief," John said.

His medical history revealed a man who had been in excellent physical health his entire life. He had never taken any long-term medications, had grown up in a Christian family, was successful in his career, and was enjoying a strong relationship with his wife and children. It wasn't until we began discussing his mother's health that the pieces of the puzzle began to fit. John's mother had suffered a "nervous breakdown" after the birth of her fifth child and for the rest of her life suffered severe bouts of depression, to the point of needing hospitalization several times.

Reserved for only the most severe and resistant cases of depression, John had even received some electroconvulsive therapy (ECT). This questionable procedure consists of causing a person to have a grand mal seizure by passing electrical shockwaves through the brain while the person is under general anesthesia. A few seem to experience some positive, albeit often temporary, emotional change. There are, however, clear risks involved in this type of treatment. For instance, it poses the danger of some short-term memory loss (and perhaps other damage to the central nervous system), particularly with repeated use. Such methods should always remain ones of last resort.

In any case, given his background, I thought, what courage it has taken for John to step forward and disclose the problem with which he had so long been privately struggling.

We know our emotions can affect our spiritual lives. Physical illness like low thyroid or hormonal changes (such as those that occur in menstruation or menopause) can affect our emotional life too. Each area affects the other. Consequently, conducting an accurate assessment of each of the areas optimizes any intervention.

The purpose of this chapter is to focus attention on the physical aspects of depression. One of the hardest questions to answer is when should medical treatment be considered? When has the line been crossed from human emotion to physical disorder? The psychiatrist Dr. Stephen Stahl, one of the world's leading authorities on the functions of brain chemistry, has said:

> Depression is an emotion that is universally experienced by virtually everyone at some time in life. . . . Stigma and misinformation in our culture create the widespread popular misconception that mental illness such as depression is . . . a deficiency of character, which can be overcome with effort. For example, a survey in the early 1990s of the general population revealed that 71% thought that mental illness was due to emotional weakness; 65% thought it

was caused by bad parenting; 45% thought it was the victim's fault and could be willed away; 43% thought that mental illness was incurable; 35% thought it was the consequence of sinful behavior; and only 10% thought it had a biological basis or involved the brain.[1]

Dr. Stahl's point that misconceptions of depression abound in our culture is well taken. Contrary to the black-and-white thinking that exists in the public mind, there is abundant evidence of a complex mind-body interaction. This interaction makes it challenging to sort out the origins of change even at the physiological level. We know that emotional and behavioral changes made in therapy—changes that involve making different choices in life—can prompt changes in brain chemistry just as much as changes in brain chemistry can prompt corresponding changes in emotions and behavior. In other words, psychological causes and brain chemistry are interrelated.

Notwithstanding the "chicken and egg" issues we discussed earlier in the book, the fact that depression involves the biochemistry of the brain is central to our consideration of the biology of any mood disorder. We have already noted that in addition to the many psychological depressions there are some predominantly biological depressions, such as bipolar affective disorder, that can be treated with a combination of psychotherapy and medication.

Before we get into some of the more specific medical issues, it might be helpful to try to explain in a simplified manner how the brain works.

NEUROTRANSMITTER RECEPTOR HYPOTHESIS

Neurotransmitters are hormones or chemicals that "hand off" or "transmit" the signal from one nerve to another across a gap called the synapse. There are many neurotransmitters, some of which have not yet been fully identified. These include serotonin, norepinephrine, acetylcholine, and dopamine.

In order to function normally, you need to have a full reservoir or "tank" of these hormones in the nerve cell ready to be released and thus communicate the message to the next nerve. The synapse is the space between the ending of one nerve and the beginning of another nerve that must be bridged by the movement of these hormones. The concentration of these hormones must be sufficient enough to stimulate or heat up the receptors at the next nerve to create a chain reaction and transmit the message to the next nerve. This is not unlike getting up in the morning and standing outside your shower and turning on the hot water, waiting for the cold water to be flushed from the pipes before you step in to take your shower with warm water.

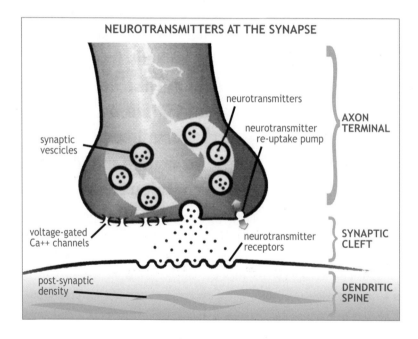

For our purposes, depression occurs with depletion of the neurotransmitter hormones, like running out of hot water. If the brain does not have an adequate amount of these hormones, it begins to malfunction. Some people have inherited a tendency to have low hormone levels because their nerve cells either break down more of the hormones than other people's do, or they don't make enough, leaving them in a deficit situation. When either of these processes is going on in the brain, the levels of neurotransmitters can become depleted either through increased demand and overuse or from inadequate production or replacement.

The brain fills up the tanks of serotonin, norepinephrine, and dopamine during sleep. Consequently, if you do not get adequate sleep for some reason, you will be starting the next day without a normal reservoir of neurotransmitters, putting you at risk for suboptimal functioning.

When people experience significant adversity, like a divorce or the death of a child or any number of other factors that create severe stress, the brain works overtime in anticipation of the worst possible situation. In this "full combat-alert state," the mind plays the what-if game, expending energy trying to anticipate the worst possible scenario and make early preparation for all of the likely or unlikely possibilities. This leads to a vicious cycle, because the more stressed you are, the less capable you are of functioning at your optimum level, which creates even more stress.

The spiral of anxiety, sleep deprivation, fatigue, and depressed mood can become progressively more severe until the person becomes incapacitated. With what's going on in the brain, it is hard to pull yourself up by your own bootstraps and reverse this cycle. This is where medication comes in to lend assistance by raising the level of neurotransmitter hormones. It does this by blocking their reuptake into the sending nerve, which will metabolize and break down a significant share of these hormones. Medication allows the levels of hormones to be sufficient enough at the synapse so the message can be sent from one nerve to the next in a more normal fashion (like having instant hot water). Antidepressant medications are *not* addictive like Valium, narcotics, or cocaine that act by directly stimulating synaptic receptors in certain areas of the brain, producing an altered state of consciousness or euphoria.

Confusion as to why some people struggle with adversity more than others can be partly answered by the concept of individual physical variability. Some people can go through divorce or lose their job and seem to manage just fine, while others seem to collapse into depression over lesser disappointments, such as not getting a new car. Just like the color of your eyes and hair, there is individual variability in your body's ability to manufacture or metabolize (break down) the brain hormones. If you inherited a tendency to have low levels of these hormones, you will be more vulnerable to experiencing a chain of events that leads to depletion and, therefore, it is more likely that medication will be necessary to provide relief.

Can significant depletion be caused by long-term emotional stress? Yes. Can significant depletion be caused by an environmental stressor? Yes. Can significant depletion be caused by family genetics? Yes. So, how should the issue of using medications be viewed? As a necessary evil? As something to avoid at all costs? Is medication a cure-all that should be given to everyone?

The good news is that most people can be helped significantly with their depression once they have found a suitable medication. And with this help, they are much more amenable to the work of psychotherapy, which is more likely to bring about lasting change.

COMMON QUESTIONS ABOUT DEPRESSION

One of the first questions people ask is when to consider depression severe enough to involve medication. In chapter 2, the basic symptoms diagnostic of clinical depression and some of their implications were mentioned. There are, of course, assessment tools (such as questionnaires, personality inventories, and various other paper-and-pencil tests, as well as clinical interviews) that increase our accuracy in confirming the diagnosis of depression. (See www.Depressionoutreach.com for an example of the Hamilton Depression Scale.) These will show the degree of severity of your depression and whether medication is advisable.

Another consideration is what factors contribute to under-diagnosis and under-treatment. It is estimated that only 30 percent of people who experience biological depression are being adequately treated. Some of the major contributing factors include: (1) stigma—it is not "OK" for people to take antidepressant medications because some consider it to be "drug abuse"; (2) lack of public knowledge as to what depression is, its various subtypes, and how it can be treated; (3) reluctance to seek help—only 17 percent of people who are eventually diagnosed with depression actually go to their doctor for their depressed mood; (4) the common occurrence of depressive symptoms being masked by physical symptoms like fatigue or associated medical illnesses, including low thyroid, heart attacks, and sleep apnea; and (5) poor medication prescribing and follow-through on the part of physicians who are not fully knowledgeable and skilled in using the newer and more-effective medications.

Some ask whether nonmedication treatments should be tried first. It's useful to do an assessment of a person's current lifestyle. Are they simply exhausted and need more sleep? Are they experiencing loneliness through death or loss of a relationship? Are they angry or bitter over an injustice? Are they physically depleted and in need of proper nutrition and exercise? Have they taken steps to nurture their spiritual life? If people have done all these things and are still experiencing significant problems in mood, then they need to talk to their doctor.

WHAT ABOUT ST. JOHN'S WORT?

St. John's Wort is an herb that has an effect on brain hormones, although its effect is considered to be milder than prescription medications. Simply because it is nonprescription, however, does not mean it is safe. Many people can experience elevation of blood pressure if they eat certain foods like cheese, beans, or wine when consuming this herb. St. John's Wort should not be taken with other prescription medications, and there may be some evidence of early cataract formation with exposure to sunlight. In my experience, taking St. John's Wort has not been all that helpful for most people and poses some risks to a person's health.

WHAT DOES AN EPISODE OF DEPRESSION LOOK LIKE?

The course of treated depression follows some clearly definable stages. The following is a graphic representation of a depressive episode with the various possible outcomes:

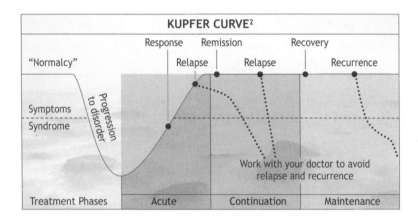

The term *response* generally means that a depressed patient has experienced at least a 50 percent reduction in symptoms as assessed by the Hamilton Depression Rating Scale. *Relapse* is the term used when a person gets worse after treatment began to work but the person had not "gotten well." *Remission* is the term used when essentially all symptoms have gone away and the person is feeling totally normal. *Recovery* means that the remission has lasted for at least six to twelve months. *Recurrence* means the symptoms of depression have returned, causing significant problems in functioning and mood.

WHICH DEPRESSIONS ARE PRIMARILY BIOLOGICALLY BASED AND THEREFORE REQUIRE SOME KIND OF MEDICAL TREATMENT?

Such depressions as bipolar disorder or those arising from hypothyroidism, hypoglycemia, rapid postpartum and perimenopausal hormonal changes, after-effects of head trauma, or depression concurrent with certain other medical illnesses or incapacitating injuries all usually involve medication and/or dietary change, together with psychotherapy.

ARE DEPRESSION AND WEIGHT PROBLEMS CONNECTED?

Depression can cause cravings and overeating behavior in some people because food is actually a mild antidepressant since food actually raises our brain serotonin levels. Therefore, some people are "treating" their depression by overeating without knowing it. There is a medication called Meridia, which is in the same class of certain antidepressant medications like Prozac, which has been helpful in curbing the appetite in some people. If you are taking Meridia, however, you cannot take other antidepressant medications at the same time.

HOW LONG SHOULD A PERSON TAKE MEDICATION?

Rule of thirds: Approximately one-third of people will experience a single episode of significant depression usually precipitated by a major traumatic event. Medication is usually required for at least six months and then it can be phased out. This is somewhat similar to a physician using a cast to hold the broken bone of the leg in proper alignment so the bone can develop a strong union. Approximately one-third of people will experience relapses of depression. If you have had more than one episode of depression requiring medication, your chances are greater than 80 percent that you will require medication at some time in the future to treat another episode. Approximately one-third of people have the more prolonged type of depression (called "chronic dysthymic disorder"), which may involve longer-term medication.

WHAT MEDICATION SHOULD I TAKE?

Just like a pair of shoes, there is no one medication that is perfect for everyone. Not only are there differences in a person's susceptibility to depression, but there is also individual variability in a person's response to medications. This makes the prescribing of antidepressants closer to "trial and error" than "one size fits all." For example, most people will be stimulated and energized by Prozac, but a minority of people will be sedated. If the medication causes significant side effects, it should be stopped and a different medication tried. Most likely, one of the medications available today will help you feel good without creating significant side effects.

If you are having mood problems as well as problems with memory, the ability to concentrate or maintain attention, or if you're experiencing fatigue, medication that would boost levels of norepinephrine should be considered. If you are having mood problems associated with anxiety, panic disorder, or phobias of multiple types, including social phobias as well as obsessive-compulsive problems, you should be considered for medication that would primarily increase your levels of serotonin.

Some of the latest scientific evidence indicates that using medications that increase *both* serotonin and norepinephrine levels are sometimes superior in helping a person improve their mood state as compared to medications that work on either serotonin or norepinephrine alone. Medications like Pristiq, Effexor XR, Cymbalta, and Fetzima raise the levels of both serotonin and norepinephrine. Many times physicians will use combinations of antidepressants to obtain full remission and lower the number of side effects. In essence, one plus one equals three in providing greater effectiveness while reducing the overall number of side effects. See www.Depressionoutreach.com for a list of the major medications currently available with assessments of the advantages, disadvantages, and personal recommendations as to the situations in which they are most likely to work best. You will also find on that site treatment guidelines regarding medication priorities that increase the chance for a successful outcome.

After learning of John's family history and his struggles with suicide (whom I mentioned at the beginning of this chapter), I had John take a Hamilton Depression Scale. His score revealed significant depression. Because John was having associated symptoms of agitation and fidgeting as well as irritability, I elected to try John on the duo-acting antidepressant Effexor XR, which enhances both the serotonin and norepinephrine neurotransmitter systems. I gave him some samples to try and asked him to return in three weeks. John's experience was somewhat unusual but not rare. He described such a dramatic change in his symptoms that he said, "It was like the clouds parted and the sun began to shine on me." It was an entirely new experience for him after he started taking the medication.

This kind of response is the exception rather than the rule but does illustrate the point that some people do have an inherited tendency that can only be adequately treated with medical intervention. John's prognosis is excellent, but he will probably require a maintenance dose of medication.

Even with biological depressions, the message is the same: We are exquisitely designed with emotional alarm systems to tell us when it is time to take action so that we might be restored to the fulfillment of our God-given purposes. There is no greater upside to the experience of depression than to meaningfully grow through our pain. In the end, is this not what Jesus meant when he spoke of living in the kingdom of God now? The abundant life he promised is not the easy life or necessarily the prosperous life as the world measures prosperity. It is the fulfilling life, the life of wisdom that understands the importance of what makes the difference for eternity.

FINDING HOPE

1. Your emotional experience affects your theology, just as theology affects your emotional experience. Reassessing both can lead to surprising spiritual benefits.

2. Emotional and behavioral changes that involve making different choices in life can produce corresponding changes in brain chemistry, and vice versa.

3. Because we know that depression can result from a depletion of neurotransmitter hormones, we have medications that can resupply them at the synapse.

4. The good news is that 90 percent of people who are depressed can be helped with medication. This makes possible much greater gains in psychotherapy.

5. While relapses during or after treatment often occur, knowing this enables us to better prepare for (or prevent) them. Sustained remission is always the goal.

6. Medication decisions are tailored to address the particular symptoms that predominate and minimize the overall number of side effects.

13

THE PROMISE
OF TRANSFORMATION

CHANGING THE FUTURE

The real voyage of discovery consists not in seeking
new landscapes but in having new eyes.

—Marcel Proust

The best news about depression is that you can change your future. Although simply trying to will yourself out of depression is not realistic, don't be misled into thinking you're without options. You are continuously making choices in life—even if you feel helpless and are paralyzed by indecision—choices that will determine your future. Whether you are aware of it or not, choices made by default are just as real as those made by deliberation.

Passivity leads to the path of least resistance. Sadly, many choose this path by accommodating to a life of silent surrender to meaningless living. You can see it in their lack of intentionality and in their vacant, faraway look that betrays any words of false cheer. It's evident in nearly every choice they make.

Once they've decided to drop anchor inside the protective breakwater of resignation, the ship of their human spirit loses its seaworthiness. The dry rot of apathy and despair that follows soon reduces their vessel to a shadow of what it once was. Gone is the means of travel on the high seas of adventure in personal growth. Gone, too, is the joy of redemption or even the appreciation of the sacrifice that made it possible.

God never intended our lives to be this way, though he knows, of course, how we got there. From the beginning, his intentions for us were almost breathtaking: We were created a little lower than the angels and crowned with glory and honor (Ps. 8:4–5), which was made evident when he gave us authority over the rest of creation.

Benevolence on this scale reveals the splendor of God's design and the full sweep of his commitment to give us an unforgettable life. Although we may be marred by the fall, we have this inheritance from him no less now than when we were first conceived. Nowhere is this more manifest than in his Son's sacrifice on the cross. Still, his love can be obscured, even sabotaged, by the depressing pessimism of our pain.

After many years in the pastorate, listening to church members pour out their heartaches, one minister came to the conclusion that if we touch *anyone's* heart it will bleed a little. This is no doubt true. We have said that suffering is a part of every life—man or woman, rich or poor, sophisticated or untutored.

It doesn't help that we have the tendency to cover it up. To disguise what we feel, we routinely tell others "everything is just fine." Many of us are convinced this disguise is necessary to avoid the attention we don't want for a state of mind we can't accept. The irony is that this dishonesty is itself an occasion for still further isolation and only guarantees the loneliness that comes from a lack of connection.

When we've exchanged the malleability of life for a rigid compulsion to keep repeating the same things over and over again, we've sacrificed our ability to successfully adapt. We often seem mesmerized by debilitating habits spawned by our irrational beliefs (see appendix B), such as all-or-nothing thinking, overgeneralization, jumping to conclusions, emotional reasoning, and self-blame. Yet, despite this endless repetition, we still seem surprised and disappointed that things don't change.

Psychiatrist Viktor Frankl pointed out that precisely because life is transitory, we have a responsibility to make the most of it while we can.

Remember, your choices are, in effect, the aces that trump the other playing cards of life you've been dealt. How you play them will largely determine the final outcome.

In this chapter, we will discuss practical strategies for achieving what you want, which in combination present hope for real change.

HELPING TO END LEARNED HELPLESSNESS

Consider any book you have read. How did the author communicate his or her meaning? Which word pictures set a peaceful tone and which established a dark, oppressive mood? Which produced feelings of excitement, fear, or despair? We can ask similar questions about the stories you are writing in your mind about events in your life. The word pictures you use as author of these stories are pivotal in determining their impact on you. We saw this in our earlier discussion on "need language."

What if your storyline assumed that you (or others) were guilty until proven innocent? Would you not become the unwitting victim of your *own* injustice? Certainly it would not be an acceptable premise on which to base society's legal system. You would not hesitate to protest such a miscarriage of justice. Yet, you are more than ready to accept this premise in the courtroom of self-evaluation. Many people are surprised to discover how often they allow such prejudicial thinking, which they would never accept in a court of law, to propel them into a state of rage or plunge them into despair.

To challenge this thinking, you must first realize its habitual nature. You tend to accept it without review. Yet, without accountability to reality, your thought-life can become stereotyped, leaving negative footprints on every conclusion you draw. So when you ruminate on pessimistic what-ifs or obsess over every injury, you end up feeling helpless and depressed. Essentially, you become a compulsive stenographer of "tragedy," victimizing yourself all over again.

This mind-set is sometimes called "learned helplessness." People who have not experienced much mastery of outcomes in their early lives are vulnerable to believing they are powerless to influence life events. Because bad things have happened to them, they believe all experiences in life are beyond their control and it is foolish to try to change them. Instead, they relinquish the power to carve out a different path to other people.

When I (Gary) asked one woman why she always turned to look at her husband before she answered a question, she became flustered and said, "Oh, I was just seeing how he was reacting to the question." When I asked her what she was looking for, she replied, "Oh, nothing I guess." In reality, she was checking to see if it was all right to answer the question or if she was expected to defer to him. In fact, he often tried to answer for her or to "clarify" her statements by substituting his own. His controlling influence was noticeable from the beginning. So was her sense of helplessness.

Meanwhile, others are so busy replaying history in their minds that they fail to see the opportunities to take charge of the present. Their past becomes, in effect, the altar on which they are sacrificing any chance for happiness in the future. But never forget, this focus is a choice.

Actively challenging these distorted thinking patterns is necessary for reducing their credibility. Suppose you went to hear a noted speaker and when he was about five or ten minutes into his speech, someone who was knowledgeable stood up and questioned the accuracy of what he was saying, citing compelling evidence for his view. You might cross out that part of the speech before resuming your note taking. Suppose further that this happened many times with others in the audience who were also knowledgeable in their fields. The likelihood is that you would quit taking notes, since you could no longer trust anything the speaker was saying. In fact, you would likely get up and leave, believing the meeting was a waste of your time.

That's what happens when false ideas are challenged. Without such challenges, you would continue believing everything you heard was true. You would do well, then, if the next time you are in turmoil, you remember that the distorted, often irrational ideas underlying it need to be challenged with the truth. You can check again the list in appendix B to help you identify which beliefs most dominate your thinking and the best arguments that challenge them.

Most people think their reactions are the direct result of the events that seem to give rise to them. For instance, say you went for a job interview and were turned down for the job. By the time you get home, your disappointment has left you depressed. If I were to ask you why you are depressed, you would tell me it was because you failed to get the job you wanted. But that would not be why you are depressed. You're depressed because of your beliefs about being turned down for the job. You would be telling yourself that not getting this job proves you'll *never* get the job you want. Now, that thought—if you believed it—*would* be depressing.

Some people might have the same experience you did, but respond differently. That's because they would be thinking that though not getting this particular job was disappointing, there are other good jobs for which they can apply; and eventually they'll get one of them—so they purpose to keep trying. The difference in emotional response is attributed to the difference in beliefs about the experience, not the activating event itself (failing to get the job), which is the same in each case.

Think of this (like cognitive-behavioral therapists do) as the ABC analysis of your response: The *activating* event (A) triggers a *belief* (B) about that event, which produces certain emotional and behavioral *consequences* (C). Understandably, then, you must challenge or *debate* the beliefs (D) if you want to change the consequences.

This is not likely to be an easy task with chronically or severely depressed people because it means challenging the constraints imposed by their straitjacket of routine. Often, just breaking new ground greatly increases the anxiety they already feel.

To overcome this fear requires minimizing the degree of threat while at the same time opening up opportunities to achieve some results. Because changing behavior first is sometimes better at altering attitudes, *doing* something different can sometimes be more effective than trying to *think* something different. In other words, sometimes you can act your way into a new way of thinking more quickly than you can think your way into a new way of acting.

So, if you want to change your behavior, begin by identifying what you are most fearful of doing and then work backward to some approximation of this activity, to something you're willing to try altering. This is less likely to induce the level of anxiety that inhibits even trying at all.

Remember, it is in the nature of experimentation that the results are not preordained. When a scientist carries out a study, regardless of the outcome (whether it supports his or her hypothesis or not) he or she has generated valuable data for the body of science. No well-run experiment proves the experimenter a failure—it can only fail to confirm the experimenter's hypothesis. Studies that produce negative results are just as valuable as studies that produce positive ones, because they direct the researcher's future study.

Likewise, personal experiments yield valuable feedback both about what works and about what doesn't—feedback that is crucial for making effective adjustments in your behavior. Such experiments are never failures. The important thing is that the new behaviors are ones *you* engage in, ones that have originated from strategies *you* have devised. This fact alone speaks volumes about your ability to participate in your own growth.

Though you may not always immediately achieve the outcomes you want, you will at least be able to define the boundaries of what's possible. Wherever those boundaries are, they can only provide indispensable information on which actions to do more and which to do less. It's this information that makes your experiments successful.

The anxiety that accompanies depression and experimentation is almost always based on grossly overinflated estimates of risk. Nonetheless, these anxiety attacks are sometimes so terrifying to people that they will go to great lengths to avoid any situation that might evoke them. They may even refuse to go to certain places or drive their car beyond a certain limited range. When that's the case, I often point out to my clients that such anxiety attacks tend to duplicate the physical effects of exercise, which we voluntarily *choose* to engage in for the sake of our health.

Think about that for a moment. Such symptoms as rapid breathing, elevated heart rate, and increased sweating—which we also describe as signs of anxiety—are the same things you consciously try to achieve when you exercise. Since you seek these experiences to improve your physical conditioning, which is good for you, why should you think that calling them "symptoms of anxiety" makes them somehow dangerous, even indicators that you might die? How can such physical symptoms appear so ominous when under other circumstances you welcome them as signs of a good workout?

Try to think of such experiences, therefore, as "aerobic moments." In fact, I challenge you to try to *increase* these symptoms when you have them. Try to sweat more, to make your heart beat even faster, and to breathe more deeply. When the episode is over, remind yourself that it was a valuable aerobic moment and that you feel even more physically fit because of it. (If these aerobic moments decrease in frequency, you can always begin supplementing them by visiting a gym or fitness center of your choice!)

EFFICIENT WORRY

Another way to overcome negative thoughts is to defer them to a designated time by scheduling a "worry hour." Instead of spreading your worry inefficiently throughout the day, you can consolidate it into one hour of your choosing. During this daily period, sit at a table and write down all of your self-rejecting worries, your guilt-inducing, depression-generating thoughts, and your obsessive concerns about social approval. If you complete the list in less than the hour allotted—and you usually will—write them over again until the hour is up.

When the hour is over, burn the list and toss the ashes away. If you start to experience worry or guilt or some other depressogenic thought before the next day's worry hour, remind yourself that you have set aside a time for this and will write it down then. You can then let the thought go, with the promise that you will pick it up later. In this fashion, you can condense all your debilitating ruminations into one sixty-minute period. Just think about how much less time you will waste doing it this way than when you worry here and there (or maybe constantly) all through the day.

If a given day is free of anxiety-inducing thoughts, you may skip the worry hour, but only for that day. Daily consistency is necessary—even when it feels like an ordeal—if you wish to gain the greatest benefit from this exercise.

Worry is, of course, simply a species of your general anxiety. As common as it is in depression, anxiety is merely a false alarm elicited by an imagined danger. It almost automatically demands a defensive response. The problem is that this strategy only makes the problem worse in the long run. It's the anticipatory dread, the blizzard of what-ifs that continues to drive the symptoms that are causing all the concern in the first place. So, in addition to your aerobic moments and your worry hours, try deliberately accepting the presence of anxiety without fanfare, simply waiting it out (since it always eventually wanes anyway) by doing some deep muscle relaxation exercises. These include alternately tensing and relaxing each muscle group in the body, beginning with the hands, moving up the arms, across the neck and shoulders, the face, back through the neck and shoulders, down through the chest, stomach and abdominal muscles, and, finally, down the legs and through the feet. While doing deep, diaphragmatic breathing between each muscle group exercise, imagine the tension draining out of each part of your body, leaving your muscles more deeply relaxed than ever before. You'll be surprised at how effective this procedure is in producing a tranquil body state. What's more, this activity involves actually doing something pleasant for yourself (which delivers a message to yourself that you matter) and at the same time ridding your body of unnecessary tension while you're waiting for the anxiety to pass. It's the "two for one" bonus for doing the opposite of what you normally do in handling the common experience of anxiety.

WHAT ABOUT GRUDGES?

Griping about someone else's mistakes in the past demands perpetual penance for something that has long since ceased to be relevant in the present. I counseled a couple where the wife spoke vehemently about some mistake her husband had made. She spoke as if it had happened only a few days before. But I discovered it had happened more than twenty years ago! She just could not let go of any perceived injustice, even though he'd apologized many times over.

Not only did bitterness destroy this woman's ability to affirm her husband, but just as important, it blocked her ability to encourage the best in herself. Since childhood, she had retreated into a fortress mentality. In her thinking, the only way she could protect herself from getting hurt was to attack first. Her grudges, then, displayed her intense fear and insecurity.

When you hold a grudge against someone, you're shackled to that person. You're trapped in a powerful, unhealthy bond that robs you of even the pretense of independent thinking. On the other hand, the ability to lay aside your resentment provides an unimaginable freedom. Paul told us that we can do this with the experience of agape love: "[Love] does not dishonor others, it is not self-seeking, it is not easily angered, it *keeps no record of wrongs*" (1 Cor. 13:5, emphasis added).

When you are released from the past and free yourself from the silent slavery of your hidden secrets and lack of forgiveness, you realize, perhaps for the first time, that those past experiences didn't destroy you after all. And what didn't destroy you then cannot harm you now. That you survived those experiences is a monumental conquest. In remembering and grieving the pain of your personal history, it's also important to honor the triumphs; in that way triumph rather than defeat can become your new theme for living.

This shift in thinking allows you to begin to let go of those who were responsible for your pain. It is one thing to have suffered by their hand in some way when you were a child or an adolescent; it is quite another to allow the memory of that suffering to control you as an adult. You didn't deserve that treatment in the past, and you do yourself no service to cling to the feelings of shame and resentment in the present.

Most people who've been badly wounded have a hard time understanding that holding on to the past is the only thing keeping them from letting go of their self-destructive behavior in the present. They cannot see this connection because the sins against them were so great. Sometimes it takes God's supernatural healing to finally understand this. For, with him, all things are possible.

Unless you are honest with yourself, there is little chance that the anger underneath will ever be processed. There are, of course, certain cultures (and certain groups within our culture) where privately "letting go" is viewed as an important family virtue. But still, it's useful to ask what happens when you are able to be more transparent.

REFRAMING YOUR APPROACH

Jim hated his job even though he was good at what he did. The workplace had become a war zone with his sales manager, Bill, who often pressed his authority. In Jim's view, Bill made poor decisions. Sensing something wrong in Jim's demeanor, his boss was always on edge around him.

A pattern developed: When Jim resisted some directive, Bill started making strident demands. It appeared that the only reason Jim had not been fired was because he was the company's top salesman. For his part, Jim had not resigned from his position because he was paid well and he knew he would take a substantial pay cut to work with one of his company's competitors. But he went home every night feeling hopeless about ever enjoying his job again. He sought professional counseling to help him determine what to do.

During one counseling session, Jim's eyebrows arched in surprise when it was suggested that his manager might feel insecure about his position and threatened by a subordinate as competent and knowledgeable as Jim. This insecurity could contribute to his poor decision making. "I never thought of that," Jim responded. "Do you suppose Bill would be open to a gentler approach, maybe if I took him out to lunch and showed some personal interest in him?" I told him that sounded like a good idea to try. "Who knows? You might get some fruitful conversation going that might lead to actual change."

When Jim returned for a counseling session a month later, he recounted his astonishment at his manager's positive response to his invitation to discuss their differences. When it was apparent that Jim was making an effort to find some middle ground, Bill proved gracious. As a result, they were able to hammer out a workable solution that eased the sense of threat to the manager while granting greater freedom to Jim to exercise his professional judgment.

Shortly afterward, Jim's depression lifted and he began to approach his work with renewed energy. The important point was not whether Jim's manager had been experiencing insecurity but that Jim needed to find another way to look at the problem, which nudged him to try a different means of solving it.

When you assume the worst about others, it's because you are protecting yourself from disappointment and rejection. Sometimes you may compensate for that fear by becoming overbearing. By making yourself as indispensable as you can, you are trying to satisfy your guilt for "being less than what you should be." But in attempting to alleviate your fear of being rejected by others, you end up rejecting yourself. It's ironic that while you're trying to be all things to all people, you're withholding all things from yourself.

Reframing the way you approach problems — including changes that relieve a stressful situation — can alter your mood. That's why it's so important to find ways to break up an entrenched but negative pattern of interaction. You can often be successful at this simply by changing your behavior in a way that surprises the other person. By introducing the unexpected, you make your relationships more interesting, even intriguing, and create a new and different context for shifting around interactions.

Keeping that in mind, try the following approach the next time someone is angry with you. Instead of getting defensive and counterattacking as most people do, excuse yourself for a moment, go to the next room, and reduce your hyperaroused state (taking deep breaths, etc.). This buys you time to cool off. Then ask yourself what the other person *least* would expect in response. When you have the answer, return to the room and carry out the course of action you have determined would take that person by surprise.

You will find that most people, when caught off guard, respond with the hesitation that the unfamiliar produces and then a reaction of increased curiosity. Sooner or later, however, they are likely to change their behavior to accommodate your new, innovative response. You may well discover, too, that the challenge of generating surprise reawakens your spirit of creativity, something that can lie dormant when a relationship has become too predictable.

WHEN YOU DON'T FEEL LIKE IT

Depressed clients will often recite with resignation many activities they used to enjoy, such as going to movies, cycling, hiking, engaging in sports, or playing cards with friends. They add that they no longer do these things because they "just don't feel like it anymore."

To counter this tendency to withdraw, ask yourself: What would I do *if* I felt good about myself and were content with my world? If you don't know, think of a person you perceive to have a healthy self-regard and base your response on the way you imagine that person would respond. Once you have determined what you would do under these circumstances, carry it out.

You may object that you can't do this because you *don't* feel that way about yourself. However, there are many things you do that you don't feel like doing. Even though you don't always feel like getting out of bed and going to work in the morning, you do it anyway. In the past, you haven't allowed your feelings to stop you from carrying out many activities or responsibilities you believed were important.

This directive is no different.

Healthy self-respect comes from the pledge to treat yourself in a valuing, tenderhearted way, regardless of how you feel. It means behaving in a way that gives you the message that you count for something, that you are worth the effort. Otherwise, your internalized messages of self-hatred will continue to flourish unopposed. By being a friend to yourself, you, not others, are in charge of changing your self-concept.

This is not the same as simply burying your feelings as some do when they want to stop hurting. It doesn't help to flatline your emotional life. Author Alane Pearce warns against this in her recent autobiography of her life with God:

One day I was so tired of crying all the time that I just decided to stop. I turned off the nozzle to the tears and told myself, "That's enough!" It worked for a while. At least I thought it did. The reality is that we cannot just turn off one set of emotions without affecting them all; the emotional nozzles are all inter-connected. Sure, I did not cry anymore, but neither did I laugh. My life turned into a flat, emotionless existence. I could not love. I had no passion. I lost touch with joy. I wasn't sad, but I wasn't happy.[1]

So you see, there is little chance that you will feel better about who you are or about the life you live by going into denial. That just makes things worse. It doesn't do much good either to merely order yourself to feel differently. It's more productive to intentionally engage in behavior that you know will send a different message to the self.

Try this experiment (doing what you would do if you felt good about yourself) for at least a month and record the changes you experience as a result. It's important to do these things on a daily basis, rather than occasionally or only when you want to. Doing them when you don't particularly feel like it demonstrates a higher level of commitment and results in greater empowerment. You will learn to revise your reasons for doing or not doing things to align more clearly with a proactive lifestyle instead of resigning yourself to a reactive coping pattern.

In time, you will discover the truth of author Paul Watzlawick's observation that "what the world does not hold, it cannot withhold . . . we cannot find out there in the world and thus can never *have* what we already *are*."[2] And what we are has already been determined by God's loving, creative hand. It is seen in how he has individually gifted each one of us.

MAKING SENSE OUT OF NONSENSE

To eighteen-year-old Suzanne, who had gone to private Christian schools all of her life, the college experience proved to be a shock. Overwhelmed by the "scholarly" arguments of agnostic professors, she concluded that her faith must be little more than self-delusion. Thereafter, she drifted into the college party scene and began living a life of self-indulgence. Without her faith as a compass, Suzanne's world was drained of all meaning, and she became depressed.

Later, trying to sort out how she got to where she was, she wondered why life had become so pointless. "I'm doing all the things that are supposed to make me happy, you know, all the stuff you were never allowed to do, what one of my teachers called *freedom*. But it isn't what it's cracked up to be. I mean, where's the real fun?" Somehow her happiness had been kidnapped. Underneath, she yearned for a God who was personal and for a future she could believe in. In time, Suzanne discovered that the empty secularism she had encountered was just that—vacant. It offered nothing more than momentary gratification.

Without the context of her faith, the world no longer made sense. The pain she experienced made no sense either. When we are stripped of our answers to life, we tend to fill in the blanks ourselves, like Suzanne did, with the assistance of those who are just as lost as we are.

God loves us in spite of the flaws in our character—but he does not ignore them. He wants us to mature and know him more intimately. Although suffering does not originate with God, he can still make it serve a useful purpose. Even *with* faith, it is sometimes difficult to see this happening in hardships. But without faith, it is impossible.

You must understand that your distress is not his goal—it is the prelude to something better. If you want to grow, you must become patient in his love and flexible in your adversity. It means asking God *how* rather than *why*, using hardship as a springboard to meaning rather than as a reason for helplessness. One client said it best: "It seems . . . like a window of opportunity to understand things that the mind can never know, only the heart." She was right to say it is primarily an issue of the heart—both your heart and God's heart. It is that unique connection with God that enables you to cope with difficult realities.

If God is to be your source of hope, you must trust that he always acts in your best interest and that he is not limited to a specific timetable.

And you must be willing to slow down long enough to hear his voice. Remember, God's aim is not instant relief from suffering (even if yours is), but a process of transformation that brings joy even in the midst of suffering. The end goal is to make you more like him.

STEPPING OUT BY WORKING OUT

One of the ways of tackling depression is also one of the simplest: physical exercise. When we become depressed, we tend to withdraw into a protracted state of lethargy. We just don't feel like doing anything—in a word, we vegetate. Even the simplest of tasks seem to require a herculean effort to complete. So, of course, the last thing we are likely to pursue is physical exercise. Yet, this is precisely one of the best things we can do to alleviate depressive symptoms.

In keeping with what we know about mind-body interaction, there is now considerable evidence that physical exercise has a significant impact on the biochemistry of the brain—in particular, on those chemicals in the brain responsible for changes in mood states. Exercise boosts the production of endorphins, those mood-elevating hormones that are part of the so-called opiate system in the brain.

Exercise also affects the supply of certain neurotransmitters, the biochemical messengers between nerve cells in the brain that we talked about in the last chapter. It just so happens that the ones affected by exercise are the same ones targeted by antidepressant medications. Author and psychiatrist John Ratey cites an impressive number of studies suggesting that physical exercise elevates the levels of norepinephrine, long known for its involvement in feelings of well-being; primes the dopamine pump, which improves mood and helps the attention span; and increases serotonin, which, as we have already discussed, is understood to be critical to the regulation of mood as well. It's not surprising, then, that the neural pathways where all three of these brain chemicals can be found also run through the "reward centers" of the brain. These are areas that are activated during experiences of personal pleasure.

Perhaps even more important, though, is the fact that we now know exercise also encourages the production of BDNF, or "brain-derived neurotrophic factor," reversing the inhibitory effect of long-term depression on this brain protein. Any increase in BDNF is significant because of its recently discovered role in renewing and restoring brain function and, above all, stimulating cell production in those parts of the brain responsible for learning, memory, and higher thinking.

We also know that exercise counteracts the effects of cortisol, a natural steroid (a corticosteroid hormone) released during stress that, if found in excess, can be detrimental to the health of the body.

So, if you want to avoid a deteriorating brain and a declining body, start exercising. It's best to start slowly and then work up to thirty or more minutes a day. Studies have shown that for some people, such exercise is just as effective as medication in reducing depressive symptoms. And when, for some reason, medication doesn't seem to be effective, exercise still is.

Though not a cure-all, what a simple, inexpensive way to begin addressing your depression! You don't have to know how the brain works to know what works for your brain. The bottom line is that if you condition your body, you will be doing one of the fastest things you can do to alter your mood and get back on track with a more sanguine lifestyle. When people say, "It's the simple things that count," they couldn't be more accurate than when they are talking about the importance of getting the body active again.

THE CONTEMPLATIVE LIFE

Aside from isolated monastic communities in some Catholic and Eastern traditions, meditation has all but disappeared from the religious culture of America. But did you know that the Bible encourages it? A busy culture like ours leaves little time for inner reflection. But meditation was and is an important strategy for keeping our spiritual eyes on God.

Biblical meditation is the act of silently reflecting on the truths of God's nature and mentally acknowledging his loving presence. It is the conscious reminder of the life we have in him now and of the life we will have with him in eternity. When I was in college, I used to drop by a church nearby the campus that was open during the day. With soft choir music playing in the background, it was a serene environment where I could catch my breath from my busy schedule and contemplate God and my life with him. I found those times rejuvenating to both the mind and the soul. With the prompting of the Holy Spirit, meditation inspires us to love more, give more, and serve more. Our relationships with others become our primary focus, and ministering to others becomes our highest priority.

It also inspires a deeper kind of contentment. King David said it best: "The LORD is my shepherd, I lack nothing. He makes me lie down in green pastures, he leads me beside quiet waters, he refreshes my soul" (Ps. 23:1–3). Think about that. He mentally nourishes us ("green pastures"), provides emotional renewal and a sense of well-being ("quiet [or restful] waters"), and spiritually revives us ("refreshes my soul")—if only we stop long enough to fully drink in his presence.

Part of this spiritually contemplative life is the communion of prayer. When we sense the nearness of God, we find that it reveals the truth about us—about things we need to learn. It also provides healing for our painful memories and losses. Personal, purifying change becomes internalized in the presence of the One we love. It is a bond that makes our faith an experiential fellowship. To pray is to linger in the presence of the Author of our worth and lovability. Indeed, prayer is the instrument for a growing life attachment to his heart.

Jesus told us to come to him with our requests—not to inform him but to sift out the supplications we make on a whim from those made from honest, lasting desire. Jesus promised that what we ask in the Spirit will be given to us—what we seek for the sake of righteousness we will find—and when we take the risk to knock with intention, he will open the door of his direction (Matt. 7:7). These verbs have tremendous significance. Our Lord was telling his listeners to keep on doing those things that are basic to knowing his will. Exercising our privilege of prayer gives us the spiritual preparation for a durable faith in hard times.

We often look up at the sky on a crisp, clear night and say, "The stars are out tonight." Although we say that they "come out" at night, they are there all the time. But we only see them after the sun "goes down" and the sky grows dark. In the same way, people who suffer in the darkness of adversity have a greater opportunity to see and appreciate the good things in life.

It was reported that an aged Jewish man was found living alone in dreadful squalor on the back streets of a small town in the northern part of Iraq. The compassionate relief worker who found him brought him out of the indescribable place he had called home for more than twenty years and took him to live in a modern assisted-living complex in Israel. Later, he spoke of his overwhelming happiness and his eternal gratitude for his rescue—things he felt so deeply because of how lonely and depressing his conditions had been for so long. The contrast was so dramatic that he wept tears of joy over every precious day of freedom.

If we are free enough and willing enough to see it, there is an upside that either accompanies or follows every downside—a light in every darkness. And just as there is a responsibility that comes with every freedom, there is a challenge that comes with every insight. The challenge here is to have a trusting faith. It is not a call to blind trust, but to a trust informed by God's gracious acts in history. Our faith depends on it. Our personal healing must likewise stem from it.

BIBLICAL NUTRITION FOR IMPOVERISHED SOULS

In what clinicians call "bibliotherapy," various books relevant to a client's problems are often recommended to augment what is happening in counseling. In the case of Christians, that includes, most importantly, Scripture itself. The Bible is indeed rich with teaching on issues of mental health. The unsurpassable wisdom contained within its pages provides valuable tools—cognitive, behavioral, and spiritual—for stimulating personal growth. There is no doubt that God's Word can transform lives. Its message is, after all, intended to fundamentally renew our minds (Rom. 12:2).

It is precisely for this reason that in this book we have made so many references to biblical passages that address critical issues involved in depression. God has given us not only a blueprint for salvation, but also a guidebook on how to live well. Effective counseling must then, necessarily, capitalize on this divine resource to bring a person's faith to the problems at hand. Pastors who counsel members of their congregations know this intimately. One client of mine put it this way: "Counseling has been so helpful to me. It has given me insights I never would have had on my own, insights which have given me true hope for a far better future. Most of all, though, it has been the passages in the Bible that you've shared with me that have helped me to realize just how relevant the Bible is in guiding me to a better place. It's so exciting that my faith can grow along with my understanding of my problems!"

Some clinicians may be hesitant to use the Bible as much because they are afraid of "overspiritualizing" the problem. But I have found that where the Bible is used—not indiscriminately but intelligently and prudently, especially at pivotal moments in therapy—it often opens my clients' eyes to the pinpoint accuracy of God's message of hope. They realize, maybe for the first time, that their faith can effectively be brought to bear on their concepts of who they are, why they function as they do, and what they can do to change. The simple fact is that biblical truth can transform lives. It is this spiritual component that generally authenticates to believers the importance of the steps they are taking.

As I have witnessed these "God moments" unfold before me, my own faith has been strengthened time and again. Indeed, it's quite impossible to be nonchalant about the unique way God powerfully intersects with the human mind!

MAKING A DIFFERENCE

We discussed earlier that reaching out to those in need is both an extension of faith and a practical means of combating depression. There is nothing quite like helping other people rise above their adversities in life to revive your own spirit.

Two things happen when you give of yourself in this way. First, you discover the principle that both the helper and the helped tend to stimulate growth in each other. This fact reflects the importance of true gratitude in relationships. Second, serving others reminds you that you can still create outcomes that make a difference. Both results challenge the depressing belief that you don't matter.

It's the gift of introspection born of emotional warfare that elegantly sets the framework for helping others. Author Andrew Solomon wrote, "The unexamined life is unavailable to the depressed. That is, perhaps, the greatest revelation I have had: not that depression is compelling but that people who suffer from it may be compelling because of it."[3] He followed these words of wisdom with a conclusion from his own suffering: "I do not love experiencing my depression, but I love the depression itself. I love who I am in the wake of it."[4]

People who have experienced depression are often led to make changes that make them more patient, understanding, and thoughtful. This is why they become more compelling. The lesson of depression invites us to cherish life more, to value greater wisdom, and to enlarge our appreciation for the deeper concerns of the human soul.

FINDING HOPE

1. If you want to change the stories being written in your mind, change your behavior first. Doing something different can sometimes be more effective than trying to think something different.

2. Try to view your anxiety attacks as "aerobic moments." Then try to increase your symptoms when you have them.

3. Increase the efficiency of your worrying. Each day, condense all your anxiety-inducing thoughts into a single hour. Use the rest of the time for more enjoyable activities.

4. Stop fighting your anxiety. Instead, send yourself a positive message by doing some relaxation exercises while you wait for it to pass.

5. Think of forgiveness as the gateway to freedom from the toxic burden of bitterness.

6. Doing the unexpected in a relationship increases its interest value and provides the context for change.

7. Emotional distress is never God's goal—maturation is.

8. By practicing God's loving presence in meditation, you initiate a growing life attachment to him and a more durable faith.

HAMILTON SURVEY FOR EMOTIONAL AND PHYSICAL WELLNESS

DR. GREGORY KNOPF, MD

Name: _____

Date: _____

Instructions: Mentally review the past two weeks and rate yourself on a scale of 0 to 4 for each question as you identify with the phrases, symptoms, and feelings (0 = none, 1 = mild, 2 = moderate, 3 = severe, 4 = extreme).

_____ 1. Depressed Mood:
   I find myself feeling sad and helpless/hopeless because of the present circumstances, or for no reason at all. I feel a sense of hopelessness that things will not get better. I find myself crying more frequently and am not able to "hold it together." I often feel worthless.

_____ 2. Guilt Feelings:
   I sometimes feel like I should be punished. I do not like myself right now, and maybe I deserve some of the things that are happening to me. Even though I can't think of specifics, I feel guilty much of the time.

_____ 3. Suicide:
   I often find myself thinking about death and sometimes wishing that I didn't have to live anymore. My life seems empty and not worth the effort it takes. I find myself wanting to avoid other people and be alone. I told at least one other

person that it would be better if I were dead. Sometimes I find myself wanting to cut myself or I think about taking a lot of pills.

_____ 4. Initial Insomnia:

I have difficulty falling asleep after I get into bed at night.

_____ 5. Middle Insomnia:

I have difficulty sleeping all night long without interruption. I wake up for no reason several times a night. I sometimes get back to sleep and sometimes not.

_____ 6. Delayed Insomnia:

I find myself waking up two to three hours before I want to, for no reason, and cannot get back to sleep.

_____ 7. Work and Interest:

My job and family are no longer enjoyable. I often find myself not caring about my job or home responsibilities. I rarely do any of the hobbies that I used to enjoy. My friends invite me to do things, but I often find reasons to say no. The things I used to enjoy don't seem to lift my spirits. People at work are noticing that the quality of my work has deteriorated. My family members are beginning to complain that I don't do the usual things around the house I did in the past.

_____ 8. Alertness:

I find myself feeling sluggish in my ability to think, communicate my ideas, and sometimes just move around.

_____ 9. Agitation:

I find myself fidgeting and feeling restless. Often I will pace back and forth or sometimes clench my fists. Sometimes I will tap my feet or hands for no reason, or bite my lips. I often find myself wringing my hands. Sometimes I will pull at my hair or pick at my fingernails or clothes.

_____ 10. Anxiety (psychological):

I often feel tense and unable to relax. I act irritably with family or coworkers. I am easily startled. Even though I try not to, I often worry over trivial matters. Often, I am fearful for no reason. I have a sense that things are going to get worse and I will be unable to do anything to change them. I feel out of control and that I could have an anxiety attack.

Add your ratings together. Use the following guide to interpret your total:

0–7	Normal
8–19	Mild "dysthymia" or sub-clinical depression
20–29	Mild to moderate major depressive disorder (MDD)
30–39	Moderately severe major depressive disorder (MDD)
40+	Consistent with severe major depressive disorder (MDD)

Appendix B

IRRATIONAL BELIEFS TEST

The following most common irrational beliefs and their rational counterparts are measured by the Irrational Beliefs Test (IBT) and are useful for identifying the dysfunctional ideologies of clients who are suffering from depression and anxiety.

IRRATIONAL BELIEFS*	RATIONAL BELIEFS
1. It is a dire necessity for me to be loved and approved of by virtually every person that is significant to me in any way.	1. While it is nice to be loved and approved of by certain select people, it is not necessary. My self-worth does not depend on the approval of others.
2. I should be thoroughly competent, adequate, and achieving in every respect if I am to consider myself worthwhile.	2. Being competent and achieving in some areas certainly has its rewards, but my self-worth has nothing to do with my level of performance.
3. Certain people are bad, wicked, or villainous, and they should be severely blamed and punished for their villainy.	3. While certain people may do bad, wicked, or villainous things, they still have personal worth. Negative consequences are used to correct the bad behavior, not to punish the person.
4. It is awful and catastrophic when things are not the way I very much want them to be.	4. It is unfortunate and disappointing when things are not the way I would like them to be, but that is not the end of the world.
5. Human unhappiness is externally caused, and I have little or no ability to control my sorrows and disturbances.	5. Unfortunate events may happen to me that are beyond my control, but I do have control over the degree to which these negative events will upset me.

continued

IRRATIONAL BELIEFS*	RATIONAL BELIEFS
6. If something is or may be dangerous or fearsome, I should be terribly concerned about it and should keep dwelling on the possibility of its occurring.	6. If something is or may be dangerous or fearsome, I will take whatever precautions are reasonable and then accept what I cannot control.
7. It is easier to avoid than to face certain life difficulties and self-responsibilities.	7. In the long run, it is easier to face than avoid certain life difficulties and self-responsibilities.
8. I should be dependent on others to give me support and make decisions for me.	8. Although gathering information from experts and support from friends is quite acceptable, I am the one who makes the final decision and deals with the unpleasant situations of life.
9. My past history is an all-important determinant of my present behavior, and because something once strongly affected my life, it should indefinitely have a similar effect.	9. My past history can have an important effect on my present behavior. However, just because something once strongly affected my life, there is no reason it should continue to have a similar effect.
10. There is invariably a right, precise, and perfect solution to human problems, and it is catastrophic if this perfect solution is not found.	10. There is seldom a right, precise, and perfect solution to human problems. It is better to choose the best of the available alternatives than to search for a nonexistent perfect solution.

*These irrational beliefs lead to a variety of agitated feelings and behaviors that block a more adaptive lifestyle. As you will notice, most of them support a life of self-victimization. The following is a breakdown of the effects specific to each irrational belief.

Irrational belief 1: Leads to a *desperate search for social approval* as a criterion for self-acceptance. It often reflects an underlying self-hatred.

Irrational belief 2: Leads to a *paralyzing fear of failure*, where performance becomes the basis for all personal worth.

Irrational belief 3: Leads to a lot of *blaming behavior*, where fault-finding and accusations are the major preoccupation.

Irrational belief 4: Leads to a lot of *frustration, anger, and even rage* because life is deemed unfair and people are seen as cruel or hurtful.

Irrational belief 5: Leads to *overwhelming sense of helplessness*, where passive resignation is the rule.

Irrational belief 6: Leads to *crippling anxiety*, where worst-case scenarios dominate one's thinking.

Irrational belief 7: Leads to a life of *avoidance and irresponsibility*, where there is little self-discipline to be proactive.

Irrational belief 8: Leads to a life of *childlike overdependency*, where searching for others to lean on is the primary motive.

Irrational belief 9: Leads to *living perpetually in the past*, where all rationales are found for passive inaction.

Irrational belief 10: Leads to *inflexible perfectionism*, where rigid compartmentalization is the norm. It's the refusal to accept imperfect reality.

MEDICATION OVERVIEW

	MEDICATION	DOSAGE	ADVANTAGES	DISADVANTAGES	NICHE
SNRI (Serotonin and Norepinephrine Reuptake Inhibitors)	Effexor XR (Venlafaxine) extended release capsules	25 mg to 375 mg	broad spectrum; few side effects; excellent efficacy; minimal sexual dysfunction; effective in anxiety	occasional nausea or stimulation; withdrawal/ rebound problems; increased blood pressure in some people at high doses	excellent broad spectrum; few side effects; can be used in combination; improves cognitive dysfunction; low sexual dysfunction
	Cymbalta (Duloxetine)	30 mg to 120 mg	"balanced" elevation of serotonin and norepinephrine; minimal sexual dysfunction; also approved for diabetic peripheral neuropathic pain, fibromyalgia, and generalized musculoskeletal pain	some nausea for the first six days when starting medicine	some advantages in reducing musculoskeletal pain from depression and fibromyalgia; may also help with some urinary problems; low sexual dysfunction
	Pristiq (Desvenladaxine)	50 mg once a day for most people; 100 mg for some people	cleanest of all antidepressants because it's not metabolized through the liver; few side effects; less rebound and blood pressure problems; with fewer sexual problems	some nausea for the first six days when starting medicine	fewer side effects than Effexor XR; very effective and predictable in people who may be either rapid or poor metabolizers
	Fetzima (levominacipran) levotioxetine	20 mg, 40 mg, 80 mg, or 120 mg	increased energy; improved motivation	potential agitation	good for those who experience a lot of fatigue
SSRI (Selective Serotonin Reuptake Inhibitors)	Prozac (Fluoxetine)	10 mg to 80 mg	time tested; increased energy and early stimulation	slower onset of action; long residual; sexual dysfunction; may cause fatigue after long-term use	good for those patients who are younger or may have problems of noncompliance
	Paxil (Paroxetine)	10 mg to 50 mg	increased energy; OCD/panic approved	side effects: nausea, sedation, sexual dysfunction, birth defects with pregnancy, weight gain	patients with anxiety, OCD, and panic disorder
	Zoloft (Sertraline)	25 mg to 200 mg	increased mood "middle of road" SSRI; OCD approved	side effects: some sedation, sexual dysfunction	good "first option" SSRI; low cost
	Celexa (Citalopram)	20 mg to 40 mg	increased mood; "pure" SSRI	possibly less potent than other SSRIs; sexual dysfunction	try when other SSRIs cause side effects; good for anxiety
	Lexapro (Escitalopram)	10 mg to 20 mg	fewer side effects than Celexa	some sexual dysfunction	try when other SSRIs cause side effects; good for anxiety

	MEDICATION	DOSAGE	ADVANTAGES	DISADVANTAGES	NICHE
Newer Antidepressant Medications	Brintellix (vortioxetine)	5 mg to 20 mg	broad range of depression and anxiety symptoms; also stimulates or modifies five other serotonin receptors; long lasting	some nausea and gastrointestinal side effects; minimal weight gain; low sexual side effects	good for those who have not improved with other medications
	Viibryd (vilazodone)	10 mg, 20 mg, or 40 mg	raises serotonin and also stimulates one other serotonin receptor	side effects: nausea and diarrhea	good for those who have not improved with other medications
Other Antidepressant Medications	Wellbutrin SR and Wellbutrin XL (Bupropion)	150 mg to 300 mg	lifts mood; approved for ADHD; used for addictions (smoking); minimal sexual dysfunction	may cause seizures in high doses or in people with eating disorders; inconsistent response	good for those with depression and ADHD, addictions (smoking, overeating)
	Desyrel (Trazodone)	50 mg to 400 mg	most sedating antidepressant	weaker at lifting mood; some morning sedation; priapism; dose titration	used in combination with other antidepressants for people with severe sleep difficulty
	Remeron (Mirtazapine)	15 mg to 45 mg	helps with insomnia; minimal sexual dysfunction	sedation in more than 50 percent; weight gain with lower dose	for depression with insomnia; patients who need weight gain (anorexia/ weight loss)
	Tricyclics (Amitryptyline, Doxepin, Nortryptyline, Imipramine, others)	Variable	help with sleep; stabilize mood; help with musculoskeletal pain and headaches	side effects include dry mouth; lethal in overdose; weight gain; drug interaction; orthostatic blood pressure changes	no longer "first line" agents; good for patients with fibromyalgia and chronic pain

MEDICAL CONDITIONS ASSOCIATED WITH DEPRESSION

M any people, including family members and even the patients themselves, are often unaware of the fact that some of the symptoms they observe or experience in an illness are due to depression. It is not uncommon for people who suffer from a chronic illness or medical condition to also suffer from depression. But it is easily concealed by other medical problems and so, as a result, depression frequently goes undetected and untreated. Nonetheless, it is one of the most prevalent emotional consequences of physical illness. Typically, it reflects the stress of coping with disease; but the disease itself can also cause it.

Some studies suggest that as many as one-third of all patients with some kind of chronic medical condition also suffer from depression. This is partly due to the limitations imposed by the illness or condition on their mobility, on their ability to engage in activities they once enjoyed, and on their expectations of the future. The severity of the depression is often proportional to the severity of the illness and the limitations it imposes.

Depression can actually further complicate the medical condition (for example, increase the risk of coronary heart disease), as well as increase the patient's fatigue and immobility. What's more, it often causes people to become isolated, further amplifying their loneliness and hopelessness. Partly because this can likewise enhance the risk of suicide, it is important to diagnose the presence of depression as early as possible.

The following are the depression rates associated with a particular chronic condition:

- Heart attack: 40–65% experience depression
- Coronary artery disease (without heart attack): 18–20%
- Parkinson's disease: 40%
- Multiple sclerosis: 40%
- Stroke: 15–27%
- Cancer: 25% (up to 45–50% with cancer of the pancreas)
- Diabetes: 25%
- Chronic pain syndrome: 30–54%*

What makes things worse is that depression and chronic illness can initiate a destructive loop: The chronic condition can trigger depression, which, in turn, can hamper effective treatment of the illness, which, as a consequence of continued (and perhaps increased) pain and disability, leads to even more depression. Add to that the fact that some medications used to treat the medical condition can themselves cause depression, and you can have a rapidly deteriorating situation. That's why it is important to seek therapeutic help as soon as possible. It is wise, too, for friends and family to make every effort to keep the chronically ill person actively engaged with life to prevent their withdrawal, something that can otherwise likely happen.

General Medical Conditions That Can Cause or Be Associated with Depression:	
Cancer Breast cancer Leukemia Lymphoma Prostate cancer	**Circulatory Disorders** Heart attack, congestive heart failure Stroke HIV-positive-AIDS Anemia
Gynecological Conditions Perimenopause and menopause Pregnancy/postpartum depression Premenstrual cycle	**Musculoskeletal Conditions** Back pain Chronic pain Chronic fatigue syndrome Fibromyalgia Rheumatoid arthritis Systemic lupus
Endrocrine Disorders Diabetes (Hyperglycemia) Hypoglycemia Hypothyroidism Hyperthyroidism Adrenal dysfunction (Addison's disease) Cushing syndrome (adrenal tumor) Hyperparathyroidism Infectious hepatitis	**Neurologic Disorders** Cardiovascular disorders Dementia Epilepsy Migraines Multiple sclerosis Parkinson's disease Lewy Body disease Traumatic brain injury Syphilis
*This list of medical conditions was adapted and modified from a compilation of medical sources.	

MEDICATIONS ASSOCIATED WITH DEPRESSION**

The following medications are known either to have a possible side effect of depression or have a likelihood of resulting in depression with their rapid withdrawal.

BLOOD PRESSURE MEDICATIONS (ANTIHYPERTENSIVES)
Reserpine (brand name: Serpasil)
Beta blockers (for example, brand name: Inderal)
Calcium channel blockers
Methyldopa (brand name: Aldomet)
Guanethidine sulfate (brand name: Ismelin sulfate)
Clonidine hydrochloride (brand name: Catapres)

SOME CONTRACEPTIVES
Progestin-estrogen combination (various brands)
Norplant (discontinued distribution after 2002, but some still have implant)

HORMONE TREATMENTS
Estrogen (for example, Premarin, Ogen, Estrace, Estraderm)
Progesterone and derivatives (for example, Provera, DepoProvera)

ANTI-PARKINSON'S DISEASE AGENTS
Levodopa carbidopa (brand name: Sinemet)
Amantadine hydrochloride (brand names: Dopar, Larodopa, Symmetrel)

ANTIANXIETY AGENTS: BENZODIAZAPINES
(ESPECIALLY WITHDRAWAL AFTER ADDICTION TO THEM)
Diazepam (brand name: Valium)
Chlordiazepoxide (brand name: Librium)

PSYCHOACTIVE SUBSTANCES

Alcohol (tends to have a masking effect with depression)

Opiates (for example, opium, heroin, codeine, Hydrocone, Methodone, Morphine, Oxycodone, Darvocet, Percocet, Percodan, Vicodin, to name some of the more common ones)

Amphetamines

Cocaine

Anabolic steroids

CHEMOTHERAPY AGENTS

Vincristine, vinblastine, procarbazine, Interferon

GLUCOSTEROIDS

Cortisone acetate

FIRST GENERATION ANTIPSYCHOTIC MEDICATIONS

Phenothiazines (for example, Thorazine, Mellaril, Stelazine, Trilafon, Phenergan)

Haloperidol (brand name: Haldol)

**This list of medications that can have depressive effects is adopted and modified from "Practical Pharmacology," professional seminars by Dr. Gollapudi Shankar, PharmD, MS, PH-C, BCPP, CGP.

NOTES

CHAPTER 1

1. Andrew Solomon, *The Noonday Demon: An Atlas of Depression* (New York: Scribner, 2001), 443.

2. Edith Schaeffer, *The Art of Life*, comp. and ed. Louis Gifford Parkhurst, Jr. (Westchester, IL: Crossway, 1987), 21.

3. Paul Brand and Philip Yancey, *Pain: The Gift Nobody Wants* (New York: Harper Collins, 1993), 6.

4. Robert Frost, "The Gift Outright," in *The Poetry of Robert Frost*, ed. Edward Connery Lathem (New York: Holt Rinehart and Winston, 1969), 348.

5. Viktor E. Frankl, *Man's Search for Meaning: An Introduction to Logotherapy* (New York: Washington Square Press, 1963), 176–177.

6. Jack Riemer, "Perlman Makes His Music the Hard Way," *Houston Chronicle*, February 10, 2001.

CHAPTER 2

1. A. W. Tozer, *The Pursuit of God* (Wheaton, IL: Tyndale, 1982), 112.

2. Theodore Rubin, *Compassion and Self-Hate: An Alternative to Despair* (NewYork: David McKay Company, 1975), 77.

CHAPTER 3

1. Andrew Solomon, *Noonday Demon: An Atlas of Depression* (New York: Scribner, 2001), 81.

2. Louis Pasteur, as quoted in Rene Vallery-Radot, *The Life of Pasteur*, trans. R. L. Devonshire (Garden City, NY: Garden City Publishing, 1919), 79.

3. John Eldredge, *The Journey of Desire: Searching for the Life We've Only Dreamed Of* (Nashville: Thomas Nelson, 2000), 9.

CHAPTER 4

1. Andrew Solomon, *Noonday Demon: An Atlas of Depression* (New York: Scribner, 2001), 432.

2. Richard E. Byrd, *Alone* (Garden City, NY: International Collectors Library American Headquarters, 1938), 105.

CHAPTER 5

1. A. W. Tozer, *The Attributes of God: A Journey into the Father's Heart* (Camp Hill, PA: Christian Publications, 1997), 42–43.

2. *Chariots of Fire*, directed by Hugh Hudson (Burbank, CA: Warner Studios, 1981).

3. Kenneth Blanchard, author of *The One Minute Apology*, interview by Laura Ingraham, *Laura Ingraham* radio show, January 21, 2003.

CHAPTER 6

1. A. W. Tozer, *The Attributes of God: A Journey into the Father's Heart* (Camp Hill, PA: Christian Publications, 1997), 8, 11.

2. Paul Tournier, *Guilt and Grace: A Psychological Study* (New York: Harper & Row, 1962), 174.

3. C. S. Lewis, *The Weight of Glory and Other Addresses* (New York: Harper-Collins, 1949, 1980), 25–26.

4. This discussion and C. S. Lewis's quote were taken from Armand M. Nicholi Jr., *The Question of God: C. S. Lewis and Sigmund Freud Debate God, Love, Sex, and the Meaning of Life* (New York: The Free Press, 2002), 106.

5. Lindsay Lee Johnson, *Soul Moon Soup* (Asheville, NC: Front Street, 2002), 106–107.

CHAPTER 7

1. Marina Marcus et al., developers, "Depression: A Global Public Health Concern" (WHO Department of Mental Health and Substance Abuse, 2012), 6.

2. Arthur Freeman, "Self-Directed Negative Behavior: Cognitive Behavioral Treatment of Depression Spectrum Disorders" (lecture, Therapeutic and Alcohol/Drug Interventions Conference, Las Vegas, NV, May 2–4, 2007).

3. Haddon Robinson, in a message delivered in Vancouver, Washington, April 1994.

4. Cristian Barbosu, report, *The Church Around the World* 35, no. 1 (Carol Stream, IL: Tyndale, 2004).

5. John Piper, *The Purifying Power of Living by Faith in . . . Future Grace* (Sisters, OR: Multnomah, 1995), 32.

6. Mark Twain, "Famous Twain Quotes," The Mark Twain House & Museum, accessed July 8, 2014, http://www.marktwainhouse.org/man/famous_twain_quotes.php.

7. Piper, *Future Grace*, 386.

CHAPTER 8

1. John Piper, *The Purifying Power of Living by Faith in . . . Future Grace* (Sisters, OR: Multnomah, 1995), 324.

2. Paul Tournier, *Guilt and Grace: A Psychological Study* (New York: Harper & Row, 1962), 185.

3. C. S. Lewis, *Mere Christianity* (New York: MacMillan, 1952), 104.

CHAPTER 9

1. Philip Yancey, *Reaching for the Invisible God: What Can We Expect to Find?* (Grand Rapids, MI: Zondervan, 2000), 16.

2. Henri J. M. Nouwen, *Life of the Beloved: Spiritual Living in a Secular World* (New York: Crossroad, 1992), 106.

3. Ibid.

CHAPTER 10

1. Alane Pearce, *Notes from the Margins: Healing Conversations with God* (Colorado Springs, CO: Corbin Press, 2009), 69.

2. Art Greco, "The Monster in My Closet: A Story of Depression," *The Covenant Companion*, September 2004, 9.

3. Ibid., 21.

4. Ibid., 9.

CHAPTER 12

1. Stephen M. Stahl, *Essential Psychopharmacology of Depression and Bipolar Disorder* (Cambridge, UK: Cambridge University Press, 2000), 2.

2. Developed by David Kupfer, MD.

CHAPTER 13

1. Alane Pearce, *Notes from the Margins: Healing Conversations with God* (Colorado Springs, CO: Corbin Press, 2009), 103.

2. Paul Watzlawick, *Ultra-Solutions: How to Fail Most Successfully* (New York: W. W. Norton, 1988), 107.

3. Andrew Solomon, *Noonday Demon: An Atlas of Depression* (New York: Scribner, 2001), 438.

4. Ibid., 442–443.

Helping Pastors Find Hope in Despair

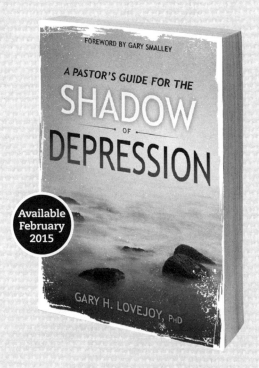

Pastors face unique challenges and unrealistic expectations that can lead to feelings of failure, deep sadness, and depression. Too often they feel no one understands, as if there's nowhere to turn.

In this book, Dr. Gary Lovejoy, PhD, comes alongside pastors to help them recognize when they may be depressed so they can find help and make needed changes. Even more, Dr. Lovejoy identifies assertive ways pastors can address critical issues before the shadows begin to envelop them.

Depression is a warning sign that won't simply go away on its own. Every pastor should read this guide, even if they've never felt depressed. It may be the lifeline you need at a critical time.

A Pastor's Guide for the Shadow of Depression

978-0-89827-830-9
978-0-89827-831-6 (e-book)

 1.800.493.7539 | WWW.WESLEYAN.ORG/BOOKS

Hope for Those Wrestling with Depression

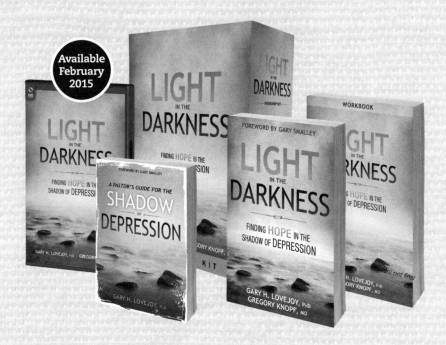

The *Light in the Darkness Workshop Kit* provides everything you need to lead a group of congregation members through an in-depth study of Dr. Gary Lovejoy and Dr. Gregory Knopf's practical and hopeful book, *Light in the Darkness: Finding Hope in the Shadow of Depression*. It's also a great way to reach out to people in your community who may be experiencing depression. The workshop kit includes:

- 1 *Light in the Darkness: Finding Hope in the Shadow of Depression* book
- 1 *A Pastor's Guide for the Shadow of Depression* book
- 1 Light in the Darkness DVD (includes 13 video segments, 1 per chapter)
- 1 copy of *Light in the Darkness Workbook*
- *Light in the Darkness* Leader's Guide (free download)

Light in the Darkness Group Resource Kit
978-0-89827-827-9